THE INSTRUCTIONAL DESIGN PROCESS

THE INSTRUCTIONAL DESIGN PROCESS

Jerrold E. Kemp

San Jose State University

1817

HARPER & ROW, PUBLISHERS, New York
Cambridge, Philadelphia, San Francisco, Washington,
London, Mexico City, São Paulo, Singapore, Sydney

121281

Sponsoring Editor: Louise H. Waller
Project Editor: Brigitte Pelner
Cover Design: Caliber Design Planning, Inc.
Text Art: Vantage Art, Inc.
Production: Debra Forrest Bochner
Compositor: Donnelley/Rocappi, Inc.
Printer and Binder: R. R. Donnelley & Sons Company

The Instructional Design Process

Library of Congress Cataloging in Publication Data
Kemp, Jerrold E.
    The instructional design process.

    Includes bibliographies and index.
    1. Curriculum planning. I. Title.
LB1570.K435   1985   375'.001   84-15813
ISBN 0-06-043589-5

88 9 8 7 6 5 4

Contents

Chapter 3

Learning Needs and Instructional Goals   25

Chapter 4

Topics, Job Tasks and General Purposes   36

Chapter 5

Learner Characteristics   45

Chapter 6

Subject Content and Task Analysis   58

Preface

"I've been teaching for some years, but never have felt I was planning my instruction with sufficient attention to detail. How can I do a better job?"

"We're a team of engineers and have been asked to plan a new training program. Where do we start?"

"I'd like to work with instructors in planning courses so the majority of their students will accomplish what is required of them. Is there a procedure I can use?"

"I've been assigned greater responsibilities for training and I need help with designing a training course in an individualized instructional format."

"As a producer of audiovisual and video materials, I am frequently asked to develop training packages. My concern is how to design a training program, incorporating my materials in it."

"I just want some useful knowledge about instructional planning procedures so that I might fill a more professional role in my organization."

Do you find yourself relating, in some degree, to at least one of these situations? If so, this book will be of value to you.

The major objectives of *The Instructional Design Process* are:

1. to establish a sound basis for systematic instructional planning;
2. to examine a practical planning method consisting of ten elements;
3. to consider other essential matters for implementing the instructional design process.

A major audience for this book is the instructional designer or a person interested in fulfilling that role. The contents guide an individual or a planning team who are designing an instructional unit or a complete instructional program.

Organized and presented on an introductory level, the content nevertheless has sufficient detail and depth so as to develop competency in instructional planning for the reader. Numerous examples and applications are included as the various elements comprising the instructional design process are considered.

Each chapter concludes with a set of review exercises on two levels. First, there are simple *recall* questions to check how well you *remember* the important facts and generalizations that have been discussed. These are followed by *comprehension* questions which test your *understanding* of the information treated in the chapter. For those chapters that present elements of the instructional design process, review exercises are supplemented with *application* problems. Following the exercises are references on the topic.

The four Appendices consist of (1) answers to the review exercises, (2) information for an application problem (sky diving), (3) a glossary of terms used in the book, and (4) two examples that completely illustrate the total instructional design process—one in an academic subject and the other in training for a skill.

The manuscript for this book was tested in four classes of an instructional design seminar and in a community college teaching methods course at San Jose State University. Reactions and suggestions were obtained from colleagues at all levels of education and from practitioners in industry. I particularly wish to thank Vinnie Apicella of the Calma Company, Barry Bratton and his graduate students Wendy Rosen and Steve Merkel-Hess of the University of Iowa, and from the School of Education at San Jose State University, G.W. Ford, Wally Thurston, and Rob Simas. Finally, I appreciate the thoughtful suggestions offered by Ron McBeath and his assistance with faculty development materials. The comments received were very useful during the "formative evaluation" phase of preparing the book.

The course offered at San Jose State University, *Instructional Design,* is organized into two parts. Part I provides learning experiences based on the content of the book. There are *no* lectures in the course. It is conducted as a series of self-paced, audio-tutorial learning activities. Audio recordings direct each student's study of the text and completion of review exercises, with feedback on answers. Part II of the course consists of individual and group assignments which require students to apply the knowledge acquired about the instructional design process in Part I. Contact me if you would like a copy of the course requirements, activities, and information on this audio-tutorial component.

Jerrold E. Kemp

THE
INSTRUCTIONAL
DESIGN
PROCESS

chapter 1

Introduction

Situation 1: On a College Campus

Comments by two college students as they leave a classroom after completing the final examination for a course:

> "I'm glad that's over. We don't have to sit through any more pointless lectures."
>
> "Dr. Brown didn't tell us that Chapter 12 would be covered on the exam!"
>
> "I really have no idea what I've learned in much of this course."
>
> "I wonder how he'll grade us."

Situation 2: At a Community Hospital

In the Learning Center, a nursing education student starts her study of a new module as preparation for her clinical practicum later in the week. Here are some of her thoughts:

> "I think I can complete the activities for these objectives in about 3 hours."
>
> "I like this module approach to learning. The content is logically organized. I'm asked to apply the information as well as study the nursing principles."
>
> "I certainly work hard, but after testing myself on the objectives, I feel confident I've learned."

Situation 3:   In a Business Company

Tom, the instructional designer in the training department of an electronics company, is reviewing results of a new safety course with two instructors. Here are the observations they make:

> "The number of accidents in handling chemicals has already decreased over 30 percent since our technicians completed the course."

> "On the feedback evaluation, most employees tell us they like the course. Some say they learned things they are even using at home."

> "This course should pay for itself within a year. Management would be pleased to hear this."

Situation 4:   In a School Administrative Office

A statewide curriculum coordinating committee is reviewing a report relating goals, curriculum, and achievement in 200 schools. The results, which dismay the committee, show that:[1]

> "Less than 50 percent of the schools have established a set of goals."

> "For those schools with identifiable goals, there was little relation between what was taught and stated goals."

> "Achievement tests emphasized only basic skills (reading, mathematics, and language), which represented only a portion of what was being taught."

Situation 5:   At a Television Production Facility

The television producer has been meeting with a potential client who is organizing a continuing education program for the professional members of a national association. The program will utilize a teleconferencing format. Each session will treat a different topic and will be introduced with a videotape presentation by a recognized expert on the topic. The client is shopping for a company to handle arrangements for producing the videotapes. The television producer has asked these questions:

> "What is the overall purpose of the educational program?"

> "What is the background of the people who will be the audience?"

> "Where will the viewing take place?"

> "What activities will comprise the instruction besides viewing a videotape each week?"

The client is impressed with the sequencing and directness of the questions being asked. He decides to further explore this company's capabilities to produce the video presentations.

Each one of these situations is related directly to the matter of instructional planning. Situations 2 and 3 illustrate satisfactory results of careful

[1]Adapted from Richard Kimpston and Harlan Hansen, "Accountability—Doing What They Say," *Educational Leadership.*

planning, while number 5 is the starting point for potential success. On the other hand, situations 1 and 4 reveal unsatisfactory results primarily because of poor planning. From your own experiences, you no doubt can relate a number of other successful and unsuccessful incidents as the outcome of satisfactory or unsatisfactory instructional planning.

Traditionally, plans for instruction have been based largely on ambiguous purposes and casual subjective judgments. The more one works in education or training, the greater is one's realization that the instructional process is complex. It is composed of many interrelated parts and functions that must operate in a coherent manner in order to achieve success.

For an instructional program to be successful, the following should occur:

- Satisfactory learning takes place so that participants have acquired necessary knowledge, skills, and attitudinal behavior patterns, and after training, perform productively in their assignments.
- The learning is accomplished with due regard for reasonable expenditures of money and time.
- The learning experiences are meaningful and interesting so that students are motivated to continue with their studies.
- The planning and implementation of an instructional program proves to be a satisfactory set of experiences for the instructor and the support staff.

A TECHNOLOGY OF INSTRUCTION

In order to relate all elements of the instructional process in building a successful program, an approach receiving increased attention is one similar to that used widely for product design, development, production, and implementation in business, industry, the military, and space exploration. This approach involves the application of an overall plan incorporating the various elements essential to accomplishing an identified goal. It is called the *systems approach* to problem solving.

This process is based on the method of scientific inquiry, whereby a problem is identified, a hypothesis for solution is formulated, experiments are conducted, and data are gathered that lead to a conclusion about the suitability of the hypothesis for solving the problem. If it is proven to be correct, the results are used to produce or improve products or services. If not, different approaches are tried until success is realized.

When the method of scientific inquiry is applied to instructional planning, a *technology of instruction* results. This means the systematic design of instruction, based on knowledge of the learning process, taking into consideration as many factors and variables about the particular situation as possible. Then, after necessary tryout testing and any revisions, successful learning will result.[2]

[2]For a consideration of science areas which have been identified as contributing to the development of a technology of instruction, see Robert C. Stakenas and Roger Kaufman, *Technology in Education.*

For many people, the term *instructional technology* means the *resources* of instruction—machines (computers, projectors, recorders) and materials (computer software, films, slides, recordings). This is but one meaning of instructional technology. Another, more important understanding of the term is as the *process* of systematic planning. This process establishes a way to examine instructional problems and needs, sets a procedure for solving them, and then evaluates the results. *Instructional design* is the procedure used to implement this process. The management of personnel, budgets, and support services to improve instruction within an organization or institution is called *instructional development.* Thus, the instructional development procedure is used to direct and control projects, while the instructional design procedure is used to plan courses.

BACKGROUND FOR THE INSTRUCTIONAL DESIGN CONCEPT

The concept of instructional design can be traced back to military training efforts during and immediately following World War II. At those times, the work of psychologists was revealing important new information about how human learning takes place, including the importance of specifying details of a task to be learned or performed, and the need for active participation by the student or trainee to ensure learning. At the same time, audiovisual specialists were developing ways to utilize the recognized learning principles in designing effective films and other instructional materials.

In the early 1950s much interest was being shown in educational applications of the learning theory known as *behaviorism.* B. F. Skinner, the psychologist, developed a stimulus-response (S→R) model based on the principle that learning takes place through a series of small steps in which the learner must actively participate. With success in learning, the student is immediately rewarded. The application of the psychological concepts of *feedback* and *reinforcement* (see page 103) leads to what is called *operant conditioning.*

This theory led to the "programmed instruction" movement in the 1960s which established useful guidelines for organizing individualized, self-paced instruction in precise ways so that learning would take place successfully. Of all the developments in recent years, the theoretical view of learning proposed by Skinner and its applications through programmed instruction have been most influential for the emergence of the instructional design process. During this period, practitioners identified a number of elements that require attention for designing comprehensive instruction. These include: writing objectives (see Bloom, Krathwohl, Mager, Popham); organizing subject content, analyzing tasks, encoding and decoding information, and setting conditions for learning (see Gagné, Glaser, Travers); recognizing contributions of audiovisual media and other forms of technology for instruction (see Dale, Finn,[3] Hoban, Allen);

[3] Ronald J. McBeath, *Extending Education Through Technology.*

devising self-paced and individualized learning methods (see Postlethwait, Keller); and evaluating learning (see Bloom, Stufflebeam, Popham).

As the importance of all these features is recognized, we become better prepared to answer the question: "What is the best way to plan instruction so that the goals of a program can be met effectively in the shortest period of time?" The answer is to integrate, in a systematic manner, the many elements that require attention. This leads to the use of a comprehensive instructional design plan.

REVIEW*

A. Recall

1. For instruction to be successful, *four* things need to happen. Paraphrase a statement of each one.

a. _____

b. _____

c. _____

d. _____

2. Define these terms:

a. Systems approach

_____

b. Instructional technology (two meanings)

(1) _____

(2) _____

c. Instructional development

_____

d. Instructional design process

_____

3. Check those of the following which have contributed to the emergence of the instructional design concept.
   - ___ *a.* programmed instruction
   - ___ *b.* evaluation of learning
   - ___ *c.* computer graphics
   - ___ *d.* organizing subject content
   - ___ *e.* international education
   - ___ *f.* writing objectives
   - ___ *g.* psychology of human learning
   - ___ *h.* competency-based instruction
   - ___ *i.* mastery learning
   - ___ *j.* analyzing tasks
   - ___ *k.* methods of individualized learning

B. Comprehension
1. Think back on your own experiences when you were a student.
   a. Can you recall an instructional situation that you felt at the time to be very *successful?* What do you believe made it so?

   _____
   _____
   _____

   b. Try to recall another instructional situation that was *unsuccessful.* What made it so?

   _____
   _____
   _____

2. To which one of the four indicators of a successful instructional program (the answer for question A.1) does each following situation relate?
   - ___ *a.* Reactions are very positive toward the program from instructors who teach it.
   - ___ *b.* Many students have inquired whether a followup course, employing the same self-paced learning method, will be offered.
   - ___ *c.* At the end of the course, results showed that 88 percent of the students had accomplished 95 percent of the objectives.
   - ___ *d.* For the first time, students completed their assignments consistently on time and had voluntarily engaged in optional activities.
   - ___ *e.* The program that formerly required two weeks was completed by trainees in 8 days.
   - ___ *f.* The technician and aides helping with the course have offered useful suggestions for improving aspects of the instructional program.
   - ___ *g.* When employees returned to their jobs after training, their supervisors rated each person as being highly competent in the new skills.

3. To which component of *instructional technology* does each of the following relate?
   - ___ *a.* Carrying through the procedure of: planning a new training program, producing necessary slides and printed materials, writing the student workbook and instructor's guide, trying out the program, making revisions, and preparing for full-scale use.
   - ___ *b.* Developing and using a computer/video interactive program.
   - ___ *c.* Writing objectives, deciding on activities, and preparing tests—all for a course to be taught.

REFERENCES

Allen, William H. "Audio-Visual Materials," *Review of Educational Research,* 26 (April 1956), 125–156.

———. "Media Stimulus and Types of Learning," *Audiovisual Instruction,* 12 (January 1967), 27–31.

Bloom, Benjamin S., et al. *A Taxonomy of Educational Objectives. Handbook I: The Cognitive Domain* (New York: Longman, 1956).

Dale, Edgar. *Audiovisual Methods in Teaching* (New York: Holt, Rinehart, and Winston, 1969).

Gagné, Robert. *The Conditions of Learning* (New York: Holt, Rinehart, and Winston, 1965).

Glaser, Robert. "Psychological Bases for Instructional Design," *AV Communications Review,* 14 (Winter 1966), 433–449.

Grant, Gerald, et al. *On Competence: A Critical Analysis of Competency-Based Reforms in Higher Education* (San Francisco: Jossey-Bass, 1979).

Hoban, Charles F. "Research and Reality," *AV Communications Review,* 4 (Winter 1956), 3–20.

———. "The Usable Residue of Educational Film Research," *New Teaching Aids for the American Classroom* (Stanford, CA: The Institute for Communications Research, 1960), 95–115.

Keller, Fred S. "Goodbye Teacher . . ." *Journal of Applied Behavioral Analysis,* 1 (1968), 79–89.

Kimpston, Richard, and Harlan Hanson. "Accountability—Doing What They Say," *Educational Leadership,* 39 no. 4 (January 1982), 274–275.

Krathwohl, David R., et al. *A Taxonomy of Educational Objectives. Handbook II: Affective Domain* (New York: Longman, 1964).

Mager, Robert F. *Preparing Objectives for Programmed Instruction* (Belmont, CA: Fearon, 1962).

McBeath, Ronald J. *Extending Education Through Technology: Selected Writings of James D. Finn* (Washington, DC: Association for Educational Communications and Technology, 1972).

Nickse, Ruth, editor. *Competency-Based Education* (New York: Teachers College, Columbia University, 1981).

Popham, A. James. *Criterion-Referenced Measurement* (Englewood Cliffs, NJ: Educational Technology Publications, 1971).

———. "Probing the Validity of Arguments Against Behavioral Goals," in *Current Research in Instruction,* Richard C. Anderson, ed. (Englewood Cliffs, NJ: Prentice-Hall, 1969).

Postlethwait, S.N., et al. *The Audio-Tutorial Approach to Learning* (Minneapolis: Burgess, 1969).

Shrock, Sharon A., and William C. Coscarelli. "Some Sources of the Art, Craft, and Science Views of Instructional Development," *NSPI Journal,* 20 (September 1981), 26, 27, 48.

Skinner, B.F. *The Technology of Teaching* (New York: Appleton-Century-Crofts, 1968).

Stakenas, Robert C., and Roger Kaufman. *Technology in Education: Its Human Potential (Fastback 163)* (Bloomington, IN: Phi Delta Kappa Educational Foundation, 1981).

Stufflebeam, Daniel L. *An Application of PERT to Test Development* (Columbus, OH: School of Education, Ohio State University, 1964).

Travers, Robert. *Essentials of Learning: An Overview for Students of Education* (New York: Macmillan, 1963).

————. *Research and Theory Relating to Audiovisual Information Transmission* (Salt Lake City, UT: Bureau of Educational Research, University of Utah, 1964).

chapter 2

The Instructional Design Process

How would you answer this question: "If you were about to start planning a new unit in a course or training program, to what matter would you *first* give attention? Here is how various individuals might answer:

Primary grade teacher: "I think first about the children. How important is the topic for them? Then, how well prepared are they to study it (physically, emotionally, intellectually)?"

High school teacher: "I'd start by writing down what I want to accomplish in teaching the unit. This becomes the goal around which I'll plan the instruction."

College professor: "My approach is to list the content that needs to be covered relative to the selected topic. This would include the terms, definitions, concepts, and principles that I feel need to be communicated to my students."

Industrial trainer: "It's important to start by listing the competencies I expect trainees to have after receiving instruction on the topic. These would be the outcomes or objectives to be accomplished."

Media specialist: "I always try to determine to what degree the topic might be treated with television or another media format. By doing this, I will be prepared with a suggestion if the instructor calls me for assistance."

The foregoing replies represent a sampling of possible approaches that might be taken as different individuals initiate their instructional planning. There could be other replies to the question. For example, one community college instructor always starts by writing the final examination for a new unit! He believes that passing the final exam is the students' greatest concern. Therefore, he writes questions which indicate what should receive emphasis in his teaching. His reasoning seems plausible.

As you read the above replies to the question, as well as formulate your own answer, two conclusions should become apparent. First, a number of different considerations appeal to educators and trainers as each one starts planning. Second, each of us selects an order or sequence of our own in which to treat these elements.

KEY ELEMENTS OF THE INSTRUCTIONAL DESIGN PROCESS

Of the planning elements identified in the quoted statements above, *four* are fundamental in the instructional design process. You will find them treated in almost every planning model. They can be represented by answers to these questions:

1. For whom is the program being developed? (characteristics of *learners* or *trainees*)
2. What do you want the learners or trainees to learn or be able to do? (objectives)
3. How is the subject content or skill best learned? (teaching/learning *methods* and *activities*)
4. How do you determine the extent to which the learning has been achieved? (*evaluation* procedures)

These four fundamental elements—learners, objectives, methods and evaluation—form the framework for systematic instructional planning (see Figure 2.1).

These elements are interrelated and could conceivably comprise an entire instructional design plan. In actuality, there are additional components which should require attention and which, when integrated with the basic four, form a complete instructional design model. The following section introduces ten

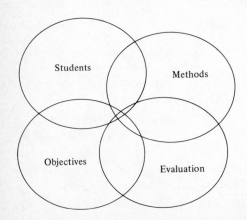

Figure 2.1

elements of the instructional design process necessary for a comprehensive design plan.

THE COMPLETE INSTRUCTIONAL DESIGN PLAN

These ten elements should receive attention in a comprehensive instructional design plan:

1. Assess *learning needs* for designing an instructional program; state *goals, constraints,* and *priorities* that must be recognized.
2. Select *topics* or *job tasks* to be treated and indicate *general purposes* to be served.
3. Examine *characteristics* of *learners* or *trainees* which should receive attention during planning.
4. Identify *subject content* and analyze *task* components relating to stated goals and purposes.
5. State *learning objectives* to be accomplished in terms of subject content and task components.
6. Design *teaching/learning activities* to accomplish the stated objectives.
7. Select *resources* to support instructional activities.
8. Specify *support services* required for developing and implementing activities and acquiring or producing materials.
9. Prepare to *evaluate learning* and outcomes of the program.
10. Determine preparation of learners or trainees to study the topic by *pretesting* them.

The ten elements of this instructional design plan can be illustrated by the diagram shown in Figure 2.2.

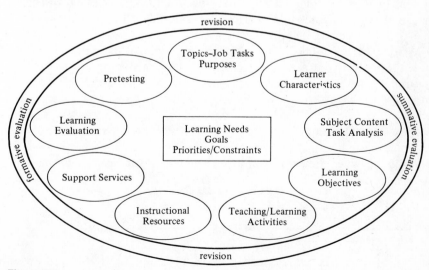

Figure 2.2

The starting place for instructional planning should be to decide if an instructional design is appropriate for a potential project. Thus, in the diagram you find the first element placed at the center of the model.

Although the list of ten elements forms a logical sequence as illustrated, the order in which you address the individual elements is not predetermined. It is for this reason that the oval pattern is used. An oval does not have a specific starting point. Recall the various answers to the question asked at the beginning of this chapter. Each person may proceed through the instructional design process in his or her own preferred way, starting with one element or another, and following whatever order is felt to be logical or suitable.

In the above diagram, the elements are *not* connected with lines or arrows. Connections could indicate a sequential, linear order. The intent is to convey flexibility in the way the ten elements may be used. Also, in some instances you may find it unnecessary to treat all ten elements. For example, in some programs assessing learning needs, pretesting, or listing subject content may not be considered necessary.

Another reason for using the oval form is that there is an interdependence among the ten elements. Decisions relating to one may affect others. As learning objectives are stated, items of subject content may be added or reordered. Or, while selecting teaching/learning activities, the intent of a learning objective may become clearer than as initially stated and require revision. Consequently, the procedure recommended permits and encourages flexibility in the selection of elements and in the order of their treatment. This procedure allows for additions and changes as the instructional design plan takes shape.

Many instructional design models identify and use features similar to those described in this book. Such models are often represented by a diagram with boxes and arrows as a series of steps in a sequence, as shown in Figure 2.3. The intent of this type of model is to establish a 1–2–3 sequential order. In actual use, the process often does not take place in such a linear way. The open, circular pattern seems more appropriate and useful.

As you gain experience with using this instructional design plan, you no doubt will establish your own arrangement of components for the design of a course. But even when following a sequence with which you are comfortable, adjustments will have to be made. Be prepared for them and handle them in stride.

The word "element" is used as a label for each of the ten parts of our instructional design plan. This is preferable to the terms *step, stage, level,* or *sequential item,* which are expressions in keeping with the linear concept.

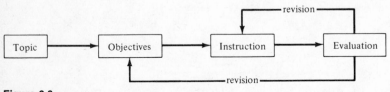

Figure 2.3

Another part of our diagram is the indication of *revision* around the elements. This illustrates the feedback feature which allows for changes in the content or treatment of elements at any time during development. The treatment of elements may require revisions when, for example, data about learning are collected during instructional tryouts (called "formative evaluation") or at the end of a course offering (called "summative evaluation"). If you want learners to be successful, which means their accomplishment of learning objectives at a satisfactory level of proficiency, then you will want to improve any weak parts of the program as they are discovered.

Various expressions have been used to label or title systematic instructional planning. In addition to the term *instructional design* (often abbreviated as I.D.) used in this book, you will find reference to the following in the literature:

- Instructional systems
- Instructional systems design
- Instructional systems development
- Learning systems design
- Competency-based instruction
- Criterion-referenced instruction
- Performance technology

PREMISES UNDERLYING THE INSTRUCTIONAL DESIGN PROCESS

In order to understand the process and to apply it successfully, a number of basic premises should be recognized. These premises can influence both your thinking and your treatment of the instructional design plan.

> *Premise 1:* The instructional design process requires attention to both a *systematic* procedure and a *specificity* for treating details within the plan.

Systematic refers to an orderly, logical method of *identifying, developing* and *evaluating* a set of strategies aimed at attaining a particular instructional goal. This is accomplished by utilizing the ten interrelating elements which comprise the instructional design plan.

The treatment of each element requires exacting mental effort. Application of each element of the plan should take place by giving attention to precise details. This means being *specific*. For example, a learning objective is a statement that includes a particular verb which both guides a learning activity and indicates how achievement will be evaluated. The details of a learning activity—with the description of certain required student participation— chosen to accomplish an objective is another indication of the specific treatment required when implementing the instructional design process.

Attention to detail is critical for the success of any instructional design work. By applying *systematic* procedures and being attentive to *specific* details, you can provide for effective learning.

> *Premise 2:* The instructional design process is most applicable at the course-development level.

Decisions about curricula and broad goals for a school or training program precede the design of specific courses. Although instructional designers can help administrators, managers, and committees to make decisions about the purposes, directions, and emphasis of a program, instructional design work usually starts with an identification of the instruction or training needs to be served. Then what follows is the selection of units or topics comprising a course. This is followed with the development of instructional components relating to the various planning elements.

> *Premise 3:* An instructional design plan is primarily developed for use by the instructor and planning team.

Some people believe that all details developed during planning (like for a lesson plan) are to be given to learners, often in the form of a study guide. This is not true. Many of the items written as elements in the plan will be used by the learners, but not always in the form or order in which they are being developed and stated. While learners should be given a list of the learning objectives for a unit, they do not necessarily receive the subject content outline or sequence steps that were important to the planning team while deriving the objectives.

Also, the order in which elements are being treated during planning may differ substantially from the order in which they are eventually used with the learners. For example, a pretest might be developed after the final examination has been devised (as shown in the diagram of the plan on page 11), but students will complete it prior to the start of instruction.

> *Premise 4:* In the instructional design process, the goal is to devise a procedure which enhances learning.

Traditionally, teaching has been the most important activity in an instructional program. An instructional design plan allows the instructor to devise methods for successful learning, while learners must take major responsibility for accomplishing the goals of instruction. Learning is accomplished individually by each learner or trainee. Therefore, whether learners are taught in a class or individually, activities should be so designed that each person is actively engaged in the learning process.

> *Premise 5:* The instructional design process is more effective when major attention is given to designing instruction for individual use rather than for group instruction.

This premise follows directly from premise 4 above. While there are times when lectures and other presentations to classes and opportunities for small group activities may be necessary, plans for individualized, learner-paced methods, like the development of self-study modules, should receive major attention. Consideration needs to be given to the use of various nontraditional approaches to instruction. This is one reason why flexibility in planning is so important.

Premise 6: While planning, every effort should be made to provide for a level of satisfactory learning for all students.

A study was made which concluded that up to 95 percent of all public school students can accomplish what is required of them if each individual has suitable academic background, appropriate instruction, and sufficient time for learning (Bloom, see footnote on page 16). It has been documented that if a student is prepared to learn and puts forth the effort to study, but is unsuccessful in learning, the shortcoming can be overcome if attention is given to a more careful design of the instructional plan. This justifies the need to test a plan before its implementation, as indicated by the outer *revision* oval shown in the instructional design model.

Premise 7: There is no single "best" way to design instruction.

By applying the instructional design process, a reliance on intuition or trial-and-error in planning can be reduced. Yet the instructional design process has not reached a level of scientific exactness. Many paths can be conceived to reach the same goals and objectives. Instructors and designers are unique individuals, just as learners are unique. Each designer will formulate activities and apply elements of the instructional design plan in an individual way. The proof of the success of an instructional design plan will be whether a satisfactory level of learning is achieved.

BENEFITS OF AN INSTRUCTIONAL DESIGN PROCESS

In order for any enterprise to be successful, those who are involved in the endeavor must derive some benefit. In a business operation this means that the owner makes a profit, the customer is satisfied with the price and quality of the product or service, and the worker or craftsman receives sufficient pay while feeling a sense of pride in workmanship. For those of us associated with teaching and learning, there must be equal benefits:

- The *administrator* or *program manager* wants evidence of effective and efficient learning within an acceptable cost base. (The time is past when we could say, "It looks like a good program" or, "It's acceptable because the students certainly enjoyed the course." We need hard evidence of success.)

- The *instructional designer* wants evidence that a satisfactory program has been designed. The best indication is the accomplishment of program objectives by learners within an appropriate time period.
- The *teacher* or *instructor* wants to see learners gain the required competencies and also wants personally to develop a positive relationship with learners.
- Learners want to be successful in their learning and also to find the experience of learning to be a pleasant, satisfying one.

When the design of an instructional program follows the procedures outlined in this book, or those of another suitable model, these benefits can be realized. In other words, by employing the instructional design process, your goals can be accomplished. The acceptance of the instructional development function as important to an organization will be recognized only when satisfactory results like those specified above are reached.

Additional evidence in support of the benefits for systematic planning comes from Bloom.[1] After analyzing numerous research studies conducted over a 20-year period that were designed to test various ways of improving instruction in schools, he reached this conclusion:

> It is possible for 95 percent of our students to learn all that the school has to teach, at a satisfactory level of accomplishment. The level of learning of a student is determined by the student's learning history (prior level of achievement and affective behaviors) and the quality of instruction received.

The implications of Bloom's conclusion is that successful learning will result for the great majority of learners if the instructional program is carefully designed and factors relating to individual learner characteristics are taken into consideration. This can be equally true for either an academic or a vocational training program.

Finally, attitudinal benefits for learners may be of equal importance to measurable, material results. Here are statements made by college students when they were asked to express their opinions after completing a new, self-paced learning program (audio-tutorial method) in general biology that had been designed in a systematic manner:

> "I appreciate the opportunity given by this course to finally learn at my own pace."

> "I thoroughly enjoy the atmosphere, as well as the approach to learning, here. If there were more like this instructor, students might really learn to like learning for their own benefit and not just for the grade."

> "I probably wouldn't even bother studying this stuff, but the way the material is presented is a very good incentive to study."

[1]Benjamin Bloom, *Human Characteristics and School Learning.*

"I really think this whole setup is great! I feel as if I am contributing to my learning instead of passively sitting in a lecture and falling asleep."

"I really learn here. Not just for the tests. I remember and understand what is covered."

APPLYING THE PROCESS TO BOTH ACADEMIC EDUCATION AND TRAINING PROGRAMS

An instructional program designed as a course for vocational preparation or on-the-job training requires a different emphasis from that required in an academic course—elementary, secondary, or college level. For vocational or specific job training, the program must stress the teaching of knowledge or skills required for the performance of specific tasks. The anticipated outcomes are easily identified and may be taught directly. On the other hand, an instructional program for academic education encompasses knowledge and skills for which the end point, or final application, may be uncertain. Learners are being prepared to use whatever they may learn for any number of personal, social, or possible future vocational needs. *Regardless of the goals of a course, instructional planning requires the same overall thought process with attention to similar design elements.*

The identical principles of learning apply to structuring experiences for individuals whether one is to study history or to become a qualified carpenter. While the emphasis, certain details, and terminology differ, both situations treat similar elements of the instructional design plan. Thus, the procedures presented in this book can be effective for either an academic or a training situation. Where particulars differ, special explanations and examples will be included in either the academic instruction or the planning for training.

WHO'S WHO IN THE INSTRUCTIONAL DESIGN PROCESS

As you prepare to study the instructional design process, you will want to view it from your own perspective. What will be your role in planning? What specific responsibilities might you have? What relationship do you have with other persons in your organization who are involved in aspects of teaching or training? These are all matters you should keep in mind as you study the elements of the instructional design process.

In Chapter 14 we will examine in detail the roles and responsibilities of those persons engaging in instructional planning, development, implementation, and evaluation. However, at this point, you should recognize that there are *four* essential roles to be performed during instructional planning. You may be expected to fill one or more of these positions.

- *Instructional designer*—A person responsible for carrying out and coordinating the planning work; competent in managing all aspects of the instructional design process.

- *Instructor*—A person (or member of a team) for and with whom the instruction is being planned; well-informed about the learners to be taught, the teaching procedures, and the requirements of the instructional program; with guidance from the designer, capable of carrying out details of many planning elements; responsible for trying out and then implementing the instructional plan that is developed.
- *Subject specialist*—A person qualified to provide information about content and resources relating to all aspects of the topics for which instruction is to be designed; responsible for checking accuracy of content treatment in activities, materials, and examinations.
- *Evaluator*—A person qualified to assist the staff in developing testing instruments for pretesting and for evaluating student learning (posttesting); responsible for gathering and interpreting data during program tryouts and for determining effectiveness and efficiency of the program when fully implemented.

ANSWERING THE CRITICS

"Doesn't the instructional design process discourage creativity in teaching?" "Isn't it actually a mechanistic rather than a humanistic method of instructional planning?" These and similar questions are frequently raised and need to be realistically answered. You should make up your own mind about how to answer them after completing your study of this book. Here is the author's position in answering these questions.

If *creativity* means formulating, developing, and expressing new ideas and original thoughts as ways to solve problems, then the instructional design process allows for creativity. The process is flexible, meaning that the elements can be developed in many different orders or arrangements. Numerous opportunities are available for expressing one's own ideas and independent thinking in unique ways while planning. Creativity can apply to both the planning that takes place while designing instruction and the selection of learning activities. In this process, you can be as creative as you wish, even to the extent of providing open-ended learning experiences for learners.

A *humanistic* method of instruction is one that recognizes the individual learner (student or trainee) in terms of his or her own capabilities, individual differences, present ability levels, and personal development. It should be apparent that these matters do receive attention in the instructional design process. Elements of the process include an examination of learner characteristics and an identification of readiness levels for learning. Furthermore, the application of systematic planning for designing various forms of individualized or self-paced learning also can allow for various individualized styles of learning.

Philosophically, as the planning starts, the instructional designer or instructor should mentally say this:

> "I am designing a program of learning experiences for learners so that *together* we will be successful in accomplishing the stated goals and objectives. While it is important for each person to learn, it is equally important for *me* that the learner becomes proficient."

Therefore, the approach taken should be one of cooperation among learners (and with the instructor) rather than of competition. Grading is determined by accomplishment against a standard set by the objectives.

The ideas expressed above certainly are unconventional. Many persons in education and training would react strongly to such statements. Both present beliefs and past experiences would cause these persons to deny the argument. Only when an individual becomes dissatisfied with present practices (or results) and starts to identify the need to change might the criticism cease. Only by expressing either an interest or a readiness to try something new can the door be opened to experimentation. Then the person can be informed of potential benefits for applying the instructional design process, with its many options.

By providing explanations and offering opportunities, as described in this chapter, criticism of the instructional design process can be countered. Then receptivity to this method of instructional planning might be encouraged.

QUESTIONS . . . QUESTIONS . . . QUESTIONS

As you read and study the following chapters, you will frequently see questions being raised or referred to in relation to the topic under consideration. Such questions may appear at the beginning of a chapter to indicate the important matters that will follow. Then, as the discussion proceeds, other questions help to direct thinking toward decisions that must be made.

An instructional designer continually probes for clarification, explanations, and details. You must help the persons with whom you carry out instructional planning to communicate effectively with you. This can best be done by the use of questions. Therefore, pay particular attention to the questions raised throughout the book. Then let questioning become a common part of your behavior as you explore and eventually practice the instructional designer role.

REVIEW*

A. Recall
    1. What are the four essential elements in instructional planning?

      a. _____
         _____
         _____

      b. _____
         _____
         _____

      c. _____
         _____
         _____

      d. _____
         _____
         _____

*See answers on page 249.

2. List the additional six elements that are in the Kemp instructional design plan.

   a. _____
   _____
   _____

   b. _____
   _____
   _____

   c. _____
   _____
   _____

   d. _____
   _____
   _____

   e. _____
   _____
   _____

   f. _____
   _____
   _____

3. What is the other feature that appears in the diagram of this plan? What is its purpose?

   _____
   _____
   _____

4. The author states that the design plan is "flexible" in its use. For what three reasons is it considered so?

   a. _____
   _____
   _____

   b. _____
   _____
   _____

   c. _____
   _____
   _____

5. What word best describes how the order of elements is treated in many other design plans?

   _____
   _____
   _____

6. What does *I.D.* mean? _____
   _____
   _____

7. There are other terms used in place of I.D. What might these abbreviations mean?

   a. CRI _____
   _____
   _____

    b. ISD _____

_____

_____

    c. LSD _____

_____

_____

    d. CBI _____

_____

_____

8. Which statements are *true* with respect to the premises underlying the instructional design process?

  _____ *a.* A good design plan should result in satisfactory student learning.

  _____ *b.* The process starts with broad curricula decisions being made by the instructional designer for a training program.

  _____ *c.* Do not get bogged down with details.

  _____ *d.* Devising good teaching methods is the main purpose of instructional planning.

  _____ *e.* Because the Kemp plan is a "good" one, everyone using it should follow the same sequence of steps.

  _____ *f.* Some parts of an I.D. plan are not shown to students.

  _____ *g.* The I.D. process can be most effective when designed primarily for student self-paced study activities.

9. What are the two most common arguments against using the I.D. process for instructional planning?

    a. _____

_____

_____

    b. _____

_____

_____

10. Which statements refer to *education,* which to *training,* and which are related to *both* education and training?

  _____ *a.* immediately applicable objectives

  _____ *b.* more task oriented

  _____ *c.* may serve one's personal needs

  _____ *d.* for student's future needs

  _____ *e.* goals more easily identified

  _____ *f.* requires attention to most elements in an I.D. plan

11. What are four primary roles that need to be filled for carrying out the I.D. process?

    a. _____

_____

_____

    b. _____

_____

_____

    c. _____

_____

_____

d. _____

_____

_____

12. According to information in this chapter, what is one of the important practices that an instructional designer uses when working with an instructor or client?

_____

_____

_____

B. Comprehension

1. After reading this chapter and seeing the instructional design diagram on page 11, with what element would you like to start your instructional planning? Then, with which other elements, in what order, would you proceed?

_____

_____

2. On a separate piece of paper briefly note the content of each of the seven premises underlying the I.D. process. To which premise does each of the following relate?

_____ *a.* Examining training needs in a company can be the starting point for using the I.D. process.

_____ *b.* At the end of a training program you conclude that satisfactory learning took place for most students.

_____ *c.* Carefully spelling out detail when planning an element of the plan.

_____ *d.* As a designer you are working on two projects. You find it necessary to use the plan differently with each team of instructors.

_____ *e.* Going through the planning process in a logical way.

_____ *f.* The emphasis in a course is shifted to activities for student self-paced learning.

_____ *g.* You developed what you felt to be a good design plan (with evidence from the tryout). The first two semesters of use were satisfactory. Then you had a class with members who put out little effort. As a result, learning was low.

_____ *h.* Decisions about reasons for selecting activities and resources in order to accomplish objectives are important only to those engaged in planning.

_____ *i.* Relating the facts in one element of planning to fine points in another element.

3. What are some of the things you would do in planning an instructional program in order to overcome the positions some people take relative to the following:

a. I.D. eliminates instructional creativity.

_____

_____

_____

_____

_____

b. I.D. is more mechanistic than humanistic.

_____

_____

_____

_____

4. Which one or more of the roles described near the end of the chapter do you expect to fill?

_____

_____

_____

5. What benefits to you personally would you anticipate by becoming involved in I.D. work?

_____

_____

_____

_____

_____

6. In broad terms, what would you expect to do differently if you were an instructional designer planning in these two situations?
  a. Working with a teacher to develop a course for use in an elementary school.

_____

_____

_____

  b. Working with a subject specialist to develop a sales training program for a company.

_____

_____

_____

REFERENCES

Andrews, Dee H., and Ludwika A. Goodson. "A Comparative Analysis of Models of Instructional Design," *Journal of Instructional Development,* 3 (Summer 1980), 2–16.

Bloom, Benjamin. *Human Characteristics and School Learning* (New York: McGraw-Hill, 1976).

Briggs, Leslie, ed. *Instructional Design: Principles and Applications* (Englewood Cliffs, NJ: Educational Technology Publications, 1977).

Butler, F. Coit. *Instructional Systems Development for Vocational and Technical Training* (Englewood Cliffs, NJ: Educational Technology Publications, 1972).

Cannon, John R., et al. *Training Delivery Skills: I. Preparing the Training Delivery* (Amherst, MA: Human Resource Development Press, 1984).

Davies, Ivor K. *Competency Based Learning: Technology, Management, and Design* (New York: McGraw-Hill, 1973).

Davis, Robert H., Lawrence T. Alexander, and Stephen Yelon. *Learning Systems Design: An Approach to the Improvement of Instruction* (New York: McGraw-Hill, 1974).

Diamond, Robert M., et al. *Instructional Development for Individualized Learning in Higher Education* (Englewood Cliffs, NJ: Educational Technology Publications, 1975).

Dick, Walter, and Lou Carey. *The Systematic Design of Instruction* (Glenview, IL: Scott, Foresman, 1978).

Feldhusen, John F. "The Three-Stage Model of Course Design," volume 39, in *The Instructional Design Library,* Danny Langdon, ed. (Englewood Cliffs, NJ: Educational Technology Publications, 1980).

Gagné, Robert M., and Leslie J. Briggs. *Principles of Instructional Design* (New York: Holt, Rinehart, and Winston, 1979).

Grant, Gerald, et al. *On Competence: A Critical Analysis of Competency-Based Reforms in Higher Education* (San Francisco: Jossey-Bass, 1979).

Mager, Robert F., and Kenneth M. Beach. *Developing Vocational Instruction* (Belmont, CA: Pitman, 1967).

Nadler, Leonard. *Designing Training Programs: The Critical Events Model* (Menlo Park, CA: Addison-Wesley, 1982).

Nickse, Ruth, ed. *Competency-Based Education* (New York: Teachers College, Columbia University, 1981).

Posner, George J., and Alan N. Rudnitsky. *Course Design: A Guide to Curriculum Development for Teachers,* 2d ed (New York: Longman, 1982).

Reigeluth, Charles M., ed. *Instructional-Design Theories and Models: An Overview of their Current Status* (Hillsdale, NJ: Lawrence Erlbaum Associates; 1983).

Romiszowski, A.J. *Designing Instructional Systems* (New York: Nichols, 1981).

chapter 3

Learning Needs and Instructional Goals

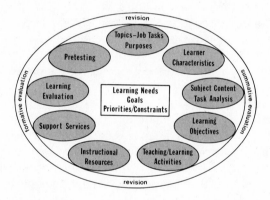

"What problems do you face with a present course, or company operations or services?"

"How well are the goals for a training course now being met?"

"Is there an immediate need for any new courses in your program?"

"How do you decide whether education or training is the solution for a problem?"

"Once an instructional need is identified, how do you initiate a plan for serving it?"

We learned in school that human beings have a number of basic needs which must be satisfied. These needs are food, water, clothing, shelter, and economic security. Most daily activities are devoted to satisfying these needs.

Beyond the basic needs, the motivation for action in various endeavors is based on a desire to satisfy interests and needs at a higher level. Political polls, census reports, market surveys for commercial products, and studies on aspects of the future all reveal trends and identify needs which serve as the bases for various actions that may lead to the introduction of new programs. The procedures that have been established through social research and similar information-gathering methods provide the patterns for identifying problems and needs which may justify initiating instructional design projects.

Questions like those raised above are often the starting point for deciding whether the instructional design process should be applied. The expressions *learning needs, learning assessment, learning needs analysis,* or *front-end analysis* are used to represent this initial planning activity.

WHY INITIATE AN INSTRUCTIONAL DESIGN PROJECT?

You might simply answer this question by stating, "Because I want to!" Or someone from management might say, "We need a new course on safety. You develop it." Sometimes there is a *wish* expressed, rather than an identified need, such as "I wish to teach a new course in radiotherapy simulators." These are all subjective reasons why an instructional planning project might be initiated. Each statement expresses a legitimate reason for starting a project, yet decisions based on opinions, preferences, and arbitrary positions need to be examined carefully before being accepted. Objective, justifiable reasons, often with quantitative data, should be found to support a proposed project. Only by carefully establishing the validity of a *wish* can the purposes for the project be clarified and become rationally acceptable to those who must make the decision for proceeding. How is this done?

A preferable way for deciding whether to initiate an instructional project is to do two things. First, find out what (if anything) is going on now in the area of your concern or interest. This may include an examination of present courses or an analysis of what is taking place elsewhere (within the organization or outside). Second, match the data collected against what should be happening. The discrepancy between *what is* and *what is desired* or *ought to be* (or, saying it another way, as a question—"How well are the purposes of a course now being met?") can be the best reason for deciding whether or not to proceed with planning an instructional design project.

Some of the reasons that justify an instructional design project are:

- Levels of student learning and/or performance are below what is expected.
- Costs for an instructional program are too high.
- Training period or time required by trainers is longer than desired.
- A wish to change methods of instruction is expressed (often from conventional classroom lectures to more flexible, individualized, self-paced learning methods).
- Students or trainees express consistent dissatisfaction with a course or program.
- Evidence from the literature, recommendations from recognized experts, and reports from other programs indicate the need for changes.
- Present content in a course or program needs additions or revision.
- A large number of new employees, without sufficient experience, are to be assigned to a working group.

- Job requirements in an organization or in the field have changed, or new equipment and procedures are to be used.
- A course or program is now being conducted at a level which assumes that students are better prepared than they are in actuality.
- Program changes are required for administrative reasons (budget limitations, training mandated, personnel cutbacks, and so forth).

Any one or more of the above reasons, with supporting evidence, can justify the need for an instructional design project.

WHEN MAY A NEED *NOT* BE AN INSTRUCTIONAL DESIGN NEED?

When changes or growth are required in knowledge, skills, or attitudes of students or employees, an education or training program often becomes important. However, there are times when, on careful examination of the situation, the need cannot be clearly identified as one primarily requiring an instructional solution. What is revealed, however subtle, may be:

- A personnel matter (instructor's attitude, poor teaching skills or lack of preparation by the instructor, low employee morale, poor supervision, a communication failure).
- A procedural matter (production bottleneck, inadequate directions for work, inappropriate work standards).
- Lack of suitable recognition (low pay, few benefits or rewards for individuals).
- An organizational or management problem (unclear staff responsibilities, poor management attitude toward the value of training).
- Insufficient support for training caused by inadequate money, facilities, personnel, equipment, or instructional time.
- External influences or situations beyond immediate or local control (policies, regulations, accreditation requirements).

If you find evidence that any of these conditions are influencing either the request for a new instructional program or hindering the success of a program underway, then steps should be taken to overcome the existing problem by appropriate action *before* spending time to apply the instructional design process. Unless these underlying deficiencies are corrected, any program—old or new—could be destined to failure.[1]

GATHERING DATA IN SUPPORT OF A NEED

There are various ways of gathering information, either to determine whether the need for a new instructional project does exist, or to support the modification of a present program. Kaufman groups assessment procedures into two

[1] For help in recognizing when a problem is not a training problem see Robert F. Mager and Peter Pipe, *Analyzing Performance Problems or "You Really Oughta Wanna!"*

categories—*internal* assessment procedures and *external* assessment procedures.[2]

Internal Assessment Procedures

Data may be gathered from sources within the institution or organization by various means, which include:

- Analyzing student test results and performance ratings.
- Interviewing instructors and other staff members as to their observations and impressions about student competencies and attitudes.
- Talking with former students and employees concerning their own impressions and judgments as to the value and success of a program and also the needs they recognize which could be served through training.
- Obtaining recommendations or receiving "orders" from management or other staff for initiating a training effort.
- Examining company records to determine efficiency of operation, production and sales levels, personnel turnover rate, safety records, and other evidence as indicators of training needs.

Interpretation of internal assessment data must of necessity be done carefully. There is a tendency toward subjective analyses by individuals who are often directly involved in the program being assessed.

External Assessment Procedures

By visiting programs underway at other institutions and analyzing required knowledge, skills, and attitudes of individuals at work in an organization detailed external assessment can be made to supplement internal ones. The methods used may include:

- Interviewing education and/or training persons at other organizations, or managers, supervisors, and employees in job situations.
- Analyzing instructional programs at other institutions or on-the-job activities, and comparing them with the requirements of local training and educational objectives.
- Distributing a questionnaire to survey present practices and recognized needs in the field.

For an academic-type program, use of internal assessment procedures is most common. These should be supplemented with data collected from external sources, such as persons at other institutions, parents, business leaders, and legislators.

For job-oriented technical fields, useful information can be gathered from all sources, both internal and external. Particular attention should be given to

[2]Roger Kaufman, "Needs Assessment."

external assessment sources because of the continual need to be competitive and completely up to date relative to required knowledge and skill competencies of employees.

Regardless of the methods by which information is obtained, it should be analyzed for training (and other) needs as previously explained. This analysis requires reviewing, classifying, interpreting, and evaluating the data gathered and then judging what action will best serve the need or solve any problem found. This data-gathering process can be very brief and informal, or it can be extensive, requiring detailed summaries and statistical treatment. You must decide on the value, importance, and level of complexity for doing a needs assessment in your own situation.

SELECTING A TITLE AND SETTING INSTRUCTIONAL GOALS

Once a needs assessment is completed and the decision is made to proceed with instructional planning, give your project an identifying title or name. Then, one or more *general goals* should be set which briefly state, for both the members of the planning team and the anticipated learners, the intent of the course or program that would satisfy the identified needs.

A **goal** is a broad statement about the learning that will take place. It helps you determine the parameters of the course and, in general terms, informs others of the major aim of the program. Here are some goal statements for specific courses:

Financial Planning for Retirement   This course is designed for persons nearing retirement age who would like information about various types of investments and how to acquire stable, secure income for later years.

Nursing Care   This course, for first-year nursing students, includes the study and practice of basic psychomotor, observational, and cognitive skills used in providing direct care to individuals in a wide variety of settings. Emphasis is placed on assessment and maintenance of human functions using preventive and therapeutic techniques.

Art History   In this program, the general education student will become familiar with the important developments and key monuments in the history of Western art from the Renaissance to the present.

In these examples, notice that each instructional goal is expressed in broad terms, often with reference to the student group which is to be served. This is the general introduction for the program. It sets a direction for those who will carry out the planning. Specific purposes and objectives for the individual topics that will comprise the course will be treated in subsequent elements.

PRIORITIES AND CONSTRAINTS

Once the needs assessment is completed and goals for the program have been set, what is to be done should be clear: Revise portions of a program or course; redo or modify a completed program; plan a new program; or decide to continue with the present program as is. If the decision is made to revise or plan a new course, then consideration should be given to any priorities or limitations that can influence the planning and the resulting program.

Consider answering these questions:

- How will this program relate to other activities of the institution or the organization?
- By what date must the program be completed for use? (the time frame)
- What funds will be available for planning and development? (the monetary limits)
- What personnel will be available for planning and development? (See categories of personnel on page 150.)
- What services will be available for program development? (media needs, printing, etc.)
- What will be the anticipated level of administrative or management support for planning and development?

By seeking answers to these questions, you will determine their importance for the proposed course or program and the degree of support that can be anticipated. Thus you will be able to identify both the program's priority ranking and any constraints within which it must be designed.

SUMMARY

This chapter introduces a way to answer the fundamental question, "Where are we?" This leads to the next question, "Where do we want to be?" Assessing needs, recognizing that an educational or training need does exist, stating goals, and facing constraints are all important initial efforts as the start of the instructional design process.

In this instructional design plan, these matters are grouped together as parts of a single element. In the diagram on page 11, they are shown at the center of the plan. They provide a foundation upon which the other elements of the instructional design process can be structured.

REVIEW AND APPLICATIONS*

A. Recall
  1. What *two* things should be done before deciding to start an instructional design project?
  a. _____
  _____
  _____

*See answers on page 250.

b. _____
_____
_____

2. State five reasons you feel are important for which an instructional design project might be undertaken.

a. _____
_____
_____

b. _____
_____
_____
_____

c. _____
_____
_____

d. _____
_____
_____

e. _____
_____
_____

3. When evaluating the merits of a request to initiate a training course, list *four* reasons that might reveal training as *not* being the primary answer.

a. _____
_____
_____

b. _____
_____
_____

c. _____
_____
_____

d. _____
_____
_____

4. Indicate the *two* groupings into which ways of obtaining information relative to a training need can be placed. Then for each group list at least *two* data-gathering procedures.

a. _____
_____
_____

(1) _____
_____

(2) _____
_____

b. _____
_____
_____

(1) _____

_____

_____

(2) _____

_____

_____

5. What name is given to the first part of the element in the instructional design process to which all above questions relate?

_____

_____

_____

6. Based on your answer for question 5, what *two* things should then be done?

   a. _____

   _____

   _____

   b. _____

   _____

   _____

7. Which of the following are *goal statements?*

   ____ *a.* To improve the abilities of bank employees in handling emergency and security situations.

   ____ *b.* To discriminate by sound the calls of 12 local bird species with 80 percent accuracy.

   ____ *c.* To install wiring and component parts in electronic assemblies.

   ____ *d.* To gain an understanding and appreciation of the roles and expertise of health workers in the community who act on teams with community health nurses.

   ____ *e.* To master the fundamentals of data processing and be prepared to make applications of new information technologies.

   ____ *f.* To understand the organization and teaching methods of the course in American history.

B. Comprehension

Situation 1: As the result of a meeting attended by district managers of your company, in your role as training specialist you have been asked to look into a problem. A great deal of dissatisfaction was expressed at the meeting with the ineffective ways that department supervisors conduct meetings and make presentations before their staff. Most meetings, reportedly, took too long, were boring, and did not seem to give employees the necessary and correct information. These conclusions were drawn from three sources: lack of employee action on information requested by the personnel office, comments made on staff evaluation forms, and informal remarks received from employees.

You then attended some monthly staff meetings to confirm the conclusions. It was apparent that many department supervisors did conduct their meetings poorly and did not communicate effectively. A short time later you visited with a friend who held a training position with another company. When you mentioned the problem you were investigating, your friend explained that his company recently initiated a training program for middle managers and supervisors to overcome some of the same shortcomings you had identified. That program is proving to be effective.

The information you gathered led you to prepare a recommendation for planning a training program so that department supervisors would become capable of conducting staff meetings more effectively in a shorter period of time.

Questions:

1. What considerations make this a problem?

_____

_____

_____

2. In your judgment, does this problem properly lend itself to being solved through training?

_____

_____

_____

3. What supporting information was gathered from *internal* sources?

_____

_____

_____

4. Was information gathered from *external* sources? If so, what was it?

_____

_____

_____

5. What *goal* was established for the proposed training program?

_____

_____

_____

6. Were any constraints or priorities set?

_____

_____

_____

Situation 2: You coordinate the instructional development office at your college. A faculty member in the English department has proposed that a new course on technical writing be offered. It would treat the organization of specialized subject matter, and the writing of technical reports and other documents. He showed you the results of a survey he conducted among industrial companies in the community. There was a high level of interest in having many employees take such a course. Also, the curriculum committee of the English department strongly recommended initiating the course as an elective for students in the Schools of Business and Engineering.

The professor indicated he would like to design the course, with your help, in a nonconventional way by using self-paced learning methods in place of lectures. He would like to spend his time meeting with small groups of students to review and discuss their writing assignments. If the course could be developed for tryout next summer, he believes a financial grant might be obtained from a foundation to defray some developmental costs.

You contact the deans of Engineering and Business and received encouragement as to the value of the course for their students. The dean of the Engineering School would consider making it a required course for certain majors.

Questions:

1. Was a learning needs assessment made?

_____

_____

_____

2. If so, organize the results as if you were presenting a recommendation to proceed (*or* not to proceed) with the design of a new course in technical writing.

_____

_____

_____

3. What might be a statement of the goal for such a course?

_____

_____

_____

4. Are there any constraints or priorities that need consideration?

_____

_____

_____

Situation 3: You are the director of educational services for a large hospital. The hospital administrator has received a number of complaints, from both doctors and nurses, that custodians do not know their responsibilities and many do not have the necessary skills to perform their jobs properly, although each person completed an orientation session when first employed. You have been directed to design a complete training course for the custodians immediately so it can be used within a month. The course should be one day (8 hours) in length. There are no funding restrictions.

In conversation with the supervisor of custodian services, you are told that he also has heard some of the complaints. But he disagrees that the custodians do not know their jobs. He says the problem is that their pay is low and that other hospital personnel have such little respect for his people, that morale is poor and turnover rate is high.

Question:
How do you proceed?

_____

_____

_____

C. Application

This section of the review provides you with opportunities to apply the principles you learned from your study of the chapter. There are two activities for you to complete.

1. Sky Diving

In Appendix B (page 277) is descriptive information on the subject of sky diving. It will serve as the basis for this application activity and those in the following chapters. Glance through the information presented. It is not necessary to read those pages carefully at this time. Complete your work on separate paper.

a. Assume you are an instructional designer and have been asked to explore the possibility of developing a training program on sky diving. To what *two* matters would you possibly give attention for establishing a need as justification to initiate a training program?

_____

_____

_____

b. State a general goal for designing a program to teach the subject of sky diving.

_____

_____

_____

2. *Your Subject*

Select a subject or area of interest you would like to develop into an instructional course or training program. Explain how you would carry out a *learning needs* assessment. Include information and explain how you would gather data relative to as many sections of Chapter 3 as feasible to your situation. Include a statement of the *goal* for the course or program and specify any *constraints* or *priorities* to which attention should be given.

REFERENCES

Harless, Joe. *An Ounce of Analysis* (*Is Worth a Pound of Objectives*) (McLean, VA: Harless Performance Guild, 1974).

Kaufman, Roger. "Needs Assessment: Internal and External," *Journal of Instructional Development,* 1 (Fall 1977), 5–8.

Kaufman, Roger, and W. English Fenwick. *Needs Assessment: Concept and Application* (Englewood Cliffs, NJ: Educational Technology Publications, 1979).

Mager, Robert F., and Peter Pipe. *Analyzing Performance Problems or "You Really Oughta Wanna!"* (Belmont, CA: Pitman Learning, 1970).

Rossett, Allison. "A Typology for Generating Needs Assessment," *Journal of Instructional Development,* 6 (Fall 1982), 28–33.

Zemke, Ron, and Thomas Kramlinger. *Figuring Things Out: A Trainer's Guide to Needs and Task Analysis* (Menlo Park, CA: Addison-Wesley, 1982).

chapter *4*

Topics, Job Tasks and General Purposes

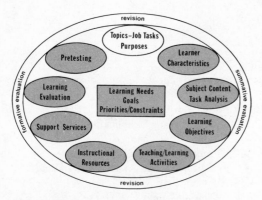

"What topics should receive attention in the course?"
"In the training program, what tasks are necessary to insure proficiency for the job?
"What will be the purpose for each topic or task?"

If you were planning to build a house (a goal) what is one of the first things you would do? Your answer is probably to decide on the kinds of rooms that will comprise the house. With instructional planning, a similar procedure is used. The goal statement, as developed in Chapter 3, normally leads to a list of topics or job tasks which establishes the structure of the course or program. A **topic** is a heading for a unit or a component of a course that treats subject content knowledge to be learned. A **job task** is a heading that relates to a physical skill that is to be performed.

SELECTING TOPICS AND JOB TASKS

The subject specialist should be able to list the topics to be treated within the content areas expressed by the goal. Here are some examples:

Course: Human Biology

Goal: To interest college students in studying the systems that comprise the human body and thereby to gain a better understanding of themselves.

Topics: 1. The Skeleton
2. The Muscle System
3. The Breathing System
4. The Digestive System
5. The Circulatory System
6. Nerve Impulses and Consciousness
7. The Senses
8. The Autonomic Nervous System
9. The Biological Background of Mental Phenomena
10. Reactions of the Organism as a Whole
11. Reproduction

Seminar: Women at Work

Goal: To help career-oriented women prepare to advance in business to leadership positions.

Topics: 1. Present Status of Women in the Workplace
2. Stereotyping Women in the Workplace
3. Responding to the Stereotyping of Women
4. Insights Gleaned from Successful Men and Women
5. Goal Setting and Career Planning
6. Skills Necessary for Success
7. Problems for Women in the Workplace
8. Balancing Multiple Roles

In the above two examples, only informational topics had to be listed for the course. In order to accomplish the goal specified for a job, the vocational job expert should be able to list *both* the topics to be learned *and* the tasks to be performed. Here are some examples:

Course: Business Machine Transcription

Goal: To provide community college students with skills to type copy from transcription machines and to apply language skills in order to produce acceptable business letters.

Tasks/Topics: 1. Operating Transcription Equipment
2. Transcription Techniques and Procedures
3. Spelling and Punctuation
4. Language Use for Transcribing
5. Business Letter Styles
6. Proofreading

Course: Therapeutic Nursing

Goal: To present essential information and skills required for basic nursing care.

Tasks/Topics: 1. Personal Hygiene
2. Comfort Measures
3. Respiratory Care
4. Dietary Assistance
5. Elimination Measures
6. Administration of Medicines
7. First Aid
8. Postmortem Care

Course: Automotive Mechanic

Goal: To gain proficiency in maintenance and repair of automotive systems.

Tasks/Topics: 1. Engine Tune-up Procedure
2. Brake Installation and Repair
3. Transmission Overhaul
4. Cooling System Cleaning and Repair
5. Electrical System Repair
6. Wheel Alignment
7. Steering Adjustment

Both topics and tasks have been listed in the above three examples. Can you identify the major differences between a *topic* and a *task?*

Topics relate to subject content knowledge. The learner or trainee is to learn certain facts, concepts, and principles; then he or she is to use the information by making applications and solving problems. Thus the sample units for the Human Biology course and the Women at Work seminar are listed as topics. In each unit the major emphasis is on acquiring and applying information. As we will see in Chapter 6, when knowledge is acquired and used, *cognitive learning* takes place.

In learning a task, the main emphasis is on accomplishing a set of physical actions—performing a skill with proficiency. Many of the units listed for the Business Machine Transcription, Therapeutic Nursing, and Automotive Mechanics courses require physical activity and are called tasks. When a task is accomplished by using muscles of the body, *psychomotor learning* (page 80) results.

Notice that in the latter three course examples, the two headings—Tasks/Topics—are used. For many tasks it is necessary that information also be learned, often before the task can be performed properly. For example, in the Business Machine Transcription course, in order to operate a typewriter, the student first must have learned to recognize letters of the alphabet and the symbols used on keys. The units on spelling and punctuation, language use, and letter styles are knowledge based. Operating transcription equipment and transcription techniques are tasks requiring performance skills. Most of the units listed for the Automotive Mechanic course call for *both* knowledge and task skills.

As you develop a list of topics and tasks relating to a goal, you might ask yourself these questions:

- What must the learner *know* to accomplish the goal?
- What must the learner *do* to accomplish the goal?

Then list both the cognitive and psychomotor learning units, or a combination of the two, that are required.

There is a third category of learning related to almost all topics and tasks, although this type may not be taught directly. It is the important area of attitudes and values, which influences the motivation and feelings of learners or trainees toward learning itself as well as toward behaviors required by each topic or task. If such units as *improving maintenance performance, applying energy conservation measures,* and *taking corrective action with employees* were to be considered for a topic, attention must be given to attitude-forming matters as well as to instruction for information and skills. This is *affective learning* (page 82).

You might add a third important question to the above two:

- What *attitude* should the learner be helped to develop when accomplishing the goal?

At this stage of planning, include all feasible topics relating to the job. Some may be combined or eliminated as you proceed. In order not to leave out or forget something that may be important, attempt to be as inclusive as possible with topics and tasks at this time.

The topics and tasks should be listed in a logical sequence. There are various ways to do this:

- By chronological, numerical, or other natural arrangement
- By proceeding from treatment of simple to more complex content
- From an overall view or study of the whole subject to a detailed consideration of the components
- By proceeding from the concrete, which is easy to explain and observe, to the abstract, which is more verbal and intellectually demanding

Consideration should also be given to organizing topics and tasks so that they build on knowledge and skills learners have acquired in previous courses or at earlier stages in the present course sequence. The selection of each topic or task becomes the starting point for detailed planning within the instructional design process.

SETTING A GENERAL PURPOSE

As you already know, writing objectives is one of the essential elements in the instructional design process. Some planning approaches encourage or require the writing of objectives right after topics and tasks have been identified. This is a difficult job, and very few of us can specify objectives clearly at this time. Even when objectives are initially being written, such terms as these are used frequently: *understand, learn about, develop a feeling for, acquire the skill to,* and *enjoy engaging in.*

Such expressions are ambiguous and are *not* suitable for stating precise learning objectives. Yet at this early planning stage they can help clarify your own thinking and allow you to indicate broadly what should be learned or accomplished in the topic or task. These statements express the planner's (or instructor's) own aim or purpose as the major outcomes for the topic or task. They do *not* indicate what learners specifically should be able to do.

Do not confuse a *goal statement,* which is expressed in broad terms for the overall course or program, with this **general purpose** written for a topic or task. While the latter is also rather unspecific, it is related directly to anticipated learning on the level of each topic or task. A general purpose consists of an inexact verb and the broad content of the topic or task. Some of the terms commonly used to express a general purpose—and also a goal—are:

to acquire a skill	to enjoy
to appreciate	to grasp the significance of
to become aware of	to know
to become familiar with	to learn
to become proficient in	to like
to be introduced to	to master
to believe in	to perceive
to comprehend	to understand
to determine	to value
to develop the ability to	

Stating one or more general purposes may be necessary for describing each topic or task. Here are some examples:

Course: Human Biology

Topic: The Skeleton

General Purpose: To become familiar with the divisions of the human skeleton and the functions they serve.

Topic: Nerve Impulses and Consciousness

General Purpose: To understand the makeup of the central nervous system and how bodily actions are controlled by nerve cells.

Course: Women at Work

Topic: Responding to the Stereotyping of Women

General Purpose: To understand how various kinds of behavior can overcome the stereotype image.

Course: Business Machine Transcription

Task: Transcription Techniques and Procedures

General Purposes: 1. To gain proficiency in converting dictated correspondence from an electronic instrument to typewritten copy.
2. To master the operation of five common transcribing machines.

Topic: Language Skills for Transcribing

General Purpose: To review basic rules for grammar important in transcribing.

Course: Therapeutic Nursing

Task: Respiratory Care

General Purpose: To become skilled in providing interventions that will prevent or overcome respiratory problems.

Task/Topic: Administration of Medications

General Purposes: 1. To acquire knowledge about drugs that are commonly dispensed.
2. To gain skills in preparing medication for administration.
3. To become proficient in administering medications.

SUMMARY

An instructional course or training program consists of a number of topics and/or job tasks. Topics are knowledge-based, while tasks are physical-skill-based. The latter may also require the learning of information for satisfactory performance of the skill.

Along with each topic or task, it is desirable to write a statement of what the instructor hopes to accomplish. This becomes a general purpose, expressed from the instructor's point of view.

Once a list of topics and job tasks, along with the general purposes for each, have been drawn up, these become the framework within which the instructional program can be designed. A number of items of content and several learning objectives should be listed for each general purpose.

REVIEW AND APPLICATIONS*

A. Recall
   1. After a goal statement is written, what planning matters next need attention?

_____

_____

_____

*See answers on page 252.

2. Which phrases refer to a *topic* and which to a *task?*
   _____ *a.* Names and definitions
   _____ *b.* Rules and principles
   _____ *c.* Affective learning
   _____ *d.* Following a procedure
   _____ *e.* Cognitive learning
   _____ *f.* A skill activity
   _____ *g.* Psychomotor learning
   _____ *h.* Attention to an attitude

3. In what three ways can topics or tasks be organized for a course or training program?
   a. _____
   _____
   _____
   b. _____
   _____
   _____
   c. _____
   _____
   _____

4. Are general purposes specified for *instructor* use or for *learner* use? Why are they written?
   _____
   _____
   _____

5. How is a goal statement both different from and also similar to a general purpose?
   a. Different: _____
   _____
   _____
   b. Similar: _____
   _____
   _____

B. Comprehension
   1. The following units are part of a course on **Electrical systems.** Indicate which units are *topics,* which are *tasks,* and which are a *combination* of the two.
   _____ *a.* Fundamentals of basic electricity
   _____ *b.* Principles of electronics
   _____ *c.* Using batteries and building DC circuits
   _____ *d.* Using transformers and building AC circuits
   _____ *e.* Safety practices for protection against misuse of electricity
   _____ *f.* Operating DC equipment and controls
   _____ *g.* Understanding AC control equipment
   _____ *h.* Troubleshooting electrical problems

   2. Refer to your answer to Recall question 3 and to page 39, which list ways that topics and tasks for a course can be organized. For each course below, indicate the way the corresponding set of topics is organized.
   _____ *a.* Management for First Line Supervisors
   Supervisor's role in organization
   Supervisor's responsibilities in department

Work authorization techniques
Improving worker performance
Controlling resources
Effective spoken communications
Effective written communications
Understanding labor relations
_____ *b.* Wars Engaged in by the United States
American Revolution
Civil War
Spanish-American War
World War I
World War II
Korean conflict
Vietnam war
_____ *c.* Using Mathematics
Whole numbers
Fractions
Decimal fractions
Ratios and proportions
Powers and roots
Algebra
Using formulas

3. Which of the following are stated as *general purposes?*
   _____ *a.* To know the effects of each vitamin on the human body
   _____ *b.* To make a 15-minute presentation on a selected topic, using necessary resources and receiving a mark of at least 8 on a 10-point rating scale
   _____ *c.* To become aware of the writings of Ernest Hemingway
   _____ *d.* To acquire skills in playing the piano
   _____ *e.* To understand the procedures for closing a sale
   _____ *f.* To identify five functions social workers perform
   _____ *g.* To plot and interpret a drug dose response curve

C. Applications
   1. *Sky Diving*
      a. Refer to the descriptive material on the subject of sky diving in Appendix B. Continue your work on separate paper. If you were to plan a course based on this material, what *topics* and *tasks* would you include?

      _____
      _____
      _____
      _____
      _____

      b. In what order would you prefer to treat the topics?

      _____
      _____
      _____

      c. For each of *two* topics, state a *general purpose.*

      _____
      _____
      _____

2. *Your Subject*

   Refer to the subject you selected for the Application project at the end of Chapter 3 (page 35). Carry out the following:

   a. List topics and tasks to be learned relating to the subject.

   _____
   _____
   _____
   _____
   _____

   b. For *two* topics and/or tasks, state general purposes to be served. (*Note:* Plan to use these topics/tasks as the basis for Application projects in following chapters.)

   _____
   _____
   _____

REFERENCES

Butler, F. Coit. *Instructional Systems Development for Vocational and Technical Training* (Englewood Cliffs, NJ: Educational Technology Publications, 1972), chapter 6.

Gael, Sidney. *Job Analysis: A Guide to Assessing Work Activities* (San Francisco: Jossey-Bass, 1983).

Mager, Robert F. *Goal Analysis* (Belmont, CA: Pitman, 1972).

chapter *5*

Learner Characteristics

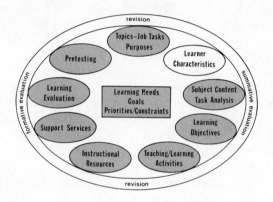

"Why is it important to give attention to learner characteristics when planning?"

"Which characteristics are most useful, and how is information about them obtained?"

"What characteristics of special learner groups may have an important impact on instructional planning?"

"What are student learning styles, and how can information be gathered about them?"

Suppose that you had never heard about the instructional design process, and you start giving your lecture at the first class meeting of your course. You have put a lot of work into developing this new introductory unit in order to impress students with the value of the subject. The lecture contains detailed statistical content from recent research and complex explanations.

As you proceed, you sense reactions: A few students are listening intently and rapidly taking notes. Others look puzzled; and some appear completely indifferent. This is a one-time opportunity for all of them to get this important information! What is wrong?

It may be that in your preparation, you have given little consideration to the nature of the student group, their aptitudes and preparation levels, degree of motivation, or other traits which contribute to interest and success in learning.

One of the key elements of the instructional design process mentioned in Chapter 2 was the need to consider the learners for whom a program is being developed. Obviously, the measure of success of an instructional plan will be based principally on the learning level accomplished by the learners involved. Learner populations, from elementary levels through high school and college, and in training areas—whether industrial, business, health, government, or military—are composed of varied types of people. Therefore, it is essential, early in planning, to give attention to the characteristics, abilities, and experiences of the learners—as a group and as individuals.

It is well recognized that all persons differ in many respects, including the ways in which they learn. Some of these differences are evident in the kinds of experiences each person requires in order to learn, and if competence in a skill is to be acquired, in the amount of time and practice each person requires. To serve either an academic class or a training group, the instructional planner must obtain information about the capabilities, needs, and interests of the learners. This information should affect certain elements in planning, such as the selection of topics (and the level at which topics are introduced), the choice and sequencing of objectives, the depth of topic treatment, and the variety of learning activities.

When designing an instructional plan, decide early in the initial design stages which characteristics of your learners or trainees it would be most useful to identify. Then decide how to acquire the necessary information.

ACADEMIC INFORMATION

Probably the most easily obtainable and the most often used category of information about individual learners is an academic record. This record would include:

- School grade or training level completed and major subject areas studied.
- Grade-point average or letter grades for academic studies.
- Scores on standardized achievement tests of intelligence and in basic skills like reading, writing, and mathematics.
- Special or advanced courses completed relating to the academic major or area of training.

Much of this information can be obtained from student records on file in a school's administrative office. Some of it is available on employment applications or in a personnel file. If you find the need for a specific kind of information about learners and it is not available, specialized tests can be obtained and administered through a testing or personnel office.

Closely associated with the academic information about learners are the knowledge and skills that learners may already possess which directly relate to the subject content or skills to be learned. Obtaining knowledge and skills information is one of the purposes for the pretesting element of the instructional design process (see Chapter 12). Thus, there is a close relationship between the information obtained about learner characteristics and the data to be acquired from pretests.

PERSONAL AND SOCIAL CHARACTERISTICS

In addition to academic information, it is desirable to be aware of personal and social characteristics of the learner for whom the program is to be planned. To design a procedure for teaching a person anything, an instructor needs the following knowledge about the learner:

- Age and maturity level
- Motivation and attitude toward the subject
- Expectations and vocational aspirations (if appropriate)
- Previous or current employment and work experience (if any)
- Special talents
- Mechanical dexterity
- Ability to work under various environmental conditions—noise, outdoors during inclement weather, high elevations, and so on.

Such useful data may be obtained by observation, interviews, and informational questionnaires, as well as from attitudinal surveys completed by learners. (See Chapter 11 for further discussion about these information-gathering methods.) If special groups comprise a significant percentage of the student population, social characteristics peculiar to each group should be given due consideration.

CHARACTERISTICS OF NONCONVENTIONAL LEARNERS

While it is important to gather and use during planning the usual kinds of information—academic, personal, and social—about all learners, attention also should be given to the special characteristics of those individuals termed here *nonconventional learners,* whose preparation, behavior, and expectations may not be conventional. These groups include individuals from ethnic minorities, learners with special disabilities, and learners categorized as adults.

Ethnic Minority Learners

Learner groups may include members of ethnic cultures with backgrounds and behaviors that differ markedly from those of the majority of learners or trainees. Therefore, consideration should be given to their special characteristics during planning.

One obvious problem may be deficiency in the English language. If this is the situation, remedial training in English (or the language in which the instruction will be conducted) must be provided as needed. Cultural and social differences should be recognized because they can affect such things as the ability to take responsibility for individualized work or to engage in creative activities. In some cultures an accepted strong authority figure, like the father in a family, influences the freedom and decision-making abilities of children. If background experiences are limited, there can be a naiveté and lack of sophistication that may affect a learner's readiness for and participation in a program.

In order to build confidence in their ability to succeed, individuals from minority cultural groups may need to experience more than routine teaching procedures. Such consideration can be essential whether the learners are in an academic or a vocational training program. Some of the considerations that may be employed in helping these learners become successful in learning are:

- To provide incentives, such as personal recognition, monetary awards, or free time, as motivators for engaging in and continuing with learning.
- To provide for cooperative activities, since many minority learners gain satisfaction from group projects and from assisting others.
- To employ a more visual than verbal treatment for presenting elements of a topic.
- To provide extra examples as illustrations of generalizations.
- To allow more time than normal for study and for completion of assignments, within reasonable constraints, and more opportunity to practice a skill.
- To provide many occasions for a learner to check his or her success in learning and progress toward a goal.

Some of these considerations may just seem to be common sense, but they are important for all learners. Furthermore, they are of particular value when preparing instruction for learners with a cultural background that differs from that of the instructor.

Information about the abilities of learners in ethnic groups can be obtained through the usual testing, interview, and questionnaire procedures. In addition, consider obtaining help from counselors in an organization or from the community who have had direct experience in working with such individuals.

Disabled Learners

The category of disabled learners includes physically handicapped individuals and others with learning disabilities such as hearing and vision loss, speech impairment, and mild mental retardation. Each type of handicapped learner has unique limitations and requires special consideration. While some physically handicapped persons can participate in regular classes, others cannot. A careful analysis of individual abilities should be made through observation, interviews, and testing.

Many handicapped learners require special training and individual attention. Therefore, an instructional program may require extensive modification in order to serve handicapped learners appropriately. Specialists who are capable of working with disabled individuals should be a part of any instructional planning team.

Adult Learners

An important factor reducing the homogeneity of learner populations is the increasing number of adults who have become learners in these settings: returning to colleges and universities, engaging in community adult education programs, and participating in job training or retraining for new skills in business, industry, health fields, government service, and the military.

The field of adult education, known as *andragogy,* has been studied at length.[1] A number of generalizations regarding adults and their accommodation in the educational process are recognized:

- Adults enter a program with a high level of motivation and readiness to learn. Often they clearly know what goal they want to reach. They appreciate a program that is structured systematically, with elements clearly specified.
- Adults bring to a course extensive background experience from both their personal and professional lives. These experiences should be used by an instructor as major resources by helping adults relate their experiences to the topics being studied.
- Adults may be less flexible than younger learners. Their habits and methods of operation have been developed into a routine. Before they will accept change, they must see an advantage in doing so.
- Adults want to be treated as adults. They want to participate in decision making. They want to act with the instructor in mutual assessment of needs and goals, in the selection of activities, and in deciding on evidence for evaluation of learning.
- Most mature adults are largely self-directed and independent. While some adults lack confidence and need reassurance of their ability to learn, the great majority prefer to engage actively in their own learning. They would prefer that the instructor serve as informal facilitator to guide, assist, and provide encouragement as necessary.
- To adults, time is an important consideration because they may have outside responsibilities. They do not like to waste time. They do want to be sure that the purpose of an instructional event will be of value to them. Therefore, purposeful and carefully structured activities are important.

For adults, as well as for other learners, the same principles of human learning and behavior must form the bases of an instructional program. These

[1] R.H. Knowles, *The Modern Practice of Adult Education.*

principles will be given attention in Chapter 8. There are differences in degree and specificity as to how the principles should be applied with certain groups. By being sensitive and alert to the characteristics of special groups of learners, you can plan programs especially effective for them.

LEARNING STYLES

Some learners find certain methods of learning more appealing and effective than others. For a long time it has been known that, in preference to attending verbal lectures and reading textual material, some individuals learn better from a visual approach to studying, and others from physical activities and the manipulation of objects. The attempt to identify a person's unique learning styles can be beneficial during instructional planning.

There are three aspects of learning styles for which evidence and substantial research are providing information useful for setting learning conditions. These aspects are human brain hemisphere functions, learning conditions, and cognitive learning styles.

Human Brain Hemisphere Functions

The human brain is divided into right and left halves called *hemispheres.* From studies of persons who have suffered brain damage, it has been found that the two hemispheres contribute differently to the way an individual perceives and organizes information during the process of learning. The *left* hemisphere is more efficient in handling information in a *logical, sequential,* and *analytical* way. This side is especially well-suited to the functions of language (reading, speaking, and interpreting written symbols).

The *right* hemisphere interprets information in a holistic or all-inclusive manner. This side gives attention to the *synthesis* of information, *visual-spatial* relationships, and *problem solving.* The right hemisphere is considered to be the side of the brain used for *creative thinking* that can result in, for example, writing music, designing a work of art, or engineering a structure.

For an individual, one hemisphere of the brain may predominate, with a minimum contribution being made by the other hemisphere. For example, learners with the right hemisphere dominant may have delayed language development or have reading and spelling problems. Individuals with left hemisphere dominance can more likely be inventors or otherwise nonconventional thinking persons. Therefore, attention should be given to diagnostic methods that can identify persons with such a dominance so as to better guide those having greater strengths on one side of the brain than the other. (See suggested references on this topic at the end of the chapter.)

Learning Conditions

Many environmental factors in the classroom or study area can affect a person's ability to concentrate and to absorb and retain information. For example, we all know of teenagers who can best study with popular music blasting at full volume from a nearby radio. They feel comfortable with a noise background, and ignore it when they concentrate. Therefore, how each person responds to sound, as one factor in the learning environment, may be an important consideration for that person's successful learning.

Dunn and Dunn[2] have designed a Learning Style Inventory for school-age learners and a second instrument for adult learners. These questionnaires contain statements to which an individual responds (by acceptance or rejection). The result is an analysis of the conditions under which the person prefers to learn. The assessment of individual preferences is in the following areas:

1. Immediate *physical environment,* in relation to sound, light, and temperature levels, and choice or arrangement of furniture.
2. Individual *emotionality,* in relation to motivation, taking responsibility, and being persistent in completing a task.
3. Individual *sociological* needs, in relation to being self-oriented, peer or group-oriented, adult-oriented, or of combined orientations.
4. Individual *physical* needs, in relation to perceptual preferences, need for mobility, daily use of time, or biorhythm for efficient functioning.

The following are sample items to which a learner reacts by selecting those preferred:

I study best when it is quiet.

I concentrate best when I feel cool.

I really like to mold things with my hands.

It's hard for me to sit in one place for a long time.

I study best at a table or desk.

The things I remember best are the things I read.

I can ignore most sound when I study.

I like to study by myself.

The things I remember best are the things I hear.

When I can, I do my homework in the afternoon.

Since an individual makes a personal selection of preferred items from the lists in a Learning Style Inventory, there may be a tendency to choose a "proper" or "expected" answer. This is one criticism of such testing instruments. The authors claim to overcome this shortcoming by including more than a single statement relating to a factor, each of which is stated in a different way so that a bias can be avoided.

By examining the individual profiles of learners after completing an inventory, the instructor, in consultation with the learner, can offer suggestions

[2]Rita Dunn and Kenneth Dunn, *Teaching Students Through Their Individual Learning Styles.*

and help to create a suitable learning environment. This can be of particular value when students are engaged in an individualized or self-paced learning program.

Cognitive Learning Styles

Another approach to analyzing the factors which affect how a person is most likely to learn is by *cognitive style mapping*. The initial work in this area was performed at Oakland Community College in Michigan by Hill.[3] This method provides a framework for describing and diagnosing an individual's way of searching for meaning when confronted with a particular educational task. Three sets of behaviors are examined.

The first set of behaviors indicates the extent to which the learner tends to gather information by using qualitative and theoretical symbols (words and numbers), the five senses, and cultural codes (sources of subject meanings). The second set indicates the influences a learner brings to bear on deriving meaning from the information gathered in the first set. (Does the learner structure meaning in an individual fashion, or primarily in terms of associates—for example, on the basis of the family's or other authority's ideas?) The third set indicates the manner in which the learner reasons to derive meaning—that is, how the learner approaches a problem in the process of drawing a conclusion by analyzing, questioning, or otherwise appraising that which is under consideration.

In the Hill technique, a Cognitive Style Interest Inventory, based on the three sets of behavior, measures the ability of a learner to deal with visual, tactile, and auditory perceptions, motor coordination, abstractions, and social interactions.

Here are sample statements for determining one's cognitive style. The learner responds by rating each statement as *rarely, sometimes,* or *usually:*

> I can listen to a song and recognize the "tune" the next time I hear it.
> I would feel the material in a suit before buying it.
> I live my life according to my own moral values.
> I know how long it will take to complete most tasks.
> I learn something better when I can discuss it with friends.
> I enjoy an activity more if my friends do it with me.
> I like to make up my own mind about what is right and wrong.
> I would rather take a written English test than an oral test.
> I prefer to follow spoken directions rather than written ones.
> I can fix things without looking at my hands.

The results of a learner's preferences are diagrammed as a map to show the cognitive characteristics of the individual, thus identifying the learner's

[3]Joseph Hill, et al., *Personalized Education Programs Utilizing Cognitive Style Mapping.*

strengths and weaknesses. The map serves as the basis for the learner and instructor to develop a Personalized Education Plan that matches the learner's preferred learning style with educational tasks.

Another type of learning style inventory uses sets of words which the learner rank-orders as "best to least" preferred.[4] The patterns that result measure the learner's relative emphases in four learning modes—concrete experience (feeling), reflective observation (watching), abstract conceptualization (thinking), and active experimentation (doing).

As with the Learning Style Inventory described in the previous section, cognitive style mapping can be a useful technique for finding out more about a learner's preferred ways to learn. The results of this testing should be considered along with other data and not be used as the sole basis for determining an individual's learning style.

SUMMARY

When plans are to be made for classroom or group instruction, obtain general indications of the academic and social characteristics of potential and actual learners. This range of capabilities, interests, and needs can guide the planning decisions relative to the selection of objectives for a topic or task, the depth of treatment of the topic, the number and variety of activities to be recommended, the examples and resources needed, and other pertinent considerations. Special attention should be given to the unique characteristics of nonconventional learners, such as individuals from ethnic groups, learners with disabilities, and adults.

For designing individualized learning programs, data about each learner can further aid in the selection of alternative activities, resources, and the most appropriate study environment. In planning for individual learners, the matters of learning styles, including brain hemisphere dominance, preferred learning conditions, and cognitive learning can all profitably receive attention.

REVIEW AND APPLICATIONS*

A. Recall

    1. What are the *two* main categories for obtaining information about learner characteristics? List at least *three* kinds of information that would be important under each category.

       a. _____

         _____

         _____

         _____

         _____

       b. _____

         _____

         _____

         _____

         _____

[4]David A. Kolb, *Learning Style Inventory.*

*See answers on page 253.

2. Answer *true* or *false* for the statements in each grouping.
   a. Relative to *minority* culture learners:
      ____ *(1)* Allow additional time for study.
      ____ *(2)* Permit learners to work together on assignments.
      ____ *(3)* Provide specific kinds of incentives to motivate learners to study.
      ____ *(4)* Provide few opportunities for learners to test themselves as they advance through a program.
      ____ *(5)* Use verbal methods in preference to visual ways for presenting content.
   b. Relative to *adult learners:*
      ____ *(1)* They prefer to be told what to do and expect to be directed by instructor.
      ____ *(2)* They have much time to devote to learning.
      ____ *(3)* They are self-motivated to learn.
      ____ *(4)* They are often set in their ways and do not easily accept change.
      ____ *(5)* Their previous experiences can be of value during learning.
   c. Relative to *learning styles:*
      ____ *(1)* Solving a complex problem in an entirely new way makes use of the right side of brain.
      ____ *(2)* Level of *economic* need is one of the learning conditions recognized by Dunn and Dunn.
      ____ *(3)* Information about learning styles is more useful in planning for individualized learning than for regular classroom instruction.
      ____ *(4)* Kinds of furniture a learner prefers to use is an illustration of a physical need.
      ____ *(5)* The right side of the brain is the logical, analytical hemisphere.
      ____ *(6)* An example of a sociological need is a student's preference for being told what to do by the teacher.
3. What is the meaning of "cognitive style mapping" and its significance relative to learner characteristics?
   _____
   _____
   _____

B. Comprehension
   1. To which one of the listed categories does each of the following relate?
      a. Academic information
      b. Personal and social characteristics
      c. Ethnic minority learners
      d. Disabled learners
      e. Adult learners
         ____ *(1)* The plan and pattern for how the program will be conducted is set. The instructor will maintain this arrangement since the students prefer that things continue as established.
         ____ *(2)* A class of 5th grade students.
         ____ *(3)* A questionnaire is used to determine the level of student interest for taking the course.
         ____ *(4)* To allow employees free working time to successfully complete the introductory unit of the training course.
         ____ *(5)* Determine need for special desks and equipment so students can successfully carry out lab work.

     (6) Trainee background: 3 from sales, 5 from office staff, 8 from production.

     (7) Reading levels—8th through 11th grades.

     (8) Students are 20 to 30 years of age.

     (9) You plan to take little time on introductions so students can get right to work on projects.

     (10) Illustrate concepts on overhead transparencies rather than describe them verbally.

     (11) Discussion reveals that most students hope to attend college.

     (12) The course will be so organized that few lectures will be given and most activity will be by groups, with the instructor available for help as needed.

     (13) Allow students to work on homework assignments with friends.

     (14) Information gathered shows that 80 percent of students have completed the basic electronics course.

2. Relate the following to:
   a. Predominantly right hemisphere learner
   b. Predominantly left hemisphere learner

     (1) Writing an unusual short story

     (2) Carefully following steps in a cooking recipe

     (3) Thinking up a new way to carry out an operation

     (4) Easily learning a foreign language

     (5) Doing detective work to locate a lost item

     (6) Applying the instructional design process

3. The following items refer to elements that might be included in a *cognitive style mapping inventory*. They relate to one area—*sensory stimuli*. To which of these categories does each item refer:
   a. To perceive meaning through sight
   b. To perceive meaning through hearing
   c. To perceive meaning through touch
   d. To perceive meaning through smell
   e. To perceive meaning through taste

     (1) I can identify familiar foods by their odor.

     (2) When I listen to music, I can tell one instrument from another.

     (3) I can button my coat in the dark.

     (4) I feel that the aroma of a store has a lot to do with its sales.

     (5) I tune a radio by the sounds I hear and not by the numbers on the dial.

     (6) Pictures in textbooks help me to understand what the book is saying.

     (7) I can tell a nickel from a dime in my pocket with my fingers.

     (8) I can feel the difference between cotton and silk.

     (9) It bothers me when the radio is not tuned exactly right.

     (10) The taste of food is more important to me than the way it looks.

     (11) I would pick up and feel vegetables in a store before buying them.

     (12) I think the "scent" of a new car is one of the nicest things around.

     (13) I choose clothes mostly because of the way they look on me.

     (14) Outside noises take my attention from what I am doing.

     (15) I can identify familiar flowers or plants by their aroma.

_____ *(16)* I can concentrate better when I have something on which to chew or eat.

_____ *(17)* I learn more from a picture than I do from a written description.

_____ *(18)* I enjoy new foods because I like new flavors.

_____ *(19)* I can identify the difference when drinking Coke and Pepsi Cola with my eyes closed.

_____ *(20)* I like looking at art works.

Now relate the above items to yourself. Place a check mark before each one that you feel applies to your own preferred behavior. After you check answers, see if there is a pattern. This can give an indication of your own cognitive style relative to the use of your senses for learning.

C. Applications

   1. Sky Diving

Select and describe the student group for this training program. Specify the characteristics for which you would want information and how you would obtain the date. Make up your own decisions as necessary.

_____

_____

_____

_____

_____

   2. Your Subject

Specify the student group and the characteristics you feel are important and helpful in planning.

_____

_____

_____

_____

_____

REFERENCES

Berman, Bennett H. "The 4MAT System: Exploring Relationships Between Left/Right Brain Dominance, Learning Styles, and Implications for Training," *Performance and Instruction,* 21 (February 1982), 9–12.

Contreras, Gloria, and Ana Maria Rodriguez. "What Trainers Should Know About Multicultural Education," *NSPI Journal* 14, (May 1980), 17–19.

Cross, K. Patricia. *Adults as Learners: Increasing Participation and Facilitating Learning* (San Francisco: Jossey-Bass, 1981).

Dunn, Rita, and Kenneth Dunn. *Teaching Students Through Their Individual Learning Styles: A Practical Approach* (Reston, VA: Reston Division of Prentice-Hall, 1978).

Grabowski, Stanley M. "What Instructors Need to Know About Adult Learners," *NSPI Journal,* 14 (July 1980), 15–16.

Hill, Joseph E., et al. *Personalizing Educational Programs Utilizing Cognitive Style Mapping* (Bloomfield Hills, MI: Oakland Community College, 1971).

Hunt, David E. "Learning Styles and Student Needs: An Introduction to Conceptual Levels," in *Student Learning Styles: Diagnosing and Prescribing Programs,* James W. Keefe, ed. (Reston, VA: National Association of Secondary School Principals, 1979), 27–38.

Kidd, J. R. *How Adults Learn* (New York: Association Press, 1973).

Kirby, Patricia. *Cognitive Style, Learning Style and Transfer Skill Acquisition* (Columbus, OH: National Center for Research in Vocational Education, 1979).

Knowles, Malcolm. *The Adult Learner: A Neglected Species* (Houston, TX: Gulf, 1978).

Knowles, Malcolm. *Andragogy in Action: Applying Modern Principles of Adult Learning.* (San Francisco: Jossey-Bass, 1984).

Knowles, R. H. *The Modern Practice of Adult Education: Andragogy versus Pedagogy* (New York: Association Press, 1970).

Kolb, David A. *Learning Style Inventory: A Self-Description of Preferred Learning Modes* (Boston: McBer, 1978).

Lewis, Rena B. "Performance Technologists and the Needs of Special Learners," *NSPI Journal,* 14 (May 1980), 20–21, 31.

Manteuffel, Mary S. "The Satisfied Learner: A Review of the Literature," *Performance and Instruction,* 21 (May 1982), 15–18.

McCarthy, Bernice. The 4MAT System (Oak Brook, IL: Excel, Inc., 600 Enterprise Drive, 1980).

McLagan, Patricia A. *Helping Others Learn* (Reading, MA: Addison-Wesley, 1978).

chapter 6

Subject Content and Task Analysis

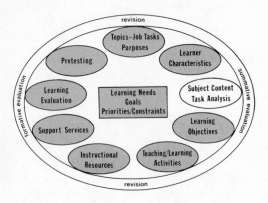

"What items of subject content, relating to the topic should be taught?"
"In what ways can the subject content items be organized?"
"How is a task analyzed to identify its components and then to sequence the actions required?"
"To what other elements of the instructional design process are subject content and task analysis most closely related?"

Assume you are a student attending a lecture. As the instructor delivers the lecture, what are you doing? Probably taking notes so you will capture the essence of the content being presented. You may do this in detailed sentences, or more frequently in outline form like this:

Topic: *The Circulatory System*
  I. Types of vessels in closed circulatory system
    A. Arteries—carry blood away from heart
    B. Veins—carry blood toward heart
    C. Capillaries—final division of arteries unite to form first small veins

   II. Circulation
      A. Systemic—supplies most of body (aorta)
      B. Pulmonary—supplies lungs
      C. Coronary—within heart
  III. Heart
      A. A double organ
         1. Right side—pump for pulmonary circulation
         2. Left side—pump for systematic circulation
      B. Flow of blood
         1. Right atrium (earlike flap on heart)—from body
         2. Right ventricle—to pulmonary artery
         3. Left atrium—from pulmonary vein
         4. Left ventricle—to aorta and body
         5. Valves permit passage of blood in one direction
         6. Systole—flow from ventricles
         7. Diastole—relaxation of heart muscle and expansion of chambers

We are all familiar with this procedure of outlining information as it is being presented to us.

Now, reverse the procedure. You are the person who will deliver the lecture. What is your preparation? You either write out the lecture in a narrative form to be read as written, or with experience, you prepare an outline consisting of the main headings, supporting details, and examples. This outline becomes the framework for reference as a guide to your presentation.

Change your role. You are preparing a group of instructors who, in the training they will conduct, will be using videotape recordings. Your task is to provide instruction in the use of a videocassette recorder. What do you do?

If you are familiar with the equipment, you can prepare an outline of the steps to be followed in operating the recorder. If you are unfamiliar with the equipment, you should check the manual or obtain guidance from an experienced person. In either case, you will need to consider information about the machine and also detail the steps to follow when using the recorder to play videocassettes. This outline procedure for a skill to be learned is called a *task analysis.* One example follows:

  Objective: *To Operate the Videocassette Recorder*
  A. Nomenclature—parts and controls
    1. Front of recorder
      a. Program selection switch
      b. Power switch
      c. Control buttons—eject, play, pause, fast forward, rewind
    2. Back of recorder
      a. VHF OUT terminal
      b. Tape speed switch
      c. VHF OUT/IN connector cable
    3. Television receiver
      a. ON/OFF switch
      b. Channel selector
      c. Volume control

    B. Operating Procedure
        1. Plug recorder into 110v outlet
        2. Plug TV receiver into 110v outlet
        3. Attach cable from VHF OUT on recorder to VHF IN on TV receiver
        4. Set PROGRAM SELECT to VTR
        5. Set TV receiver on channel *3*
        6. Set *tape speed* switch to *B1*
        7. Turn POWER to ON on recorder and TV receiver
        8. Press EJECT button; insert videocassette; press lid down
        9. Press PLAY button
      10. Adjust VOLUME control on TV receiver
      11. and so on . . .

The examples of the circulatory system and videocassette recorder operation illustrated above comprise the components of an element in the instructional design process—outlining subject content for learning the knowledge representing a topic (cognitive learning), or performing a task analysis for a skill (which may include both cognitive and psychomotor learning). In the sequence of planning, enumerating subject content or performing a task analysis leads to the formulation of learning objectives (see Chapter 7). At other times you might find it preferable to state objectives first and then deduce the details of content or of the task from the objectives. Employ either procedure:

subject content/task analysis → objectives

or

objectives → subject content/task analysis

depending upon which seems appropriate to your situation or to your preferred method of planning.

There is a natural, close relationship between objectives and subject content. Each one can help you to develop and refine the other one. Later in the planning process the content and task details become useful for: (1) accomplishing teaching and learning activities, (2) developing instructional resources like questions on worksheets and scripts for audiovisual materials, and (3) providing content for test questions when evaluating learning.

SUBJECT CONTENT

Subject content provides the substance of information for any topic. Information in turn leads to knowledge, which is the structure of relationships among factual details. The ultimate result is intellectual thought and understanding.

Selecting and arranging the information for the purpose of learning requires an understanding of how content may be structured and how logical sequences result. Robert Gagné, a psychologist, has described a useful method for structuring and sequencing content in terms of learning outcomes.[1]

[1]Robert Gagné, *The Conditions of Learning.*

Organizing Subject Content

The lowest level of learning is called *verbal information* by Gagné. It requires only the memorization, recall, or ability to identify specific facts.

- Names, symbols, labels, places, dates
- Definitions
- Descriptions of objects or events
- Other facts essential to a topic

Any topic includes many details relating to one or more of the above categories. These are the building blocks or tools of any subject—the "vocabulary" that must be learned. Verbal information is preparation for more complex ways of organizing the content. Unless the facts are arranged in structured patterns, they will be of limited use to a student and may be quickly forgotten.

The patterns or generalizations that are developed by organizing and structuring facts comprise Gagné's *intellectual skills*. They may be grouped on two levels: (1) *concepts;* and (2) *principles, rules,* or *laws.*

Concepts—relating together facts, objects, or events that have common features and assigning them a single name.

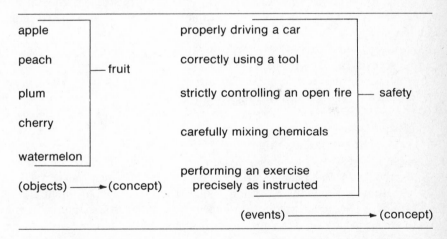

"Fruit" is a *concrete* concept, since it results from the direct observation of specific objects (apples, peaches), all of which have common features (round shape, edible, product of a tree or bush, and so forth). Also, the individual fruit subcategories can represent separate concepts which include lower-level objects (apple varieties—winesap, red delicious, Jonathan, pippin). "Safety" is an *abstract* concept. It is built from a series of related events, each of which exhibits the characteristics of *safe operation.*

Within any subject topic, concepts lead to a higher level of generalization. This can be a *rule, law, principle,* or well-established *procedure.* These are statements consisting of the relationship between two or more concepts.

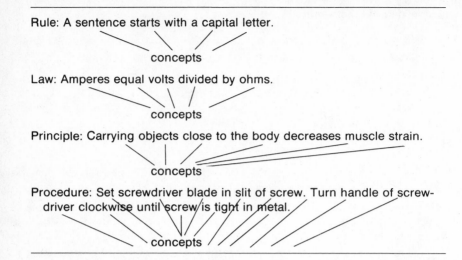

Rule: A sentence starts with a capital letter.

concepts

Law: Amperes equal volts divided by ohms.

concepts

Principle: Carrying objects close to the body decreases muscle strain.

concepts

Procedure: Set screwdriver blade in slit of screw. Turn handle of screw-driver clockwise until screw is tight in metal.

concepts

Each generalization above is derived from a particular set of concepts. Therefore, it is important to recognize that when a principle is to be taught, both the underlying facts *and* the concepts must be communicated together. The relationship between concepts and principles is so close that often the terms are used interchangeably. For example, we may refer to the structure of the atom, "work" as measured by force $\times$ distance, Newton's second law of motion, and Archimedes' principle of buoyancy as "concepts" in physics, although each actually is a principle or a law.

However, it is not so important that you be able to differentiate between a concept and a principle. The implication is that any generalizations *above the factual base level,* be they concepts or principles, need to be recognized and considered when selecting and organizing subject content.

The ultimate value of information is its practical use. Therefore, a major purpose of most instructional programs is to prepare learners or trainees to apply the facts and generalizations (concepts and principles) learned. This preparation is done by requiring the learner to solve problems, explain situations, infer causes, predict consequences, and so forth. Gagné calls this the *cognitive strategy* level of treating subject content. The term *problem solving* is commonly used to indicate this type of activity as the highest level of intellectual activity.

If subject content is carefully organized and suitable learning activities are provided, learners and trainees can become capable of solving problems and making applications such as those expressed in these sentences:

- You need to drive an automobile with which you are entirely unfamiliar.
- A hospital patient in intensive care exhibits a rapidly varying pulse rate. What do you do?
- You are directed to design a new, more attractive way to package a food product.

- Solve this problem: There is among dogs a recessive gene for deafness. Suppose you had a kennel of dogs, including some deaf ones. How would you develop a reliable breeding stock by completely eliminating all genes for deafness?

This treatment of the levels of subject content organization has been brief and greatly simplified. For further details and explanations, you are encouraged to study the chapters in Gagné.[2] Another useful treatment of much of this material is that by De Cecco and Crawford.[3]

Diagramming Subject Content

Usually subject content is outlined under a series of headings—as sequential subtopics, a chronological arrangement, a procedural order, or by facts-to-generalization relationships. While this procedure may be suitable for many topics, there are times when a visual treatment, in graphic form, may be more appropriate.

By using a diagram or chart instead of a formal outline, the planner is better able to see relationships among elements of content. This procedure facilitates smooth transitions or may reveal that the content is incomplete for the development of a topic.

During English grammar lessons, you may have learned how to diagram sentences. By doing this, you were better able to see clearly the structure and parts of a sentence (subject, predicate, object, adjectives, modifiers) and their relationship.

Example: The quarterback made the touchdown.

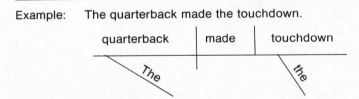

Example: I have heard programs from Germany on my shortwave radio.

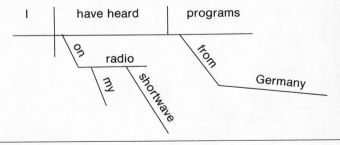

[2]Gagné, *The Conditions of Learning.*
[3]John DeCecco and William Crawford, *The Psychology of Learning and Instruction.*

A similar procedure can be employed to map the structure of content relative to a topic.

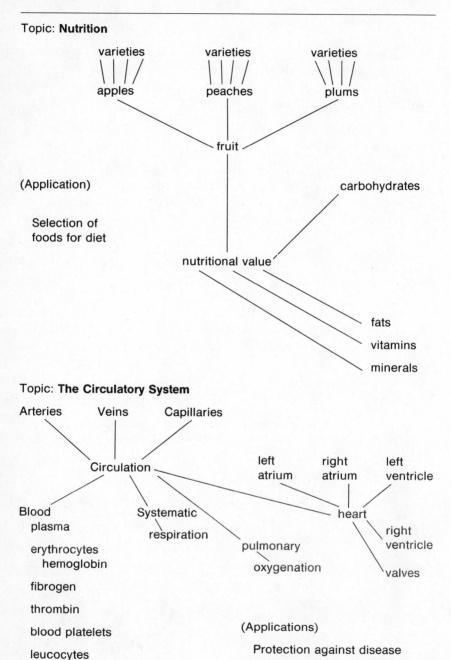

Topic: **Nutrition**

varieties   varieties   varieties

apples   peaches   plums

fruit

(Application)   carbohydrates

Selection of
foods for diet

nutritional value

fats

vitamins

minerals

Topic: **The Circulatory System**

Arteries   Veins   Capillaries

Circulation   left   right   left
                                     atrium   atrium   ventricle

Blood   Systematic   heart
  plasma   respiration   right
                                       pulmonary   ventricle
erythrocytes
  hemoglobin   oxygenation   valves

fibrogen

thrombin

blood platelets   (Applications)

leucocytes   Protection against disease

                                      Transport of food to cells

                                      Process of heart transplant

As you see from these two examples, the mapping of subject content can be relatively simple or complex, depending on the topic and the level of treatment. This procedure can help you to answer two important questions about the subject content for a topic:

- Have all necessary elements of content been included?
- Are the elements properly arranged for satisfactory learning? (See the suggestions for sequencing topics and tasks on page 39. Similar procedures can apply to sequencing content.)

If you find this procedure of diagramming subject content useful, here are suggestions for applying it:

1. List the facts (names, symbols, definitions), concepts, and principles which you or the subject specialist feel (or references indicate) should receive attention as components of the topic.
2. Arrange the components of information in a sequential order. This may start with any level (facts, concepts, principle) and add other parts as you identify associations.
3. As you arrange the items, it is natural to connect them with lines. The lines show relationships and indicate sequence order for treatment.
4. As the diagram takes shape, for full treatment of the topic, you may find breaks in the continuity which indicate the need to add missing elements, be they facts, concepts, or principles.
5. Examples, applications, and problem-solving suggestions might be added to complete the framework for acquiring knowledge and understanding.

When a diagram or your outline of subject content is completed, you then need to decide the method for treating the components of content when instruction is to be planned. This decision may affect the order for developing learning objectives. There are two common categories of content treatment:

- *Deductive method*—Starting with generalizations (concepts or a principle) and leading to facts, then to observations, applications, and problem solving.
- *Inductive method*—Starting with facts, details, and observations, leading to the formulation of concepts and a principle, and finally to applications and problem solving.

The treatment of most topics does not necessarily follow a simple deductive or inductive sequence. Deductive and inductive elements are often intermixed to determine a sequence based on the instructor's preference or the emphasis for the topic in terms of the general purpose.

TASK ANALYSIS

In Chapter 4 you learned that a job consists of a number of tasks. These are comparable to topics in a subject area. In examining topics we gave attention to the subject content. With tasks, we must consider *both* content and physical movements which are combined as the skill.[4]

The planning at this stage is guided by the question "What must be learned by the student or trainee to perform the task?" The answer requires a **task analysis**—a detailed inventory of the "knowing" and "doing" components of the skill. Such content matters as names and functions of parts, order of assembly and use of parts, and operating procedures, all may require attention. The skill part of the performance is concerned with the step-by-step description of bodily actions, performed with precision and appropriate timing.

Resources for Information

In order to carry out a task analysis, it is necessary to have correct and detailed information about all aspects of the job and each task. The best source for this information might be a subject expert who is not only thoroughly familiar with details of the job and its tasks, but has also practiced the skill. Such a person, as a professional or a craftsmen, has up-to-date information and familiarity with the latest techniques and equipment.

Other resources may be used to supplement or verify the knowledge and skill of the expert:

- Reference books, manuals, and other literature either from a library or available from the manufacturer
- Films or video and other audiovisual materials on trades and jobs that illustrate the task to be performed
- A visit to a location in which the job is practiced (in an up-to-date manner); interviews and observations of the task being performed.

Of the above resources, the most useful is interviewing and observing a person at work. First prepare yourself for the visit by reading available materials as background. Make an outline or a list that will prepare you for what you will see and hear. Think of questions you might want to ask the person who explains or demonstrates the task. Questions such as these can guide you in doing a thorough task analysis: What is done? How is it done? What is used (equipment, materials, special clothing)? Why are things done as they are? Are special conditions required (working alone, high noise level surroundings, handling hazardous materials)?

Often an experienced person forgets the details and simple procedures that must be learned by a trainee. Or the assumption is made that everyone has certain knowledge or skills. Asking questions like those stated above can help you to overcome learning obstacles.

---

[4]*Note:* A third element, attitudes or human relation factors, as referred to on page 39, may also be important as part of the learning required for a task. This matter is more appropriately considered with learning objectives in Chapter 7. For a discussion of approaches to task analysis which include social relationships, see Ivor Davies, "Task Analysis: Some Process and Content Concerns."

During the interview and observation, identify and record every fact, detail, or movement the person indicates or makes. Remember that every task has both "knowing" and "doing" components. Identify these two aspects at this time. Note any special difficulties, or tricks learned through experience on how to do certain things, as well as any safety warnings that should be emphasized. Ask the expert to "think aloud" while performing the task and to indicate *decision points* that can affect what is to be done next. Each job that requires more than routine use of manual skills involves decisions, choices, judgments, and other discriminations as well as simple-to-complex problem-solving behavior. Find out about as many of these matters as possible while gathering data. Sometimes recording explanations on audiotape and taking photographs or shooting videotape can be the best record of what you see and hear.

Detailing a Task

In analyzing a task, attention is given to all the steps or elements that comprise the task. Mager and Beach call this procedure "task detailing."[5] These are the specific things that must be learned, or skills that must be performed, for accomplishing the task. The lists prepared through experience, research, interview, and observation, as described in the previous section, provide the material for listing the steps or details of a task.

The sample outline on page 59, To Operate the Videocassette Recorder, is an example of detailing a task. Here is another example:

Task: Making a Hospital Bed
A. Terminology
    1. Closed bed.
    2. Drawsheet.
    3. Miter
    4. Toe pleat.
B. Preparatory Steps
    1. Wash hands.
    2. Assemble linen supplies.
        a. Mattress pad.
        b. Sheets (2).
        c. Cloth-covered plastic drawsheet.
        d. Blanket.
        e. Spread.
        f. Pillows (2).
        g. Pillow cases (2).
    3. Place bed in high position.
    4. Move mattress to head of bed.
C. Make Bed on One Side
    1. Place mattress pad on mattress.

[5]Robert Mager and Kenneth Beach, *Developing Vocational Instruction.*

2. Place bottom sheet over mattress and pad with center fold at center of bed.
3. Unfold sheet onto lower half of bed with lower hem even with edge of mattress at foot and smooth out.
4. Unfold rest of sheet to top of mattress and smooth out.
5. Tuck excess sheet under mattress at foot.
6. Miter corner where sheet has been tucked under mattress.
7. Tuck sheet under side of mattress to foot of bed.
8. Place drawsheet over middle section of bed.
9. And so on.

Flow Charting

The details of some tasks form a single, linear sequence. This means that each step or stage of the procedure is performed in 1–2–3 order without any decisions having to be made or alternative actions chosen. The details for Making a Hospital Bed, as enumerated above, illustrate a single, linear sequence.

When elements or steps within a task may follow different paths, based on choices or decisions that must be made, it is useful to prepare a *flow chart*. Visually the chart shows the sequence for performing the task in accordance with the data previously collected. This is similar to the visual diagramming method presented for handling subject content on page 63. Some authorities use the term *decision tree* when the procedure includes decision points with

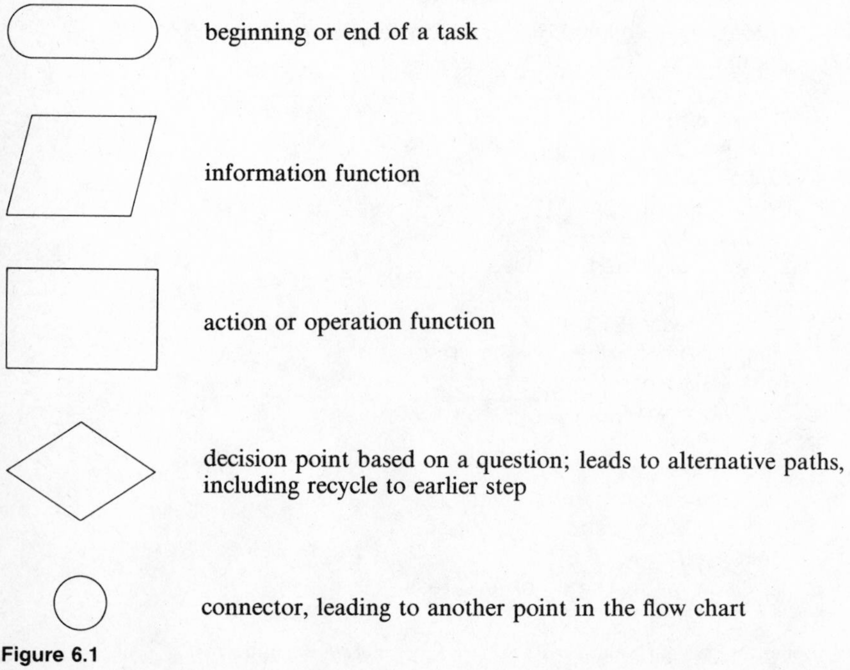

beginning or end of a task

information function

action or operation function

decision point based on a question; leads to alternative paths, including recycle to earlier step

connector, leading to another point in the flow chart

Figure 6.1

alternative paths. Another expression, *algorithm,* borrowed from mathematics and computer science, is widely used to describe a basic diagrammatic procedure for successfully soving complex problems.[6] An algorithm is prepared by a programmer as an aid or map when developing a computer program.

Regardless of the terms used, graphic methods are very useful for communicating the sequence of actions required for a task, along with associated knowledge. In order to understand and be able to apply the flow charting procedure, you need to give attention to the following:

- Skill elements shown in appropriate boxes (as indicated above)
- Knowledge elements written alongside the appropriate skill boxes

The symbols that are used in flow charting include those shown in Figure 6.1 on the previous page.

A sample flowchart for a task is shown in Figure 6.2 on the following page.

Even for a task as simple as preparing a soup, this visual display shows that there are numerous steps and details which need attention. You can imagine the effort required to prepare a flow chart for a complex task! However, preparing it can certainly help you to indicate all parts required for a procedure. Especially note the decision diamonds and the arrows for feedback loops to ensure that the procedure will be completely and accurately accomplished. Although the soup preparation example required little supporting knowledge, there will be many instances for which much essential information should be listed as accompanying elements in the flow chart.

Instead of describing the details of a task on paper, index cards could be used. They allow for greater flexibility and ease in rearranging or adding items. (See the information in Chapter 13 on using cards in planning.)

SUMMARY

A listing or description of the subject content relating to a topic is an important aspect of instructional planning. The content should be organized in some logical, sequential way. The three levels described by Gagné or a diagramming method can be used.

When examining a task, the "detailing" method of Mager and Beach or flow charting can be used. These methods should include all steps or elements that comprise the task along with decisions, choices, or judgments that need to be made and their implications.

The value of specifying subject content and analyzing a task will be recognized when other elements of the instructional design are planned. Subject content and task analysis can be used as the basis for stating objectives, as content for audiovisual materials and other instructional resources, and for designing testing instruments to evaluate learning.

[6]Paul Merrill, "Representations for Algorithms," *Performance and Instruction.*

Task: Prepare Noodle Soup for Four Persons

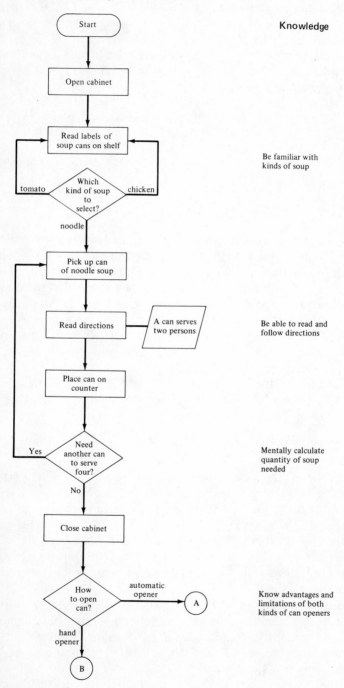

Figure 6.2

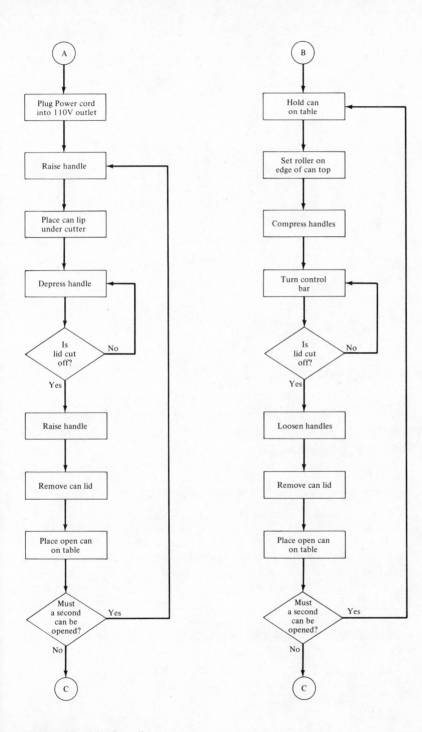

Figure 6.2 (continued)

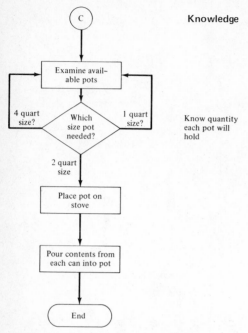

Knowledge

Know quantity
each pot will
hold

Figure 6.2   (continued)

REVIEW AND APPLICATIONS[*]

A. Recall

   1. Which elements of the instructional design plan directly influence the choice of
   subject content?

   _____

   _____

   _____

   2. To which other elements of the plan is subject content important?

   _____

   _____

   _____

   3. Who is the psychologist that has contributed to our understanding of the
   structure of subject content?

   _____

   _____

   _____

   4. a. What three categories comprise Gagné's sequential structure of subject
   content?

   _____

   _____

   _____

[*]See answers on page 253.

    b. To which category in (a) does each of the following relate?
        (1) Concepts _____
        (2) Definitions _____
        (3) Rules _____
        (4) Problem solving _____
        (5) Dates _____
        (6) Principles _____

5. Another method of organizing subject content is to do it visually. This is called _____ .

6. Briefly describe a procedure that may be used in your answer to question 5.

7. What are the two ways subject content may be treated during instruction?
    a. _____

    b. _____

8. How does a task analysis differ from a listing of subject content?

9. What are three resources you might use when carrying out a task analysis?
    a. _____

    b. _____

    c. _____

10. What is the difference between *detailing* and *flow charting* a task?

11. Draw the symbol for each function used in a flow chart.

    a. _____   information

    b. _____   decision point

    c. _____   action

    d. _____   connector to another point

    e. _____   beginning or end of task

B. Comprehension

1. Listed below are planning steps for part of a unit to be titled Overhead Transparencies. Which of these items would you include under the subject content heading?

_____ *a.* Some felt pens used to make transparencies are water based, others are permanent color.

_____ *b.* To apply three methods for preparing transparencies.

_____ *c.* To become more interested in using the overhead projector.

_____ *d.* Methods for making transparencies: on clear acetate, photocopy process, thermal method.

_____ *e.* Opening of the cardboard frame is 7½×9½ inches.

_____ *f.* Make a transparency using felt pens on clear acetate.

_____ *g.* To identify the five main parts of the overhead projector

_____ *h.* Steps used to prepare a transparency on clear acetate: (1) prepare rough drawing on paper, (2) transfer drawing to acetate using felt pens.

_____ *i.* Overlay technique allows instructor to show sections of a transparency sequentially.

_____ *j.* Lamp used in the overhead projector is 500 watts.

_____ *k.* Follow the procedure demonstrated on the videotape to prepare a transparency with a photocopy machine.

2. For your answers in question 1, categorize the items selected as subject content according to Gagné's levels.

3. Identify the levels of Gagné's content structure for the following subject content items. They relate to the topic of Alphabetical System of Filing used in a commercial business course. (Use abbreviations: *is*—intellectual skills, *vi*—verbal information, *cs*—cognitive strategies.)

_____ *a.* Indexing is the process of selecting the heading under which a record is to be filed.

_____ *b.* The alphabet runs from A through Z.

_____ *c.* Assignment: Transpose a list of names and index them.

_____ *d.* For indexing efficiency, rearrange the names of individuals so the last (surname) name may be considered first.

_____ *e.* Alphabetical filing is used in 90 percent of all filing systems.

_____ *f.* Names should be arranged in alphabetical order, one name at a time, beginning with the surname.

_____ *g.* Transposing means to rearrange so the last, or surname, precedes the first name.

_____ *h.* Always place an incomplete name in front of a more complete name.

_____ *i.* When you are ready, evaluate a file box of name cards for proper indexing. Mark errors.

4. Here is a task analysis for making a telephone call to a person whose name and address you were given. You do not have a phone number. The steps may not be in correct order. Rearrange them into proper order by placing numbers before each item. Also, *add* any important steps that are not included. (*Suggestion:* Write each item on a card or slip of paper, then rearrange.)

_____ Listen for dial tone.

_____ Locate first name of person.

_____ Write phone number on slip of paper containing name.

_____ Refer to slip of paper containing person's name and address.

_____ Listen for phone ring.

_____ Close telephone book and return it to storage place.
_____ Start conversation.
_____ Locate last name of person on page in alphabetical order.
_____ Place telephone book on table for use.
_____ Point to telephone number beside name.
_____ Dial each of the seven numbers.

_____ _____
_____ _____
_____ _____
_____ _____

5. On the left below is a partial list relating to the task Self-service Gasoline Pumping and Checking Air in Tires. On the right side (or on a separate sheet) develop a flow chart using *all* items of information. (It is not necessary to add any new items, but you can if you wish.)

Pull into station

Is an unleaded gas pump available?

If none available, decide whether to wait or go to air pump to check tires.

Align car beside pump.

The price is $1.25/gal.

Decide on amount of gas to buy.

Prepay attendant.

Remove gas cap.

Put nozzle in tank opening.

Set pump lever to ON.

Do all dials turn back to zero?

If not, notify attendant.

Pump gas.

C. Applications

  1. Sky Diving

    a. Select a topic and outline the subject content as described on page 277 in Appendix B.

    _____
    _____
    _____
    _____
    _____

    b. Select a task and prepare a task analysis by either *detailing* or *flow charting.*

    _____
    _____
    _____
    _____

  2. Your Subject

  Select one of the topics or tasks you identified in the Application project for Chapter 4 on page 44. Proceed to list subject content and/or do a task analysis.

REFERENCES

Cram, David D. "Flowcharting Primer," *Training and Development* Journal, 24 (July 1980), 64–68.

Davies, Ivor K. "Task Analysis for Reliable Human Performance," *NSPI Journal,* 20 (March 1981), 8–10, 31.

———. "Task Analysis: Some Process and Content Concerns," *AV Communications Review,* 21 (Spring 1973), 73–86.

DeCecco, John, and William Crawford. *The Psychology of Learning and Instruction* 2d ed. (Englewood Cliffs, NJ: Prentice-Hall, 1974), chapters 10,11.

Gael, Sidney. *Job Analysis: A Guide to Assessing Work Activities* (San Francisco: Jossey-Bass, 1983).

Gagné, Robert. *The Conditions of Learning,* 3d ed. (New York: Holt, Rinehart, and Winston, 1977), chapters 2, 4–8.

Harless, J.H. "Task Analysis—A Clarification of the Term," *NSPI Journal,* 19 (February 1980), 4–5.

Horabin, Ivan, and Brian Lewis. "Algorithms," volume 2, in *The Instructional Design Library,* Danny Langdon, ed. (Englewood Cliffs, NJ: Educational Technology Publications, 1978.

Mager, Robert, and Kenneth Beach. *Developing Vocational Instruction* (Belmont, CA: Pitman, 1967), chapter 3.

Merrill, M. David, and Robert D. Tennyson. *Teaching Concepts: An Instructional Design Guide* (Englewood Cliffs, NJ: Educational Technology Publications, 1977).

Merrill, Paul F. "Task Analysis—An Information Processing Approach," *NSPI Journal,* 15 (March 1976), 7–11.

Merrill, Paul F. "Representations for Algorithms," *Performance and Instruction,* 14 (October 1980), 18–24.

Miller, Robert B. "Task Description and Analysis," in *Psychological Principles in System Development,* Robert Gagné, ed. (New York: Holt, Rinehart, and Winston, 1962).

Mitchell, M.C. Jr. "The Practicality of Algorithms in Instructional Development," *Journal of Instructional Development,* 4 (Fall 1980), 10–16.

chapter 7

Learning Objectives

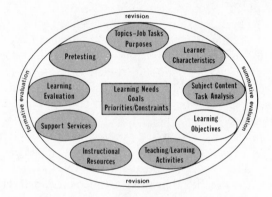

What do the following situations have in common?

Students find it difficult to take notes during the lecture because they are unaware of what is important.

Trainees did not know they were to learn how to operate all components of the equipment after the lab session was completed.

After the exam was concluded, a number of students realized they had studied the wrong content.

While observing the youngsters at work, it became evident they were having a lot of fun, but seemed to be learning little of value.

When an evaluation of the training program was made, it became obvious that learners had been confused because they did not know exactly what the instructor expected of them.

The professor reported that scores on the midterm test were very low. He had done all that he could by covering the content that he knew to be important. His conclusion: "This was probably a particularly dumb class of students."

Each of the above situations indicates the lack of a clear statement of what learners are expected to learn. Unless the requirements are specifically defined, the learner does not know precisely what to study or what activities to perform. Also, without such definition, the instructor has difficulty in measuring the specific learning. These deficiencies can be overcome if the instructor writes precise statements for learners in the form of tangible benefits expected to result from the instruction. The benefits are indicated in terms of what the learner is to accomplish, hence the expression *learning objectives.*

By knowing what is expected from the stated learning objectives, learners can better structure their study procedures and prepare for examinations. Also their self-confidence to proceed with the forthcoming learning activities will be improved. On the other hand, writing learning objectives serves important functions for the instructor. First, the stated objectives provide a basis for the selection and organization of instructional activities and resources so that effective learning can take place. Second, learning objectives provide a framework for devising ways to evaluate student learning. Since written tests and performance activities are the major means to measure student learning, objectives should guide the design of relevant testing items and procedures.

Only by stating learning objectives do we know what we want to teach and can later determine the extent of our accomplishment. Thus the writing and use of learning objectives can have a worthwhile impact on improving both teaching and the resultant learning.

Some instructional designers insist that learning objectives be stated carefully early in planning, specifically right after the goal or statement of general purposes is formulated for a topic. Sequentially, this may sound correct, but in actual practice it does not often work. While some instructors can write their learning objectives immediately, many people cannot enumerate detailed objectives at this point. The reason is that their own thinking about what to include in the unit may not yet be clear. It is for this reason that the subject content and task analysis element is placed in the instructional design plan preceding the element of learning objectives.

Writing learning objectives is a developmental activity that requires changes, refinements, and additions as the writer develops subsequent planning steps. Sometimes it is not until learning activities are being selected or evaluation methods stated that the "real" objectives for teaching a topic become clear. Therefore, expect to start with loosely worded objectives, move ahead in the planning sequence, and then return to spell out the learning objectives in specific detail as each one becomes evident.[1]

CATEGORIES OF OBJECTIVES

Objectives for learning can be grouped into three major categories—**cognitive, psychomotor,** and **affective.** These areas (or *domains* as they are generally called) are widely referred to in the literature that discusses objectives. Your

---

[1]Robert F. Mager, *Preparing Instructional Objectives.* This author very capably makes the case for objectives in an instructional program. If you are not familiar with his brief, fascinating book, be sure to read it.

understanding of the levels within each domain is important when planning a unit of instruction or a training course.

Cognitive Domain

The domain to which we give most attention in educational programs is the *cognitive domain.* It includes objectives concerning information or knowledge, and thinking—*naming, solving, predicting,* and other intellectual aspects of learning. Bloom and his associates developed a taxonomy for the cognitive domain that is widely used.[2] (A *taxonomy* is a method of sequential classification on progressively higher levels.)

The taxonomy is organized within two major groups: (1) simple recall of information, and (2) intellectual activities. Bloom labels the lowest level as *knowledge,* while the higher mental abilities are classified into five increasingly more intellectual levels—*comprehension, application, analysis, synthesis,* and *evaluation.*

Here are examples of learning objectives on each of the six levels in the cognitive domain:

Course: History

Topic: Conflict in the 20th Century

Knowledge: Define the term Cold War.

Comprehension: Describe five battle fronts on which the Cold War has been fought.

Application: Illustrate through examples the pace of the Cold War as it developed between 1946 and 1968.

Analysis: Distinguish between the policies of the Warsaw Pact nations and members of NATO.

Synthesis: Organize information that summarizes the nature and extent of the Russian–Red Chinese split.

Evaluation: Assess the evidence presented for and against a thaw in the Cold War.

Course: Fundamentals of Electricity

Topic: Connecting a Three-way Switch

Knowledge: List the tools required to wire a three-way switch.

Comprehension: Explain the purpose for each of the three wires used in connecting a switch.

Application: Sketch the procedure used when wiring a three-way switch.

Analysis: Calculate the lengths of wire needed in connecting a three-way switch to a junction box.

Synthesis: Collect all materials needed to carry out the wiring of a three-way switch.

[2] Benjamin S. Bloom, et al. *A Taxonomy of Educational Objectives. Handbook I.*

Evaluation: Compare the result of three-way switch connections with that of a standard product.

Too often major attention is given in a course to the lowest cognitive level—memorizing or recalling information. One of the challenges in instructional planning is to devise learning objectives and then related activities that can direct students to accomplishments on the five higher intellectual levels. Later on in this chapter, when we examine both the verbs used in expressing objectives and the sequencing of objectives, we will give further attention to all six levels.

Another taxonomy, attributed to Gagné, as described on page 60, comprises a cognitive sequence—*facts, concepts, principles,* and *problem solving.* In sequence, each higher level is dependent upon the learner's having mastered the preceding related lower level. Thus, a student uses *facts* to identify *concepts,* then builds relationships among concepts to identify *principles,* and ultimately applies principles to develop *problem-solving* skills.

Some relationship can be found between the categories Gagné proposes and the taxonomy of objectives listed by Bloom in the cognitive domain. They both start with simple factual learning and move to higher intellectual levels. They both include, according to each writer's interpretation, the important mental processes that are essential to learning.

Gagné explains which conditions are most appropriate for facilitating the learning of each type of performance. This method helps the planner answer these questions: "In order to be able to do or to understand this *concept* (principle or rule), what must the learner first be able to do, know, or understand?" Then, "Have I provided for this lower level of behavior?" Both Bloom's and Gagné's materials suggest systematic ways of grouping and sequencing objectives within a topic.

Psychomotor Domain

The second category in which learning objectives may be grouped is the *psychomotor domain.* It treats the skills requiring use and coordination of skeletal muscles, as in the physical activities of *performing, manipulating,* and *constructing.* Although no taxonomy is universally accepted for this domain, the most comprehensive classification is by Harrow.[3] Six major classes of physical behavior are recognized:

1. *Reflex movements*—Involuntary muscle responses to stimuli. Such movements are instinctual and not learned. *Examples:* Stiffen, extend, flex, or stretch arms and legs.
2. *Basic fundamental movements*—Body movement patterns developed during early life. They build upon reflex movements and are basic to all normal psychomotor activities. *Examples:* Crawl, walk, run, jump, reach, grasp.

[3]Anita J. Harrow, *A Taxonomy of the Psychomotor Domain.*

3. *Perceptual abilities*—Observing and interpreting stimuli in the environment to which a person is exposed, requiring a movement for adjustment. Perceptions involve kinesthetic awareness, like a change in body balance, visual or auditory discrimination, tactile or sense of touch discrimination, and coordination of eye–hand and eye–foot movements. *Examples:* Turn, bend, balance, catch an object, kick a ball, perform a simple dance.

4. *Physical abilities*—Includes endurance, strength, flexibility and agility of movements. Highly skilled movements cannot be developed without a satisfactory foundation in these abilities. *Examples:* Endure physical activity for a long time, make quick motions, stop and restart a movement, move heavy objects.

5. *Skilled movements*—Performing complex actions efficiently. Actions are based upon basic fundamental movements and use both perceptual abilities and simple, compound, or complex physical abilities which, with practice, result in skilled movements performed with ease and proficiency. *Examples:* Play a musical instrument, use a hand tool, assemble parts, operate a vehicle, adjust a machine.

6. *Nondiscursive communication*—Physical movements that communicate feelings which are both reflexive and learned. They include expressive movements like posture, gestures, facial expressions, and interpretive movements that are aesthetic or creative in form. *Examples:* Ballroom dancing, changes in facial expression, physical expressions of emotions and feelings.

Most muscular movements required for performing a task, be it a physical skill like tumbling or using a screwdriver to assemble components of equipment, can be derived from this taxonomy. Note the sample activities that relate to the four higher levels. No objectives are written for the lowest two levels which, rather than being learned, are reflexes and skills naturally developed with maturity.

Another grouping of psychomotor skills (although it is not a sequential taxonomy) is the following:[4]

1. Gross bodily movements of arms, shoulders, feet, and legs. *Examples:* Throwing a ball for a distance, picking up a heavy object so as not to strain the body, performing a back dive.

2. Finely coordinated movements of hands and fingers, hand and eye, hand and ear, and of hand, eye, and foot. *Examples:* Knitting a scarf, guiding wood through a table saw, using a typewriter, driving a car, sightreading music while playing an instrument.

3. Nonverbal communication through facial expression, gestures, bodily movements. *Examples:* Showing emotions through facial expressions, employing gestures to communicate directions; pantomiming a message.

4. Speech behavior in producing and projecting sound, coordinating sound and gestures. *Examples:* Giving instructions in a foreign language or presenting a literary reading, with gestures for emphasis.

[4]Robert J. Kibler, et al. *Objectives for Instruction and Evaluation.*

The value of the groupings of Kibler and associates is the recognition of different separate gross and fine movement skills in the first two psychomotor behavior categories. Because each one requires the use of different sets of muscles, the teaching of such skills can better be organized with attention first being given to gross movements and then to fine movements.

From either of the two above lists of psychomotor behavior, you can classify physical skills relating to athletics, the performing arts, the manipulation of tools, and the operation of equipment. Psychomotor behaviors generally are easy to observe, describe, and measure. The details resulting from a task analysis (page 65) permit you to determine the specific muscle coordination required in a physical activity and then to state the appropriate learning requirements as objectives.

Affective Domain

The third category of learning objectives is the *affective domain.* This involves objectives concerning attitudes, appreciations, values, and emotions—*enjoying, conserving, respecting,* and so on. We talk about this area as being of great importance in education, but it is the one area in which we have been able to do the least, particularly in writing useful learning objectives. Krathwohl and his associates[5] have organized the affective domain into five levels.

1. Receiving—Willing to give attention to an event or activity. *Examples:* Listen to, be aware of, perceive, be alert to, be sensitive to, show tolerance of.
2. Responding—Willing to react to an event through some form of participation. *Examples:* Reply, answer, follow along, approve, obey, find pleasure in.
3. Valuing—Willing to accept or reject an event through the expression of a positive or negative attitude. *Examples:* Accept, attain, assume, support, participate, continue, grow in, be devoted to.
4. Organizing—When encountering situations to which more than one value applies, willingly organize the values, determine relationships among values, and accept some values as dominant over others (by the importance to the individual learner). *Examples:* organize, select, judge, decide, identify with, develop a plan for, weigh alternatives.
5. Characterizing by a value complex—Learner consistently acts in accordance with accepted values and incorporates this behavior as a part of his or her personality. *Examples:* Believes, practices, continues to, carries out, becomes part of his or her code of behavior.

The levels of the affective domain, like those of the cognitive domain, form a continuum for attitudinal behavior, from simple awareness and acceptance to internalization as attitudes that become part of an individual's practicing value system. The problem of translating these feelings into identifiable and observable behavior makes the writing of attitudinal objectives

[5]David R. Krathwohl, et al. *A Taxonomy of Educational Objectives. Handbook II.*

very difficult. This matter receives more attention later on in this chapter under the heading, "Writing Objectives in the Affective Domain."

During planning, keep in mind all three domains, and attempt to treat the higher levels as they affect your topics and general purposes.

Interrelation of Domains

Even though we are examining the three domains separately, you should recognize that they are closely related in two ways. First, a single major objective can involve learning in two or even all three domains. For example, when a technician learns to mix chemicals, first, he or she must acquire knowledge about the different chemicals and their relationships as well as the psychomotor skills of performing the mixing operation. To this we might add the affective behavior of neatness and the practice of safety in the mixing procedure.

Second, attitudinal development may even precede successful learning in the other domains. It is often necessary to motivate learners to want to learn subject matter before instruction can be successful. This may be particularly true in a self-paced learning program, since the learner must take responsibility for his or her own learning, and both receptiveness and cooperation can, in some measure, determine the learner's level of achievement. Once motivation is established, a well-organized program in which the learner participates successfully usually produces positive attitudes in the learner toward the subject and the instructor.

WRITING COGNITIVE AND PSYCHOMOTOR LEARNING OBJECTIVES

A learning objective is a precise statement that answers the question, "What should the learner have learned or be able to do, relative to the subject content, upon completing this topic or unit?" Ask yourself this question each time you start to formulate an objective. Your answer will help give direction to your efforts. To answer the question satisfactorily, write learning objectives that consist of at least *two essential* parts and *two optional* parts.

Essential Parts

Start with an *action verb* that describes the learning required by the learner or trainee:

to *name*   to *operate*   to *arrange*   to *compare*

Follow the action verb with the *subject content reference* that describes the content being treated:

To name the *parts of speech used in a sentence*
To operate a *videotape recorder*

To arrange *parts in order for assembly*

To compare *points of view expressed on political issues*

Taken together, the action verb and the subject content reference indicate essentially what the student is to achieve. No doubt, you or the subject specialist on a planning team can easily choose the content for an objective. The selection of the appropriate action verb to describe the learning behavior required from the learner is the difficult part of objective writing. For learning objectives developed in the cognitive domain, a "shopping list" of verbs that express behaviors on each of the six levels in Bloom's taxonomy can be helpful. Such a list is found in Table 7.1, below. These verbs can assist you in recognizing (and giving attention to) the higher intellectual levels in your planning.

You should have little difficulty in deciding on the action verb for a psychomotor domain objective, since the skill to be performed is usually directly definable. Sample verbs are included with the categories for the Harrow taxonomy on page 80.

Table 7.1   SHOPPING LIST OF VERBS
Verbs Applicable to the Six Levels in The Cognitive Domain*

1. Knowledge Recall of information		2. Comprehension Interpret information in one's own words		3. Application Apply knowledge or generalization to new situation	
arrange	name	classify	recognize	apply	operate
define	order	describe	report	choose	prepare
duplicate	recognize	discuss	restate	demonstrate	practice
label	relate	explain	review	dramatize	schedule
list	recall	express	select	employ	sketch
match	repeat	identify	sort	illustrate	solve
memorize	reproduce	indicate	tell	interpret	use
		locate	translate		

4. Analysis Break down knowledge into parts and show relationship among parts		5. Synthesis Bring together parts of knowledge to form a whole and build relationships for new situations		6. Evaluation Make judgments on basis of given criteria	
analyze	differentiate	arrange	manage	appraise	evaluate
appraise	discriminate	assemble	organize	argue	judge
calculate	distinguish	collect	plan	assess	predict
categorize	examine	compose	prepare	attack	rate
compare	experiment	construct	propose	choose	score
contrast	inventory	create	set up	compare	select
criticize	question	design	synthesize	defend	support
diagram	test	formulate	write	estimate	value

*Depending on the meaning for use, some verbs may apply to more than one level.

Optional Parts

You may feel that stating the action verb and the content reference completely express a learning objective. This may be true in many situations. But there are times when it is desirable or necessary to be more specific and include other parameters as part of the learning requirement. This is particularly important when a training course has specific or minimum outcome requirements for proficiency. Objectives for such a competency-based program require these additional parts.

A Level of Achievement   This is the *performance standard,* which indicates the minimum acceptable accomplishment in *measurable terms* and which answers such questions as these: "How well?" "How much?" "How accurate?" "How complete?" "In what time period?" Here are ways in which the performance standard can be stated:

- In proper order
- At least 8 out of 10 correct (or 80 percent correct)
- With an accuracy of 2 centimeters
- Within 3 minutes
- Meeting the criteria stated in the manual (or established by the instructor or the class)

Here are examples of learning objectives, each of which includes a performance standard:

To arrange the six steps of water purification *in proper order.*

To troubleshoot circuit problems with *a correct solution rate of 90 percent.*

To measure a client's blood pressure within *±5mm Hg accuracy as determined by the instructor.*

To design a display which received a *rating of at least 4 against the criteria discussed in class.*

One or More Conditions   As necessary for learner understanding and in order to set evaluation requirements, add any *conditions* under which the evaluation will take place. Conditions result from answers to questions like these: "Is special equipment to be available?" "Is access to a certain book, chart, or other reference allowed?" "Are time limitations imposed?" "Are other specific factors set as conditions for testing?"

Here are examples of learning objectives, each of which includes a condition and also a performance standard, as appropriate:

Using the hospital's floor map as a guide, to locate all fire extinguishers and emergency exits on the floor with 100 percent accuracy.

Based on assigned readings, to compare the cultures of two past civilizations, enumerating at least five characteristics of each.

Given the chart showing the normal growth rate of a redwood tree, to predict within 15 percent accuracy the size of a tree over a 5-year period.

Within an 8-minute period, to set up, zero in, and operate a multimeter tester.

All learning objectives should be written in forms similar to those illustrated in the examples above. Where appropriate, include either or both of the optional parts. When no performance standard is included, the assumption is usually made that only a 100 percent correct reply or performance is acceptable. Keep your statements simple and brief. Avoid including so much detail that the effort of writing the objectives becomes discouraging and the requirements sound overwhelming to learners.

A caution: When instructional planners first start to write objectives, they sometimes tend to write descriptions of what is to occur during the instruction and consider the statements to be learning objectives. For example, "to view a videotape on ecological safeguards," or "to read pages 45 to 70 in the text." These are *activities,* not indications of learning outcomes. If you are not sure whether what you are stating is an objective, ask yourself: "Is this what I want the learner to know or be able to do after completing the topic or unit?"

WRITING OBJECTIVES IN THE AFFECTIVE DOMAIN

When we turn to the affective domain—attitudes, feelings, and appreciations— we find difficulty in specifying objectives in clearly observable and measurable terms. Most often we can indicate these objectives only indirectly by *inferring from what can be observed.* What a learner does or says can be assumed evidence of behavior relating to an objective.

Some behaviors in this area are difficult to identify, let alone to name and measure. How, for instance, do you measure an attitude of *appreciating the importance of good nutrition,* or *developing a positive relationship toward company clients?* Such attitudes can be recognized only indirectly from secondary clues. For example, if the learning objective is *To appreciate the importance of good nutrition,* evidence of accomplishment can be shown if the learner:

- Is observed eating only foods of high nutritional value (no junk foods or refined products).
- Readily advises other persons about the value of nutritious foods.
- Voluntarily reads books and articles describing good nutrition practices.
- Signs up for and attends lectures and workshops presented by nutrition authorities.

If the learning objective is *To develop a positive relationship toward company clients,* evidence of accomplishment can be shown if the employee:

- Is prompt for appointments with clients.
- Calls each client by name, is courteous, and speaks in a friendly tone.
- Shows an interest in the client as a person by talking about matters, other than business, that are mutually interesting.
- Spends extra time with a client, as necessary.
- Provides requested information promptly.

Admittedly, these examples are only indicative of the possible successful fulfillment of an attitudinal objective and do not measure it directly. Mager calls these attitudinal objectives *approach tendencies* toward exhibiting a positive attitude to a subject or a situation. The learner's attitude is considered negative if he or she shows "avoidance tendencies."[6]

In general terms, to measure an approach tendency toward a positive attitude about an activity, such indications as the following could be used:

The learner says he or she likes the activity.

The learner selects the activity in place of other possible ones.

The learner participates in the activity with much enthusiasm.

The learner shares his or her interest in the activity by discussing it with others or by encouraging others to participate.

In the book *Goal Analysis,*[7] Mager helps us further to examine attitudinal goals we might select and then to specify indicator behaviors that represent positive actions relating to those attitudes. For example, Mager suggests that if company employees are to exhibit *safety consciousness,* they can be expected to practice the following behaviors: "Report safety hazards; wear safety equipment; follow safety rules; practice good housekeeping by keeping the work area free of dirt and loose tools; encourage safe practice in others by reminding them to wear safety equipment; and so forth. . . ."

The method Mager suggests can help you to refine ways of indicating attitudinal objectives and then setting a degree of measurement for them. For other specific help in identifying and writing affective-domain objectives, refer to the work of Lee and Merrill.[8]

For each of the five levels of the affective domain taxonomy of Krathwohl and associates, described on page 82, a number of action verbs are listed. Here are additional verbs you may find useful as you state learning objectives in this domain:

---

[6] For further suggestions on formulating objectives in the affective domain and for selecting measurable indicators of successful accomplishment, see another book by Robert F. Mager, *Developing Attitude Toward Learning.* Other suggestions are offered by the National Science Teachers Association in *Behavioral Objectives in the Affective Domain.*

[7] Mager, *Goal Analysis,* p. 46.

[8] Blaine N. Lee and M. David Merrill, *Writing Complete Affective Objectives.*

acclaims	cooperates	joins
agrees	defends	offers
argues	disagrees	participates in
assumes responsibility	disputes	praises
attempts	engages in	resists
avoids	helps	shares
challenges	is attentive to	volunteers

Realistically we must recognize that there are many important objectives that cannot result in measurable outcomes. Eisner[9] uses the term *expressive objectives* for those for which specific outcomes cannot readily be stated. These objectives identify situations for the learner, but they do not include measurable outcomes. An expressive objective may allow for self-discovery, originality, and inventiveness. The result may be a surprise to both the learner and the instructor. For example, "to develop a feeling of personal adequacy in athletic performance" is an expressive objective. By stating such nonmeasurable objectives during planning, you can at least identify aspects of instructional goals that have personal or social importance and thus can make a start on deciding how to achieve them.

SEQUENCING OBJECTIVES

One challenge in designing a good instructional program is to identify the sequential levels of content and tasks within a topic. This is an important matter to which careful attention should be given while working with learning objectives. Instead of writing a string of casually related objectives, learners should be directed to accomplish a range of objectives leading to higher-order behaviors. If you do not treat the more advanced, complex, or abstract objectives, you are in danger of following the easiest path by limiting objectives to the lowest learning levels of memorization and factual recall, which are often of minor importance in any instructional program.

There are a number of methods for sequencing or classifying objectives according to levels. You have already been introduced to some of them.

Terminal/Subordinate Method

A major objective for a topic or task is called a *terminal learning objective*. It describes, in behavioral terms, the overall learning outcomes expressed originally as the general purpose for a topic. More than a single terminal objective may be necessary for accomplishing a general purpose. Here are examples of terminal learning objectives:

[9]Elliot W. Eisner, "Instructional and Expressive Objectives," in *Instructional Objectives.*

Topic: Fetal Circulation

General Purpose: To acquire knowledge and understanding of the anatomy and physiology of fetal circulation.

Terminal Objective: To describe the normal circulation pattern within a fetus.

Topic: Renaissance and Reformation

General Purpose: To understand the changes that took place in European civilization during the late Middle Ages.

Terminal Objective: To interpret the significant developments taking place as Europeans broke the continental bonds and established a world hegemony.

Topic: The Automobile Distributor

General Purpose: To clean and adjust the distributor for a smooth running engine.

Terminal Objective: To service a distributor.

The subobjectives that lead to accomplishing the terminal objective are designated *enabling* or *supporting* objectives. Enabling objectives describe the specific behaviors (single activities or steps) that must be learned or performed, often sequentially, in order to achieve the terminal objective. For the terminal objectives above, the following enabling objectives are required:

Terminal Objective: To describe the normal circulation pattern within a fetus.

Enabling Objectives: (1) To name the two types of blood vessel found in the umbilical cord. (2) To locate the two shunts which are normal in fetal circulation. (3) To label a diagram of fetal circulation, indicating differences in systolic pressure between the left and right sides of the heart.

Terminal Objective: To interpret the significant developments taking place as Europeans broke the continental bonds and established a world hegemony.

Enabling Objectives: (1) To identify economic developments that emerged in medieval Europe. (2) To analyze the political, religious, social, and psychological forces that helped create the Reformation. (3) To relate the intellectual and architectural accomplishments of the 12th century to the foundations for the Renaissance.

Terminal Objective: To service a distributor.

Enabling Objectives: (1) To identify the four main parts of a distributor. (2) To remove and clean the distributor cap. (3) To remove and clean the rotor. (4) To clean and install breaker points. (5) To set breaker points.

As you list subject content or do a task analysis of your topic (Chapter 6), the relationship of major items and supportive content becomes evident in outline form. Thus, you may find the subject content element to be a good starting point for developing terminal and enabling learning objectives.

Domains of Learning

As you already know, the cognitive and affective domains comprise sequential hierarchies starting from low levels of learning or behavior and progressing through more intellectual or sophisticated levels. You may wish to review the explanations and examples given for the six cognitive levels and the five

Table 7.2 A SPECIFICATION TABLE RELATING OBJECTIVES IN *GEOMETRY* TO GAGNÉ'S COGNITIVE LEARNING LEVELS

Objective	Learning Facts	Forming Concepts	Learning Principles	Problem Solving
1. Name the common plane geometry figures.	✔			
2. Define the common plane geometry figures.	✔			
3. Identify geometric figures shown in pictures.		✔		
4. Group similar geometric figures when shown models of various sizes.			✔	
5. List dimensions of geometric figures.	✔			
6. Label significant dimensions of geometric figures.		✔		
7. Measure dimensions in sketches of geometric figures.				✔
8. Make scale drawings of geometric figures.				✔
9. Derive the formulas for areas of geometric figures.			✔	
10. Compute areas of geometric figures in diagrams.				✔
11. Compare sizes of geometric figures in diagrams.			✔	
12. Calculate areas of common objects.				✔

affective levels described earlier in this chapter. The psychomotor domain does not exhibit as consistent a sequencing pattern as do the other two domains.

Another hierarchy is Gagné's sequence of intellectual skills—facts, concepts, principles, and problem solving—as described on page 60.

One way to check that a unit includes higher-level objectives is to prepare a specification table relating objectives to learning levels (Table 7.2). List the objectives vertically and horizontally to show to which category of learning each objective relates. From left to right move to increasingly abstract levels— "learning facts," "forming concepts," "learning principles," and "problem solving."

Another way of relating objectives to learning levels is to start with subject content and place the learning objectives that apply alongside each item. Then indicate the learning level for the objective. Table 7.3 illustrates this method in terms of the Bloom taxonomy.

In preparing such tables, you will find that an objective does not always fall neatly into a single behavioral category. An objective you classify as "learning principles" might also seem to belong under "forming concepts." Differentiating between an "analysis" or "evaluation" objective can be difficult. It is not always important to identify the specific level represented by an objective. As long as you are giving attention to objectives *above* the basic levels (higher than *knowledge* for Bloom, *factual learning* for Gagné, and *receiving* for Krathwohl), then you are sequencing satisfactorily for treating higher learning requirements.

Although we have considered two methods for sequencing objectives separately, in actual practice the terminal/subordinate method and the levels within the domains fit together logically. Give attention to both procedures in your planning.

DIFFICULTIES IN WRITING OBJECTIVES

One reason many people shy away from stating precise objectives is that formulating them demands hard mental effort. Each objective, to the degree possible, should be unambiguous. It must communicate exactly the same thing to all learners and to other instructors. Many instructors are not accustomed to such exactness in instructional planning. For too long we have based our teaching on broad generalizations, often leaving it up to the learner to interpret what we actually mean.

It is not until the importance of objectives for an instructional program becomes apparent that instructors are willing to put sincere effort into preparing them. Then the difficulties and frustrations are taken in stride, and we gradually develop a habit and pattern for expressing as many of the desired outcomes of effective learning as possible in specific, meaningful terms.

PROS AND CONS OF OBJECTIVES

As you studied the content of this chapter, you no doubt considered your own feelings and attitudes relative to the importance of writing learning objectives.

Table 7.3 A SPECIFICATION TABLE RELATING SUBJECT CONTENT AND OBJECTIVES FOR A UNIT ON *WEATHER FRONTS* TO BLOOM'S TAXONOMY IN THE COGNITIVE DOMAIN

Content/Objective	Knowledge	Comprehension	Application	Analysis	Synthesis	Evaluation
Definition Write a definition of the term *weather front.*		✓				
Types and appearance Describe three types of weather fronts.		✓				
Symbols used Identify the symbols used to show fronts on weather maps.	✓					
Movement Calculate the movement patterns of each frontal type.			✓			
Associated weather Recognize the types of weather associated with each frontal system.		✓				
Locate fronts on maps Using synoptic data, draw fronts on a weather map.			✓		✓	
Predict weather Predict weather on a map containing various fronts, singly and in combination.						✓

Some people readily accept the position taken in this book that it is of value to write observable and measurable objectives whenever possible. Others have strong views against being so specific, believing that objectives are often unnecessary or that the important outcomes of a program do not lend themselves to being stated objectively. These latter individuals may feel that the more important long-term outcomes of an instructional program are hard to define and are often unmeasurable.

This should not be an either/or situation. Admittedly, most objectives we write relate to short-term goals, attainable during a course or training program. Some of them, however, may contribute to long-term goals, such as the development of analytical skills or decision-making abilities, over which the instructor has little or no control. These high-level objectives may not be fully measurable until years later. Therefore, it is reasonable at times to assume that certain objectives cannot be completely satisfied during the planned instructional program. Learners can be followed up after completing a course to determine their competencies relative to such important long-term objectives. See page 239 about how this might be done as part of summative evaluation.

If you would like to read a rationale that examines all aspects of this topic of objectives, the reference by Davies can be most helpful.[10] He puts objectives in perspective, based on his review of literature and research in the field of curriculum design.

LEARNERS AND THEIR OBJECTIVES

At the beginning of this chapter, it was indicated that learning objectives provide particular benefits to learners. Therefore, objectives for a topic should be made available to learners at the time their study of a topic is to start. Present the objectives to learners just as they are written in their final form, including the optional parts—conditions and performance standard—for success.

By following this procedure, learners will know specifically what is expected of them and by what standard they will be evaluated. They will know that you are helping them to set their paths for learning, and they will appreciate it. There is positive evidence that learners who are informed of the learning objectives they are to satisfy do progress through an instructional unit in less time and with a greater success in learning than do those not so informed.[11]

SUMMARY

We are considering a procedure for systematically planning instruction in which the specification of learning objectives plays a key role. The objectives indicate what a learner should be able to do after completing a unit of

[10]Davies, *Objectives in Curriculum Design.*
[11]James M. Lewis, "The Whens, Whys, and Hows of Behavioral Objectives."

instruction and are expressed in precise, unambiguous terms. In order to do this properly, we have given attention to these essential matters about learning objectives in this chapter:

- Objectives can be important to both learners and instructors. They help learners plan their study and prepare for examinations. They are used by the instructor as guidance for planning instruction and devising tests.
- Objectives are grouped into cognitive, psychomotor, and affective domains within which increasingly higher levels of intellectual aptitude, skill ability, and emotional behavior are recognized.
- The domains are closely related, since a single major objective can require learning in more than one area.
- Objectives consist of an action verb and subject content reference; they may also include a performance standard and/or conditions.
- Objectives on higher intellectual levels are more difficult, and yet more important, to specify.
- Objectives can be identified only indirectly in the affective domain by inferring learner acceptance of an attitude from behavior that can be observed.
- Objectives can be organized and sequenced by various methods to ensure that the more advanced objectives receive suitable attention.

The subject matter relating to learning objectives as treated in this chapter provides the essential information to guide you in developing your own objectives and in assisting a subject specialist to write learning objectives.

REVIEW AND APPLICATIONS*

A. Recall

   1. What are some values of learning objectives both for learners and the instructor?
   a. Learners: _____
   _____
   _____

   b. Instructor: _____
   _____
   _____

   2. List the names of the three domains into which all objectives can be placed. Beside each name write descriptive words or terms.
   a. _____
   _____
   _____

   b. _____
   _____
   _____

   c. _____
   _____
   _____

*See answers on page 261.

3. In what two ways are the three domains of objectives closely related?

 a. _____

 b. _____

4. List the two essential parts that comprise a properly stated objective.

 a. _____

 b. _____

5. What may be added to these essential parts to make objectives more complete?

 a. _____

 b. _____

6. What do the following terms mean in reference to attitudinal objectives?

 a. Approach tendencies _____

 b. Expressive objectives _____

7. What is meant by the expression "sequencing objectives?"

 _____

8. List three methods for sequencing objectives in the cognitive domain.

 a. _____

 b. _____

 c. _____

B. Comprehension

 1. Relate each following objective to a domain you listed in answer A.2. Use the first letter of each domain—*C, P,* or *A.*

 _____ *a.* To sketch a picture with a pencil.

 _____ *b.* To take responsibilities for organizing special activities in a club.

 _____ *c.* To drill holes in a sheet of metal.

 _____ *d.* To spell all words in an exercise correctly.

_____ *e.* To display good manners toward citizens of other countries while working in their cities.

_____ *f.* To select the correct solution in a geometry problem.

_____ *g.* To shoot free throws in basketball with 80 percent accuracy.

_____ *h.* To judge the quality of other learners' projects.

_____ *i.* To enter into class discussion with enthusiasm about election candidates.

_____ *j.* To apply a scientific concept when performing a lab experiment.

_____ *k.* To write your name smoothly and legibly.

_____ *l.* To list six important points when applying for a job interview.

_____ *m.* To take blood pressure with a sphygmomanometer.

_____ *n.* To identify the work of influential Renaissance artists.

_____ *o.* To compare the British political system with the governmental system of the American colonies.

2. Write below the letter for each of those objectives in question 1 above that you classified in the *cognitive* domain. Beside each letter indicate whether the objective is on the *knowledge* level or on a *higher* intellectual level. Also, if you wish, state to which of the higher levels each of the latter objectives relate.

_____

_____

_____

_____

_____

3. Which of the following words would you select for use in writing specific learning objectives?

_____ to know   _____ to summarize   _____ to become aware of

_____ to relate   _____ to learn   _____ to list

_____ to compute   _____ to understand   _____ to apply

4. Check each statement that is complete and correct as a learning objective. If it is *not* acceptable, then correct or rewrite it so it becomes complete and acceptable.

_____ *a.* To reduce fractions to lowest terms.

_____ *b.* To administer medication to the proper patient with 100 percent accuracy.

_____ *c.* Given the names of three composers we study in class, to list the title of one composition for each name.

_____ *d.* To express reasons for studying the Bible.

_____ *e.* To master the area of rectangles.

_____ *f.* To exhibit an open-minded attitude by listening carefully when others are speaking.

_____ *g.* Given orally or on tape a list of words which have affixes, the learner will write the root of each word.

_____ *h.* To view the videotape on "Good Form in Tennis."

_____ *i.* To practice good work habits in the science lab.

_____ *j.* To diagram two basic communication models and write an explanation of the components of each one.

_____ *k.* To demonstrate knowledge of proper procedure for installing a zipper in a skirt.

_____ *l.* To write an adventure story.

_____ *m.* In a half-hour test at the end of this week, each student will be able to list the steps a bill follows through Congress, specifying the requirements for the passage at each step. All steps must be included in the correct order and the passage procedure must match the ones in the textbook.

_____ *n.* Given the five steps of the injection molding machine cycle, arrange them in proper order.

_____ *o.* To develop skill in proofreading material that is typewritten.

5. What are some "approach tendencies" for each of these objectives?
    a. Junior high school students to develop a positive attitude toward their peers.

    _____

    _____

    _____

    b. A factory worker to take pride in jobs he is assigned to complete.

    _____

    _____

    _____

6. For each group of objectives relating to the same topic, indicate which one is the *terminal objective.*
    a. _____ *(1)* To use a wood lathe machine.
       _____ *(2)* To construct a desk lamp in the wood shop.
       _____ *(3)* To wire an electric socket.
       _____ *(4)* To identify the uses for various kinds of wood in construction.

    b. _____ *(1)* To exhibit a positive attitude toward persons with differing religious beliefs.
       _____ *(2)* To relate similarities and differences among the leading religions.
       _____ *(3)* To identify the essential elements of each leading religion.

    c. _____ *(1)* To build up endurance for swimming by exercise.
       _____ *(2)* To coordinate arm and leg movements in swimming.
       _____ *(3)* To develop breathing in synchronization with body movements.
       _____ *(4)* To swim 50 yards in less than 40 seconds using the butterfly stroke.

    d. _____ *(1)* To list four types of invertebrates.
       _____ *(2)* To select one group of invertebrates and study its members.
       _____ *(3)* To relate all groups of invertebrates to their respective positions in the evolution of animals.
       _____ *(4)* To recognize the differences between invertebrate and vertebrate animals.

    e. ____ *(1)* To recognize how special interest groups make demands on the rest
            of society.

       ____ *(2)* To interpret how our system of government has been adapted to
            changing values and interests.

       ____ *(3)* To identify the guarantees of civil rights by the 5th and 14th
            amendments to the Constitution.

       ____ *(4)* To describe how voting rights have been extended to new groups
            over the years.

C. Applications

  1. *Sky Diving*

    a. For the topic for which you listed subject content in the Application project
    for Chapter 6 (page 75), now write learning objectives. Include a terminal
    objective and some supporting objectives above the knowledge level in the
    cognitive domain.

        _____

        _____

        _____

        _____

    b. For the task analysis you prepared in the Application project for Chapter 6,
    write learning objectives. Include a terminal objective.

        _____

        _____

        _____

        _____

        _____

  2. *Your Subject*
  Write learning objectives for your topic.

REFERENCES

Behavioral Objectives in the Affective Domain. (Washington, DC: National Science
    Teachers Association).

Bloom, Benjamin S., et al. *A Taxonomy of Educational Objectives. Handbook I: The
    Cognitive Domain* (New York: Longman, 1977).

Davies, Ivor K. *Objectives in Curriculum Design,* (New York: McGraw-Hill, 1976).

Eisner, Elliot W. "Instructional and Expressive Objectives: Their Formulation and Use
    in Curriculum," in *Instructional Objectives: An Analysis of Emerging Issues,* W.
    James Popham, ed. (Chicago, Rand McNally, 1969), 13–18.

Gronlund, Normal E. *Stating Behavioral Objectives for Classroom Instruction* (New
    York: Macmillan, 1970).

Harrow, Anita J. *A Taxonomy of the Psychomotor Domain* (New York: David McKay,
    1972).

Kibler, Robert J. *Objectives for Instruction and Evaluation* (Boston: Allyn and Bacon,
    1981).

Krathwohl, David R., et al. *A Taxonomy of Educational Objectives. Handbook II:
    Affective Domain* (New York: Longman, 1969).

Lee, Blaine N., and M. David Merrill. *Writing Complete Affective Objectives: A Short
    Course* (Belmont, CA: Wadsworth, 1972).

Lewis, James M. "The Whens, Whys, and Hows of Behavioral Objectives," *Training/
    HRD,* 18 (March 1981), 60–63.

Mager, Robert F. *Developing Attitude Toward Learning* (Belmont, CA: Pitman, 1968).

——. *Goal Analysis* (Belmont, CA: Pitman, 1972).

——. *Preparing Instructional Objectives.* 2d ed. (Belmont, CA: Pitman, 1975).

chapter 8

Teaching / Learning Activities

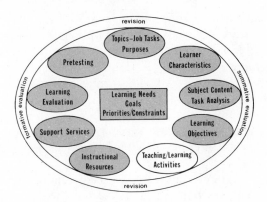

"Should I lecture on this content, or would another way to present it be better?"

"We feel a discussion is the best method to accomplish these objectives."

"I want to do role playing somewhere in this unit since my students benefit from such an activity."

"Which method of self-paced learning would be appropriate for this topic?"

"Is it better to perform the demonstration before the class, or put it on videotape for students to watch on their own?"

"They tell me it's best to include some activity for students during a lecture. How can this be done?"

These are the kinds of questions and statements that now need attention as we prepare to examine instructional methods. The purpose is to select and plan learning activities based on the content associated with the learning objectives in order to achieve maximum learner success. This is the third of the four key elements in the instructional design process—learners, objectives, activities, and evaluation.

There is a wide range of possible activities from which to make a selection. Unfortunately, there is no simple formula for matching activities with objectives. What may work for one instructor or with one group of students can be unsatisfactory in another situation. You need to know the alternatives available to you, their relative advantages, and also the various supporting materials that might be used. Then you can choose that which you feel will best serve the objectives you have established, in terms of both learner characteristics and learner preparation.

We need to provide some basis on which satisfactory decisions can be made about teaching methods and effective learning activities. This is necessary to enable the largest possible number of learners to master the learning objectives at an acceptable level of achievement, in a reasonable amount of time.

PATTERNS OF TEACHING AND LEARNING

There are many paths to learning. No doubt you are familiar with the methods of teaching and learning activities generally used. Traditionally, teachers *present* information to classes of learners through lecturing, talking informally, writing on the chalkboard, demonstrating, and showing audiovisual materials. Learners work *individually at their own pace* by reading, completing worksheets, solving problems, writing reports, working in a lab or shop, and possibly viewing films and using other audiovisual materials. *Interaction* between instructor and learners and among learners takes place by means of question and answer sessions, discussions, small group activities, learner project work, and reports.

These three patterns—presentation to a class, self-paced or individualized learning, and instructor–learner interaction—are the categories within which most methods of instruction and learning can be placed. Each instructional activity, whether teacher-controlled or for individual learner use, is related to one of these three patterns.

We cannot make use of these three patterns in a casual or haphazard manner when planning an instructional program. Why is this so? There are several reasons.

First, we know from evidence about learning styles (page 50) that both group and self-paced methods should be employed. Many learners can learn on their own, whereas other learners prefer highly structured teaching situations in which they are guided through a lesson. These variations among learners require that diverse methods of instruction be used.

Second, the conditions and principles of learning (see following section) alert us to the need for choosing methods that can provide for active participation by learners in all learning activities. As we will see, certain nontraditional methods best fulfill this requirement for some instructional situations.

Third, when we prepare to employ new technologies of instruction (television, computers, and so forth), emphasis usually is given to either group presentations or to self-paced learning activities. In either case, we may lose opportunities for face-to-face teacher-learner interactions. Providing adequately for small-group work needs to be recognized.

Fourth, there is the question of efficiency in the use of instructor and learner time, facilities, and equipment. It may be more efficient for certain purposes to present information to a class (of any size) at one time than to have each learner study the material independently. Such group instruction not only saves time, but can lessen the wear and tear on equipment and materials caused by repeated use. It also permits teachers to have maximum time to meet with groups, for individual tutoring and consultation, and for instructional planning.

From an overall viewpoint, presentations to groups and self-paced learning methods are most satisfactory for achieving objectives in the cognitive and psychomotor domains. The best way to deal with affective objectives is through cooperative group activities. In the give and take of discussions, learners can be motivated to learn, helped to sharpen their judgments, and to develop discriminations.

For these and other reasons, an understanding of the three teaching/learning patterns, their advantages and limitations, and techniques applicable within each category, are necessary for successful instructional planning. Before examining the patterns, attention is given to a number of widely accepted generalizations derived from learning psychology. Certain conditions and principles of learning can be applied, with success, to the development of activities within each of the three teaching/learning patterns.

CONDITIONS AND PRINCIPLES FOR SUCCESSFUL LEARNING

In order for instruction to be effective, learning must take place. Learning has occurred when a person now knows or can now do something that he or she did not previously know or was not able to do. Thus, learning will be evident by new behavior on either mental or physical levels.

Since the purpose of the instructional design process is to facilitate learning, you should become aware of and make use of those conditions and principles that have been shown to contribute successfully to the learning process. Each major theory of learning (for example, cognition or behaviorism) is based on evidence that has been gathered through observations and experimental research. We find agreement among these theories relative to how learning can best be achieved. A description of the more important and useful learning conditions and principles, along with a discussion of how each one may be applied to instructional planning, follows.

Prelearning Preparation

Learners should have satisfactorily achieved the learning that is prerequisite to starting a program or specific unit of study. Unless the former learning has been soundly acquired, the subsequent learning may have little meaning and can be carried out in a rote manner, but without any change in behavior.

Discussion   The pretesting element of the instructional design process (Chapter 12) can provide the data needed to determine how well prepared each student is for entering a training program or for starting a certain unit of instruction. Then, depending on the results of the pretest, arrangements should be made to overcome any apparent deficiencies in preparation.

Learning Objectives

Successful learning is more likely when objectives are clearly stated and, at the start of a topic or unit, the learner is informed of the specific objectives to be achieved. Learners can acquire more information and retain it longer when objectives for them are carefully written and systematically organized.

Discussion   The learning objectives element of the instructional design process (Chapter 7) gives full treatment to this topic.

Organization of Content

Learning can be improved when the content or procedures to be learned are organized into meaningful sequences. Then the material should be presented to the learner in segments, the size of which depends on logical divisions, complexity, and difficulty. This organization and procedure can assist the learner to synthesize and integrate the knowledge or processes personally.

Discussion   Consideration of the three taxonomies (page 78), the task analysis procedure (page 65), and the Gagné conditions for learning (page 60), determines the best sequence for the organization of content.

Individual Differences

Learners learn at various rates and in different ways. While group instruction can be beneficial for certain purposes and is preferable for some learners, evidence shows that the majority of learners can accomplish required objectives most satisfactorily if each individual, using appropriate materials, is allowed to proceed at his or her own pace.

Discussion   The attention given to learner characteristics (Chapter 5), recognizes the importance of individual differences and suggests ways to identify them, including preferred learning styles. However, it is not always easy to devise ways of serving the unique needs of individuals.

Motivation

A person must want to learn if much learning is to take place. A desire to learn requires motivation. Such a desire may be stimulated if (a) instruction is developed in such a manner as to be both important and interesting to the learner, (b) a variety of learning experiences is provided, (c) the learner knows that an early use is to be made of the material to be learned, and (d) acknowledgement of success in learning is provided to encourage further learning efforts.

Discussion   If the four conditions stated above are met and the other principles of learning presented here are satisfied, the motivation of learners and trainees can be established and then sustained.

Instructional Resources

When instructional materials, including such media forms as still pictures and video recordings, are carefully selected and systematically integrated to support activities in an instructional program, a significant impact on learner achievement can result. Such resources add flexibility to instruction and increase opportunity for adaptation to individual needs, thus improving the productivity of both learner and instructor efforts.

Discussion   Chapter 9 treats the variety, selection, and use of instructional resources that may be considered as part of teaching and learning activities in an instructional program.

Participation

In order for learning to take place, the individual must *internalize* the information and not simply be told it. Active participation by the learner is preferable to lengthy periods of passive listening and viewing. Participation means that the learner engages in mental responses or physical activities which are strategically interspersed during an instructional presentation or demonstration.

Discussion   Participation requires the learner to write answers, or make verbal replies to questions, solve problems, or engage in other types of instructional activities. Participation may also take the form of physical activity or performance. It is therefore necessary to subdivide a presentation, a demonstration, or a self-paced learning lesson into sections, each followed with immediate opportunities for participation activity to be completed by learners.

Feedback

Motivation for learning can be continued or increased when learners are informed periodically of their progress. Feedback confirms correct understandings and performance, provides knowledge of mistakes, and remedies faulty learning. For satisfactory learning, there is a close connection between feedback and reinforcement (the next principle listed).

Discussion Feedback takes place by providing correct answers against which learners can check their own replies. Also critiques of performance and informal discussions or evaluative remarks are helpful ways of keeping learners advised of their progress in learning.

Reinforcement

By receiving confirmation (feedback) on successful participating responses and actions, the learner is encouraged to continue learning. Learning motivated by success is rewarding and builds confidence. Those responses that have been positively confirmed tend to be repeated whenever the same or similar situations are faced. Thus the learner's efforts are *reinforced* to continue learning.

Discussion The value of acknowledging that a learner has answered or performed correctly requires that instruction be so designed that learning can be successful in the majority of instances. This gives the person developing a program the responsibility to do a careful, complete job within the instructional design framework.

Practice and Repetition

For a fact or skill to become a confirmed part of an individual's knowledge base or competency level, usually more than one exposure is required. Therefore, to ensure that the results of learning will be retained for a long period of time, provision should be made for *overlearning* under proper conditions. Completing written exercises, repetitive practice in a realistic setting, or drill for memorization, while employing the above described principles of participation, feedback, and reinforcement, can accomplish the overlearning and should result in long-term remembering. Practice is most effective when spaced over intervals of time.

Discussion Athletes know that if they truly want to become competent in performing a skill they must practice repetitively for long hours. A similar procedure is necessary in learning whether that be to solve math problems, to read symbols properly, or to drill holes accurately. Solving one single problem or cleaning one carburetor will not make a person proficient. Plan for activities that allow for necessary practice.

Learning Sequence

When a complex task or procedure is to be learned, it is more effective to integrate demonstration and practice periods which treat portions of the task or procedure.

Discussion A satisfactory way to integrate demonstration and practice is to: (a) demonstrate the entire procedure (live, or on film or videotape); (b) redemonstrate the first segment; (c) allow for learner practice of the first segment of the procedure; (d) demonstrate the second segment; (e) allow for practice of *both* segments, one and two; (f) demonstrate the third segment; (g) allow for practice of segments one, two, and three; and so on. The practice of each segment can be followed by a check-out procedure to be certain the action has been correctly learned. A final performance test over the complete task is advisable.

Application

An essential outcome of learning is to increase the learner's ability to apply or transfer the learning to new problems or situations. Unless a learner can do this, complete understanding has not taken place. First, the learner must have been helped to discover generalizations (concepts, rules, principles) relating to the topic or task. Second, opportunities must be provided for the learner to reason by applying the generalizations to a variety of new, realistic problems or tasks.

Discussion In order to utilize this principle, problems and real situations must be written, located, or created which will be unfamiliar to the learner or differ in some way from those used during instruction and practice. Then, when confronted with a new situation, the learner must identify elements which are similar to those found in the generalization and take action accordingly.

Instructor's Attitude

A positive attitude exhibited by the instructor and by any assistants to the subject being taught, to the learners, and to the instructional methods employed, can influence the motivation and attitudes of learners toward an instructional program.

Discussion It is important that each person involved in administering and carrying out an instructional program convey enthusiasm, cooperation, helpfulness, and interest in the subject. When learners sense or actually see such positive attitudes being expressed, they themselves will tend to behave in positive ways. The results can contribute significantly to the success of the instructional program.

The 13 principles and conditions enumerated above, if carefully applied when instructional activities are being planned, can establish a foundation that ensures satisfactory learning. You may already be familiar with many of these principles and conditions. Many of us are. But too often we either ignore them or feel too much work is required to give them suitable attention when planning instruction within the three teaching/learning patterns—presentation, self-paced learning, and instructor-learner interaction.

PRESENTATION TO A CLASS

In using the group-presentation pattern, the instructor tells, shows, demonstrates, dramatizes, or otherwise disseminates subject content to a group of learners. This pattern can be utilized in a classroom, an auditorium, or in a variety of locations through the use of radio, amplified telephone, closed circuit television transmission, or satellite communication (teleconferencing).

The teacher, in front of the group, may simply talk. He or she may utilize audiovisual materials, such as transparencies, recordings, slides, film, or video recordings, each singly or in multi-image combination. The presentation can also take place *without* the teacher being physically present if the presentation is, for example, on slides with accompanying audio recording, or in a video format.

These activities illustrate the one-way transmission of information from instructor to learners, often for a set period of time (generally a 40- to 50-minute class period). In small classes there may be some degree of two-way communication between teacher and learners, but most frequently, learners are passively listening and watching.

Advantages

The benefits of choosing a presentation method to accomplish certain learning objectives include the following:

1. A lecture or other presentation format is a familiar one and conventionally acceptable to both instructor and learners. This is the main method whereby most of us were taught. It is easy to continue this habit.
2. Generally minimal effort and thought are required to plan a lecture presentation because of an instructor's familiarity and experience with the method.
3. For some instructors, there is a feeling that in order to maintain their status or establish their authority with learners, they should be in front of the class, speaking.
4. For instructional purposes, time can be saved because more information can be presented in a given period of time by using a presentation method than by other techniques. Since the instructor controls the activity, there can be few time-consuming detours from the lesson plan.
5. Large numbers of learners can be served at one time, the group being limited only by the size of the room.
6. As the need presents itself, a presentation can be modified by deleting content, or adding new content just before or even while the presentation is being made. Also, the presentation can be adapted for a specific group of learners.

7. This is a feasible method of communicating when the information to be presented requires frequent changes and updating.

Disadvantages

The limitations of the presentation method of instruction are evidenced by the following:

1. The learner is confined to passive learning—listening and watching, taking notes—with little or no opportunity for interchange of ideas with the instructor. This method seems to violate many of the principles for effective learning previously described.
2. There is the need for an instructor to be interesting, enthusiastic, and challenging in order to maintain learner's attention during a presentation.
3. When a teacher lectures, demonstrates, shows a film, or otherwise presents subject content to a class of learners, the assumption is made that all learners are acquiring the same understanding, with the same level of comprehension, at the same time. They are being forced to learn at a pace set by the teacher. We know this is not the way learning actually takes place. Each person learns at an individual pace, according to his or her own degree of understanding. Furthermore, some learners in the group may already know some of the information to be presented and would like to skip ahead.
4. If questioning is permitted, instruction stops and all learners must wait until the question is answered before the presentation can proceed.
5. It is difficult for the instructor to receive feedback from learners pertaining to misunderstandings and difficulties encountered during the presentation. Therefore, some learners may leave the class with incorrect learning.
6. There is evidence that the content of a purely verbal presentation, with no planned learner participation, is remembered for only a short time.
7. A presentation is not the method applicable for teaching psychomotor skills, and objectives in the affective domain can be influenced only slightly.

Applications

There are specific situations and times at which a presentation to a group of learners can be of value:

- As an introduction, overview, or orientation to a new topic.
- To serve a motivational or inspirational objective in order to create interest for a subject or topic.
- To present basic or essential information as common background or necessary preparation that is not easily accessible before learners engage in small-group or individual activities.
- To introduce recent developments in a field, especially when preparation time is limited.

- To provide such resources as a one-time guest speaker, a film, or other visual presentation that can most conveniently and efficiently be shown to the whole group at one time.
- To provide opportunities for learners to make their own presentations as reports to the class.
- As a review or summary when the study of the topic or unit is concluded.

Plan for Participation

A current trend is to reduce the amount of time spent in the presentation pattern of instruction in favor of devoting more time to self-paced study and small-group activities. Carefully weigh the advantages and disadvantages of the presentation pattern in terms of the learning objectives to be accomplished. Then, if a presentation is feasible, decide on the form it should take—verbal lecture, lecture with supporting media, media only, or whatever seems appropriate.

Keep in mind that learning takes place best when learners are actively involved. Therefore, it is important to plan for including learner participation activities when the presentation format is to be used. Participation can be of three types:[1]

1. *Active interaction with the instructor.* Prepare questions to be used at various points during the verbal presentation; encourage or direct learners to answer and enter into discussion with the instructor. Decide on places at which to stop a visual presentation (often at the conclusion of a section, or the end of information presented on a concept) and bring up questions to measure understanding and to encourage discussion.
2. *Seat work.* Encourage note taking by learners so they will capture the key points being presented or provide handouts for reference and immediate use. The latter may take the form of worksheets on topics requiring the learner to fill in an outline of content, to complete diagrams that accompany visuals used in the presentation, to write replies to questions, to solve problems, and to make applications of content and concepts as the presentation proceeds. Learners may also be required to complete self-check exercises or quizzes over the content being presented.
3. *Other mental activity.* Encourage thinking along with the instructor by helping learners mentally to verbalize answers to rhetorical or direct questions and to problems posed by the instructor or another learner. Learners can also be asked to formulate their own questions relating to the materials being presented for use in followup small-group sessions.

Conditions and Principles of Learning Applied to a Presentation

Near the start of this chapter, 13 conditions and principles for effective learning were described. Following is an example of how they might be applied in a

---

[1] Dean N. Osterman, *Feedback Lecture.*

presentation situation. The application of each appropriate condition or principle is noted by name in the margin.

> Ms. Shelton is teaching an adult education course, *Health Awareness.* The emphasis is on mental attitudes toward developing habits for good health practices. The students include persons who work with senior citizen groups.

Prelearning preparation

> On the first day, the instructor distributes a questionnaire to obtain background information and areas of interest from each student. After reviewing the replies, she makes some adjustments in order of topics and depth of treatment. As an introduction, she

Motivation

> shows a series of brief video episodes that dramatically illustrate how changes in health practices can be effected among older people. These recordings stimulate much discussion and set the stage for the course work.

Objectives
Organization
Instructional resources
Participation
Feedback
Instructor's attitude

> Ms. Shelton presents an introductory lecture for each topic based on a set of objectives found in the students' study guide. The lecture is organized into segments and extensively illustrated with short video recordings. At the end of each segment she refers students to review questions printed in their study guide. Answers are discussed and misunderstandings are corrected. Because of Ms. Shelton's expressions of enthusiasm, understanding, and helpfulness, almost all students are voluntarily active during discussions.

Individual differences

Application

> Following each lecture, students work on projects, by choice either singly or in teams. They make use of the information and procedures they have learned. Their own senior citizen groups serve as the basis of some projects. Reports are presented to class, which when judged against criteria specified in the study guide, serve as evaluation measures for the course units.

SELF-PACED LEARNING

Of the three teaching and learning patterns, self-paced learning has received the most attention in instructional design plans. As the principles of learning indicate, there is much evidence to support the belief that learning must be accomplished by individuals for themselves and that maximum learning takes place when a student works at his or her own pace, is actively involved in performing specific learning tasks, and experiences success in learning.

Features

Self-paced learning methods are also called *individualized learning, self-instruction,* or *self-directed learning.* While these terms may have different meanings, the important features for the learner are self-responsibility, self-pacing, and successful learning, all based on specific learning objectives and a variety of activities with accompanying resources. As you already know, all of these are important elements of the instructional design process.

Most frequently, the instructor selects the learning objectives and sets the requirements learners must follow. A "true" *individualized learning* or *learner-controlled* program would require that a separate set of objectives and learning activities be designed for each individual, or selected by an individual, according to that individual's own characteristics, preparation, needs or interests. Through the use of computer scheduling, such individualization can be accomplished, although the programming is complex and a wide variety of activities and resources may be required.

Specific features of a quality self-paced learning program include the following:

- Learning activities for learners are carefully constructed and detailed. Self-instruction takes place best when content is organized into comparatively small, discrete steps, each one treating a single concept or segment of content. The size of the steps can vary, but it is essential that they be carefully sequenced.
- Activities and resources are carefully selected in terms of the required learning objectives.
- The learner's mastery of each step must be checked before he or she proceeds to the next step. Therefore, it is necessary to question or otherwise challenge the learner to demonstrate an understanding or a use of the content learned.
- The learner then must receive immediate confirmation (feedback) about the correctness of his or her reply or other effort. With each success, the learner confidently advances to the next step.
- When difficulties arise, further study may be necessary, or the learner may ask the instructor for help. Thus, the learner is continually challenged, completes participation activities, learns the results of his or her efforts immediately, and experiences success.

The kinds of learning objectives that may be suitably served by self-paced learning include the following:

- Learning factual information
- Mastering concepts and principles
- Applying information, concepts, and principles
- Developing basic problem-solving skills
- Developing psychomotor skills

Thus, most levels in both the cognitive and psychomotor domains, as well as those in the Gagné hierarchy, can be treated through some forms of self-paced learning activities. Many of these categories of objectives should be reinforced and supplemented by group-interaction activities. Topics or objectives that are highly abstract and are not quantifiable, like philosophical thought or human relations, may be more appropriate for study in group interaction sessions. But even with those subjects, there is usually some fundamental, factual information that should be mastered before ideas are considered within the group. Such basic content can be learned through self-paced learning methods.

Advantages

There is evidence that learners participating in self-paced learning programs work harder, learn more, and retain what has been learned better than do learners in conventional classes. Self-paced learning offers a number of unique advantages as an instructional method:

1. A carefully designed self-paced learning program will incorporate most of the principles of learning enumerated earlier. The result is improvement in both the level of learning and the degree of retention. The number of learner failures and unsatisfactory performances can be appreciably reduced.
2. This pattern allows both slow and advanced learners to pursue their studies, each on his or her own level of ability and under appropriate learning conditions.
3. The self-reliance and personal responsibility required of learners by a self-paced learning program may carry over as habits to other educational activities, job responsibilities, and personal behavior.
4. A self-paced learning program can allow for increased attention being given to the individual learner and greater opportunity for interaction among learners.
5. The activities and responsibilities of an instructor involved in a self-paced learning program change because reduced time is spent in making presentations and more time is devoted to learners in group sessions and in individual consultation.
6. While major approaches to self-paced learning may not be cost efficient immediately, as the technique and resources are employed repeatedly with following learners or trainee groups, the cost of a program can be reduced appreciably. (For a consideration of program costs and measuring program efficiency, see Chapter 16.)
7. Learners tend to prefer self-paced learning methods over traditional procedures because of many of the benefits stated above.

Disadvantages

There are also some limitations to self-paced learning that should be recognized:

1. There may be a lack of interaction between instructor and learners or among learners if a self-paced program is the sole method of instruction in a course. Therefore, it is important to plan for periodic instructor-learner small group activities as appropriate.
2. If a single-path, lockstep method is followed, learning can become monotonous and uninteresting.
3. A self-paced program is not a suitable method for *all* learners or for all instructors to employ. Observations reveal that because of learning

and teaching style differences, about 20 percent of college and adult students prefer to learn in groups through presentation and interaction activities, rather than through individualized activities.

4. Lack of self-discipline combined with procrastination can result in delaying the completion of required study by some learners. New habits and patterns of behavior need to be formed by many learners before they can be successful in self-paced learning. For these reasons, it may be desirable to set deadlines (weekly or monthly) within which learners can adjust to their own study pace.

5. The self-paced method often requires cooperation and detailed team planning among faculty involved. Also, coordination with other support services of the organization (facilities, media, reproduction, and so forth) may become necessary or even critical. All of this is in contrast to the usual single-person operation characteristic of conventional teaching.

Procedures

In planning for self-paced learning, many approaches are possible. The simplest is to design a single track for all learners and select whatever instructional materials are required from among those available commercially (printed, audio, still pictures, motion pictures, video recordings, and so forth). Such materials have been developed for conventional presentation uses, so little, if any, participation is required of learners. To provide for necessary participation, the instructor may need to develop worksheets or other aids that require learners to respond to or act upon the information in each segment of content immediately after it is presented.

We know that learners do not all learn at the same rate. Therefore, they should be allowed to study at a time convenient to them and also to pace themselves. An individual may want to linger over some material and to speed through that which is quickly understood.

A preferable way to plan for individualized learning is to start with a variety of materials serving the objectives and then plan more than one instructional sequence in order to provide for differences among individual learners. As based on preparation and need, some learners may take the fast track, even skipping ahead and using few materials before concluding their study. Other learners may require a slower track that contains a greater number of concrete illustrations or examples, more review exercises, or even smaller segments of subject content with a repetition of explanations in different contexts.

Individuals also differ in their learning styles (page 50). Some learners respond best to visual materials, while others work better with printed resources, or with hands-on experiences. Therefore, it may be advisable to collect or prepare a variety of materials to treat a set of learning objectives, and then allow each learner to select a preferred way to study. For example, if an objective requires the operation of a piece of laboratory equipment, the program for mastering this objective may include printed instructions, a set of still photographs, a short film or videotape, and the equipment itself. One learner may choose to begin with the video demonstration and then go immediately to practice with the equipment; another learner might prefer to read the instruction sheet and then examine the still pictures before attempting to practice; a third might go immediately to the equipment and learn in a trial and error fashion.

In summary, by recognizing that active participation is a key element for learning, instructional planners can design a variety of experiences for learners. These can range from a carefully structured program which allows learners to proceed at their own pace, to one that gives individuals virtually complete freedom and responsibility for choosing their own activities and materials according to their own learning styles or preferences.

Examples

Several procedures for implementing self-paced learning are described below. They range from the use of simple prepared materials, through adaptations of commercial materials, to systematically planned, full-scale programs:

Learner Contracts   The learner enters into an agreement with the instructor to achieve acceptable objectives, often by completing a project in exchange for rewards (credit points, participation in special activities, or free time). Either the teacher suggests resources, or the learner takes responsibility for deciding what to do to achieve the objectives and carry out the project.

Textbooks/Worksheets   At times, to effectively study the content of a textbook or other printed resources used as an integral part of a course, a learner may need guidance. This can happen when a learner's skills in reading or language are limited. Objectives are developed from the textbook content. A worksheet directs the study of text chapters and provides review exercises, questions, and other activities. A self-check test or a project to apply the content may conclude the review of each chapter. After completing this work, a learner should be better prepared to participate in class work which requires both an understanding and application of the textual content.

Programmed Self-Instructional Booklet or Computer-Based Instruction   A self-instructional booklet or computer program provides a sequential presentation of information on a topic in small increments. The program generally contains a statement of objectives, a pretest, and a series of "frames" in linear (straight line) or branching (alternative choice) sequences. The learner responds periodically to questions that test his or her understanding of the content. Knowledge of results is proved immediately. At the end of a sequence or program, learning is tested. This procedure of study, utilizing self-instructional booklets or computer-based instruction, is known as "interactive learning."

Such resources can serve various important purposes:

1. To provide study materials for specific portions of a course that require the learning of basic terms and particular facts
2. To direct a review or remedial study of a topic
3. To provide detailed instruction on a topic, including simulated applications of content.

Increasing use is being made of computer programs to fulfill needs formerly served by programmed self-instructional booklets.

Audiotape/Worksheets With an audiotape and worksheets, a learner reads information, refers to diagrams or other visuals, solves problems, and completes other activities under the direction of the instructor's voice on tape. The recording provides directions, information, explanations of answers, and other "tutorial" assistance.

The tape/worksheet combination can be developed to treat specific topics in a course for which other instructional materials may not exist or which require a unique approach. Tapes that contain the instructor's voice should be a personal, often informal, method of presenting course material in an interesting way. The audiocassette tape and worksheet combination form a compact package which can be conveniently used by learners wherever or whenever they choose.

Visuals/Guide Sheets Visuals with a guidesheet may be used when learners need directions or instructions in order to operate equipment, to carry out a process, or to complete a precise activity. These materials are often called "job aids." Visuals in either still or motion picture form can guide learners through the steps necessary for completing a specific task.

There is a wide range of possible choices from which selection can be made in developing new materials or adapting already existing material. These choices include: photographs, slides, filmstrips, motion picture films, videotape recordings, and/or printed guide sheets. Visuals can be displayed at work stations, in a lab or shop, or made available for pickup and study at any time. When visuals are combined with printed guide sheets that summarize an operation or provide other necessary factual or supplemental information, a complete self-instructional package on a topic can result.

Multimedia Package As the name implies, a multimedia package consists of several types of media resource materials which are used concurrently or sequentially in a self-paced learning situation. A package usually treats a single topic within a course. It can best provide the instruction for topics that require the realism of photographs or the symbolism of diagrams along with verbal explanations.

Commercially prepared multimedia packages may be in any of several forms: slides or a set of filmstrips with correlated audiocassettes and printed materials; a videocassette or motion picture film and printed materials; or an interactive computer program/videotape or videodisc system with printed materials. The printed materials may include combinations of readings, worksheets, and self-testing exercises. In addition, equipment and tools may be part of the kit with which the learner carries out performance activities.

As part of these packages, there should be a syllabus or guide for the user that describes: (a) the learning objectives of the package, (b) the directions for use, and (c) the methods for evaluating the results of use.

Personalized System of Instruction (PSI) The PSI method of self-paced learning (developed by the psychologist Fred Keller and often called the Keller Plan),[2] is an approach which may be applied to a complete course. Most frequently it is based on a textbook with study units consisting of readings, questions, and problems. Instructional resources do not have to be limited only to written material. Other media of a visual and/or audio nature may be incorporated.

After studying each increment of material and answering a related set of questions or completing activities, a learner reports to a proctor or to a tutor for a test on the particular segment of content. The test, once completed, is immediately graded by a proctor (a learner who previously had successfully completed the course), who then shows the results to the learner. With satisfactory accomplishment (often with a competency level requirement of 80 to 90 percent), the learner proceeds to the next chapter or unit. If the specified level of learning does not result (as determined by the test), the learner restudies the materials, and when ready takes another form of the test.

This procedure is repeated until the learner achieves success with the stated objectives. While some study is undertaken individually, not all learning has to occur in isolation. Some instructors meet with a class or small groups of learners to conduct special lectures and discussions. In addition, the contact between individual learners and proctors, for the purpose of evaluation and immediate feedback, can encourage further study.

Audio-Tutorial Method (AT) Another complete, systematic approach to a self-paced learning course is the audio-tutorial method. It was designed by the botanist Samuel N. Postlethwait.[3] The process usually includes three major components: (a) A large group meeting of the whole class, usually weekly, which may have any of a number of purposes—introducing a new topic, presenting a guest speaker, showing a film, or administering an examination; (b) individual self-paced learning activities in a learning lab appropriate for the course; and (c) group discussion sessions in which learners may ask questions, make reports, and engage in other forms of interaction.

A study guide is prepared which contains learning objectives, activities, exercises, and self-check tests. Audiotapes are used during the self-paced learning period to lead the learner through the learning experiences. The recording is *not* a lecture. The instructor's voice on the tape provides some

---

[2] Fred S. Keller and J. Gilmour Sherman, *The PSI Handbook*.
[3] Samuel N. Postlethwait et al., *Exploring Teaching Alternatives*.

information, tutorial guidance, and directions for the learner. Activities directed by the tape may include readings in books and from articles, studying visual materials, completing worksheet questions, and performing laboratory work as appropriate. The tape also provides the learner with answers as feedback on learning. The instructor, or a teaching assistant, usually is available in the learning lab to assist learners and to answer questions.

Self-Instructional Modules   The self-instructional module is a package which treats a single topic or unit of subject content. It includes a study guide containing all necessary information for a learner to proceed through the assigned material. Important components of a module are: (1) carefully stated directions, (2) learning objectives to be accomplished, (3) description of activities and exercises (often with alternative choices so that a learner may select a preferred method of study), (4) list of resources, and (5) one or more tests, with answers, so the learner may check progress in learning.

Learners may also be referred to materials outside of the printed module itself. Activities are not necessarily limited to the study of written materials alone. Visual and audio media resources are often used to augment, clarify, or enhance printed information. A series of self-instructional modules may comprise an entire course or may be used as part of a course to cover topical areas. Studying them may require from a few hours to a day or more of work.

Many publications relating to these self-paced learning methods provide complete information for your own explorations. Some of the more noteworthy ones are listed under "Self-paced learning" in the references.

A Planning Checklist   If you are developing a self-paced program, the following checklist of questions for evaluating your planning may prove useful:

1. To what extent does the program adapt to characteristics of the learners having different cultural and ethnic backgrounds?
2. To what extent are learners who need remedial help identified before starting on a unit or module?
3. To what extent are learners allowed to skip ahead if they already show competencies in part of the topic being treated?
4. To what extent are low-level cognitive knowledge and psychomotor skills used to provide higher-level learning experiences and practical applications of subject content?
5. How much attention is given to attitude formation?
6. Are options provided so that a learner may select learning experiences and resources?
7. To what degree are learners permitted or encouraged to progress at their own rates?
8. To what extent do learners have opportunities for checking their progress as they proceed through a program?
9. To what extent do learners have opportunities to share their learning or otherwise interact among themselves and with the instructor?

10. To what extent do instructors consult with or assist individual learners and small groups?
11. How will self-paced learning relate to other activities in the course?

Changing Roles   Finally, as a planning team designs a self-paced learning program, the instructors involved should recognize that not only will they be changing their methods of instruction, but they also must change their own roles in working with learners. These changes can become both stimulating and more demanding. Some of the changes that can be anticipated are suggested below:

- Freedom from routine teaching of basic facts and skills
- More time spent with individual learners in diagnosing their difficulties, giving help, and monitoring their progress
- More opportunities to interact with learners on higher intellectual levels concerning their problems, interests, and uses of the subject content
- More time required for preparing, gathering, and organizing materials for use by learners
- More time required to orient and supervise aides, tutors, proctors, and other assistants

Conditions and Principles of Learning Applied to a Self-paced Learning Unit

Following is an example of how the conditions and principles of learning enumerated near the start of this chapter might be applied in a self-paced learning module. The application of each appropriate condition or principle is noted by name in the margin.

Dr. Winters, a college professor, has designed an elective history course entitled *The West: Image and Reality*. It consists of 12 units on such topics as: "The Land," "Vanishing Americans," "Pioneers," "The Railroad," "Art and Songs," and "Cowboys." The content of each unit is treated as a self-paced learning module in which the instructor's voice on tape (audio-tutorial) leads students through a study of the topic. In addition, students meet in small discussion groups with the instructor for various interaction activities relating to weekly topics.

The self-paced learning format includes these components:

Motivation   1. Introduction to the topic (often in narrative story form to arouse interest)

Objectives   2. Learning objectives for the topic

Prelearning preparation   3. Pretest (if, because of taking a previous American History course, a student scores at least 85 percent, study of a unit can be omitted, but students do attend discussion group session)

Organization of content

Instructional resources

Participation

Feedback

4. Topic divided into sections
   a. Introduced on videotape with direction to complete reading or view slides, film, or videotape
   b. Content summarized on audiotape
   c. Student directed to complete review exercise which may include viewing slides
   d. Answers to exercise questions discussed on tape

Reinforcement

5. Self-check review test over complete unit

Practice, Application, Individual differences

6. Preparation necessary for discussion group and choice of individual project

INTERACTION BETWEEN INSTRUCTOR AND LEARNERS

In this teaching/learning pattern, teachers and learners, or learners themselves, work together in small groups to discuss, question, pursue problems cooperatively, and report. The importance of interaction cannot be overemphasized. For one thing, it gives learners and teachers an opportunity to get to know each other face to face. To be of maximum benefit to learners, the interaction group should consist of no more than 12 persons—from 8 to 12 participants seem to be ideal.

Small-group activities can be most effective when scheduled to follow instructor-led presentations to a class and learner self-paced learning sessions. Knowledge and skills that have already been learned can be reviewed, clarified, corrected, reinforced, and applied. Learners can report on their projects and other experiences, an activity which enables them to learn from each other as well as from the instructor. Small-group sessions may also be used to test learners' understanding of the concepts and principles they have acquired during earlier course activities.

Other areas of small group activity may be entirely student directed. These may include committee and team planning, research, construction, tryouts for performances, and self-evaluations. Learners can study films and other media materials and engage in their own interaction without having a teacher present.

For an interaction group, the instructor may have available for showing the same audiovisual materials and other resources used in group presentations and for self-paced study. Viewing such materials may be of value when questions are raised and specific points must be amplified.

Advantages

In comparison with the presentation and self-paced learning patterns, there are certain important features of the instructor/learner interaction pattern with which you should be familiar:

1. A particular strength of using small-group activities is that it helps to achieve objectives in the affective domain—attitude formation, development of appreciations, cooperation, and interpersonal relations.
2. In the cognitive domain, higher-level skills like problem solving and decision making can receive attention through interaction activities.
3. Other values of interaction include experiences in listening and oral expression when learners organize and present their ideas. The more able learners can strengthen their own learning by explaining points or principles to other learners (known as "peer" teaching). Learners can also practice leadership functions. Learners who need encouragement can be recognized, and those learners who are making poor progress can be identified.
4. During a small-group session, through discussion, an instructor may become aware of the successes or shortcomings of various phases of an instructional program and can obtain suggestions from learners for revisions.

Disadvantages

In planning for interaction activities, several problems must be faced, which, if not overcome, can render the instruction ineffective:

1. Attention to premeeting preparation can be very important; this can be done by having students complete readings, write an analysis of the topic under consideration or prepare a position paper, or engage in preparatory committee work. Thus, students will be more ready to participate during the group activity.
2. The interaction group meeting is *not* a good time for a lecture or other lengthy presentation. Instructors who are not prepared or who are inexperienced with this type of activity may fall back on lecturing for their own security. Much practice is often necessary before a teacher can successfully become a participating member of a group rather than the dominating member.
3. Getting all learners in a group to participate actively can be another important matter which needs careful attention.
4. On the other hand, an instructor should control the communication process within a group so that a discussion does not degenerate into an unproductive bull session. The instructor must be prepared to control learners who react emotionally or who tend to monopolize the discussion.
5. If it is necessary to communicate a quantity of information to the members of a group, recognize that progress in transmitting the material may be slow because of the nature of the interaction process.

Formats

A number of different techniques may be used to encourage and provide for interaction within small groups. While planning, choices can be made from among the following:

Discussion   Discussion is the most common form of face-to-face teaching in which facts, ideas, and opinions can be exchanged. As learners think about a subject under discussion and present their views, learning can take place on higher intellectual levels (specifically—analysis, synthesis, evaluation) than is possible solely with the recall of information.

Discussion can be planned in three forms:

1. *Instructor-directed*—A discussion controlled by the instructor; questions posed by the instructor are answered by individual learners; provides for a limited exchange of ideas within the group.
2. *Group-centered*—A free-flowing exchange of ideas without the controlling influence of the instructor; cooperative in that participants provide their own direction and control the pace; open-ended, as the discussion can go in any of a number of directions depending on learner interactions and reactions.
3. *Collaborative*—A discussion often focused on solving a specific problem; instructor has neither a dominant or passive role, but serves as a resource person and also as a contributor; all participants share decision-making responsibilities, and are obliged to accept and integrate ideas presented and critically evaluate alternative solutions; most difficult form of discussion to implement; best used after a group has experience with the previous two forms of discussion.

Panel Discussion   In the panel discussion, three to six qualified persons (from the community or a professional group) present information or their views on an assigned topic in front of the class. The individuals may represent different viewpoints, various interest groups, or special experiences. Learners may research topics and comprise the panels themselves to present their findings. Following the presentations, learners in the class are encouraged to ask questions of the panel members.

Guided Design   The guided design method, developed by Charles E. Wales of West Virginia University, focuses on developing the learners' decision-making skills as well as on teaching specific concepts and principles. Learners work in small groups to solve open-ended problems which require them to gather information (outside of class), to think logically, to communicate ideas, and to apply steps in a decision-making process. Learners are required to look closely at each step in the decision-making operation, apply the subject matter they have learned, exchange ideas, and reflect on solutions developed by others. The instructor acts as a consultant to the class.

Case Study   In a case study, learners are provided with detailed information about a real-life situation. All related circumstances, issues, and actions of persons involved are carefully described. Learners must study and analyze the situation as presented. They decide what was done correctly and what mistakes were possibly made in terms of principles and accepted practices in their field of specialization. During discussion, each person must explain, justify, and defend his or her own analysis of the case situation. This method is widely used in the business management field.

Role Playing   Role playing involves the spontaneous dramatization by two or more persons of a situation relating to a problem. The incident might have to do with interpersonal relations or with an operational problem within an organization. Each person acts out a role as he or she feels it would be played in real life. Other learners or trainees observe the performance and then, upon the conclusion of the performance, discuss the feelings expressed and actions observed. This process promotes an understanding of the position of other persons and their attitudes as well as the procedures that might be used for diagnosing and solving problems.

Simulation   Simulation is an abstract representation of a real-life situation that requires a learner or a team to solve a complex problem. Aspects of the situation that are close to reality are created, and the learner must perform manipulations, make responses, and take actions to correct deficiencies or to maintain a proper status. Many simulations are computer controlled, like a mock-up simulator of an airplane cockpit for pilot training. The simulator allows the instructor to set up appropriate conditions which require specific responses by the trainee. The participants become deeply involved, undergoing the same stress and pressures they would experience in reality. With the learners, the instructor discusses and evaluates the results of the activity.

Games   A game is a formalized simulation activity. In it, two or more participants or teams compete in attempting to meet a set of objectives relating to a training topic. The game takes place under a set of rules and procedures with information being provided that requires decision making and followup actions as the result of the decisions. The subjects of most instructional games are typical real-life situations as related to a training topic. Periodically, the results are evaluated by the instructor, other learners, or by a group of judges. A wide variety of prepared games is available for use in many areas of instruction.

SUMMARY

The three patterns we have examined—presentation to class, self-paced learning methods, and teacher/learner interaction activities—provide the framework within which experiences for learning can be planned. As you consider the selection of methods, the following important questions should be asked:

- Is there subject content or other material that can best be uniformly presented to all learners at one time?
- Is there subject content that learners can better study on their own, at their individual paces?

- Are there experiences that would best be served by discussion or other group activity, with or without the instructor being present?
- Is there need for individual learner/instructor discussion or consultation in private?

In considering these questions, the planning team should realize that there needs to be some degree of balance among the three teaching/learning patterns. Some enthusiasts recommend that self-paced learning, for example, is the proper method for all instruction. This method is getting increased attention as the use of computers becomes more widespread. Other persons believe that suitable opportunities also must be available for teacher/learner contact and group interaction. A major trend is to reduce the time spent in presentations by giving learners increased responsibilities for self-paced learning, but also to provide for interaction experiences as well.

In many situations, there are no clearcut divisions among the three patterns. A presentation to a regular-sized class can incorporate questions and discussion. A self-paced learning period may be supplemented periodically with tutorial interaction as one learner helps another or as the instructor replies to a trainee's question. This is how it should be. Employ each pattern for its best service to learning.

Categories of Activities

When deciding on the various kinds of teaching and learning activities which would be appropriate to accomplish the objectives of a topic or unit, consider these two questions:

1. **What will the instructor do?** Some activities are directly conducted by the teacher as when making a presentation to a class. As the instructor lectures, demonstrates, shows slides, uses a videotape, or otherwise communicates *to* the class, what is taking place is primarily a *teacher activity.*
2. **What will the learner do?** Certain activities are designed to give learners full responsibility as they work by *themselves* in self-paced learning (reading, listening to a tape, viewing audiovisual materials, working at a computer terminal, and so forth), or as they work *together* in small groups (working as a team or committee, engaging in a field trip, and so forth). These would be classified as *student activities.*

For some activities, there would be *both* teacher and learner involvement. For example, when learners attend a lecture (a teacher activity), they take notes or respond to questions (a student activity). Also, in various small-group interaction sessions both the teacher and learners are engaged so we plan for **teacher activity** and **learner activity.**

Under this element of the instructional design process—teaching/learning activities—it is of value to state who will be engaged in what specific activities. Indicate the two categories—**teacher activity** and **learner activity.** As you consider each learning objective, ask yourself whether the objective can be most satisfactorily achieved by a teacher activity, a learner activity, or by a combination of the two. Then specify details of the activity for the teacher, for the learner, or for both.

There is a natural, close association between methods of instruction and the resources that need to be used with the methods. One influences the other. Therefore, as activities are being chosen, consider also the selection of resources, discussed in the next chapter.

REVIEW AND APPLICATIONS*

A. Recall
1. Name the three broad teaching/learning patterns within which most instructional methods can be grouped.

   a. _____

   b. _____

   c. _____

2. List on the left a key word or phrase that represents each one of the *13* conditions or principles of learning described in this chapter (starting on page 101). Write them in the same order as presented in the book (for ease of checking answers). Then for each one select a definition from the column on the right and write its letter before the condition or principle.

   _____ *a.* Competencies to be accomplished

   _____ *b.* Advising student of progress in learning

   _____ *c.* Students wanting to learn

   _____ *d.* Successful learning is rewarding.

   _____ *e.* Determine previous learning level of students before starting present unit of study.

   _____ *f.* Integrating practice while learning task segments

   _____ *g.* Characteristics of learners

   _____ *h.* Convey enthusiasm and willing to be helpful

   _____ *i.* Arrange subject matter in meaningful segments.

   _____ *j.* Transfer learning to new situations.

   _____ *k.* Necessary in support of teaching/learning activities

   _____ *l.* Engaging in activities and making responses during instruction

   _____ *m.* Helps to make learning more permanent

3. Mark each statement by letter according to whether it is:
   a. *Advantage* of the *presentation* pattern
   b. *Disadvantage* of the *presentation* pattern
   c. *Advantage* of *self-paced* learning
   d. *Disadvantage* of *self-paced* learning
   e. *Advantage* of the *interaction* pattern
   f. *Disadvantage* of the *interaction* pattern

_____ *(1)* Can contribute to attitude formation

_____ *(2)* Most frequently allows only for passive student learning

_____ *(3)* Flexible for ease of adding, deleting, and updating material

_____ *(4)* Many learners need guidance before filling their participatory role.

_____ *(5)* Can serve many learners, at one time, in one location, while they proceed together through the content

_____ *(6)* Can cause an instructor to become more "learner oriented"

_____ *(7)* Requires attention to careful, detailed planning that may not be acceptable to all instructors

_____ *(8)* Makes application of most conditions and principles of learning

_____ *(9)* Limited opportunities for feedback to instructor

_____ *(10)* Students may organize and present ideas to others.

_____ *(11)* Large amount of content can be presented in given period of time

_____ *(12)* Not useful for teaching psychomotor skills and affective attitudes

_____ *(13)* Some instructors tend to dominate rather than to be a participating member.

_____ *(14)* Recognize different learning styles and learning paces of learners.

_____ *(15)* Over a period of time may reduce instructional costs

_____ *(16)* Without creative planning, instruction can become boring and mechanistic.

_____ *(17)* Activities particularly appropriate for decision making and problem solving

_____ *(18)* Assumption that all learners are learning at same pace

_____ *(19)* If overused, can become impersonal with little instructor–learner contact

_____ *(20)* May not be suitable for all learners

4. Which teaching/learning pattern would you select for each situation? Use: (1) presentation, (2) self-paced learning; (3) interaction

_____ *a.* Use a one-time guest speaker

_____ *b.* More attention can be given to principles of learning

_____ *c.* Success in learning affected by student self-discipline to complete work on time

_____ *d.* More useful for serving affective domain objectives

_____ *e.* Recognizes individual differences among students

_____ *f.* Best pattern for instructor and learners to become acquainted with each other

_____ *g.* Motivate an interest in a new topic.

_____ *h.* Simulation and games are activities for this pattern.

_____ *i.* Used to provide general information before other activities may take place

_____ *j.* For introducing a new topic

_____ *k.* May provide multiple paths for student study

5. What are *three* techniques that may be used to encourage student participation during a presentation?

a. _____

_____

_____

b. _____
_____
_____

c. _____
_____
_____

6. Differentiate between *self-paced learning* and *individualized learning*.
   a. Self-paced. _____
   _____
   _____

   b. Individualized. _____
   _____
   _____

7. Which statements are *TRUE* regarding features of a *good* self-paced learning program?
   ____ **a.** Allows learners to satisfy objectives on most levels of cognitive domain
   ____ **b.** Content organized into small segments
   ____ **c.** No need for instructor involvement with learners
   ____ **d.** Can satisfactorily accomplish highly abstract objectives
   ____ **e.** Learner should be successful in learning a section of content before studying next section
   ____ **f.** Principles of participation and confirmation continually applied

8. To which self-paced learning method does each of the following relate? Write a number from the left column for each letter.

(1) Contracts
(2) Textbook/worksheets
(3) Computer-based
(4) Audiotape/worksheets
(5) Visuals/guide sheets
(6) Multimedia package
(7) PSI
(8) AT
(9) Module

____ **a.** Gives attention to all three teaching/learning patterns described in this chapter

____ **b.** Commercial materials, often as slides or a filmstrip with audiotape and printed sheets

____ **c.** May be used as preparation for participation in regular class work so instructor does not have to review content

____ **d.** Consists of instructor's voice along with printed pages that comprise an easy-to-use package

____ **e.** Known as "job aids"

____ **f.** Study units based on textbook chapters, each of which must be successfully learned before proceeding to next one

____ **g.** May include the use of various materials, separate from the printed guide, to which a learner is directed as he or she works through the guide.

____ **h.** A portion of the course devoted to self-paced learning uses audiotape with the instructor's voice to direct learning activities

____ **i.** Learner engages in independent study project with agreement of instructor

_____ *j.* Learner receives assistance, as necessary, from tutor or proctor, and is retested until satisfactory achievement is attained; test results shown immediately to learner

_____ *k.* For remedial study of a topic to satisfy prerequisites before starting regular work

_____ *l.* Pictures with instructions that describe how to perform an operation

_____ *m.* Consists of a series of "frames" that may be in linear or branching sequences

9. What may be *three* changes in an instructor's role when using a self-paced learning method?

   a. _____
   _____
   _____
   _____

   b. _____
   _____
   _____
   _____

   c. _____
   _____
   _____

10. To which small-group interaction activity does each of the following relate? Write the number from the left column for each letter.

(1) Discussion
(2) Panel
(3) Guided design
(4) Case study
(5) Role playing
(6) Simulation
(7) Game

_____ *a.* Applying steps in a decision-making process to solve a problem while learners work in small groups

_____ *b.* Involving learners in a realistic operation that requires many actions and responses to correct errors and maintain proper status

_____ *c.* Acting out a situation relating to an interpersonal or operational problem

_____ *d.* Exchanging information and expressing different points of view

_____ *e.* Analyzing a real-life situation in terms of accepted principles and practices in order to describe correct and incorrect actions in the situation

_____ *f.* Meeting a set of objectives by following rules and procedures as teams of learners compete

_____ *g.* A number of persons present information and their views on a topic before a class

_____ *h.* Highest type is termed "collaborative"

11. In planning teaching and learning activities, it is suggested that *two* questions be asked. What are they?

   a. _____
   _____
   _____

   b. _____
   _____

B. Comprehension

1. Below are applications of the conditions and principles of learning presented in the text. Before each one, write the *most appropriate* principle it represents.

_____ *a.* Deciding to use slides to support certain activities in a unit

_____ *b.* Providing learners with a copy of the outcomes they are to satisfy for a topic

_____ *c.* Making the answers to problems available to learners immediately after they complete their work

_____ *d.* Teacher's tone of voice and visible manner toward the subject as exhibited in front of learners

_____ *e.* Having learners complete a worksheet as they listen to a lecture

_____ *f.* Allowing learners to progress through a unit at their own study pace

_____ *g.* Giving a test over content a learner should already know before starting new unit

_____ *h.* When teaching a skill, learner is given a number of opportunities to perform the manipulations involved in the skill

_____ *i.* Having learners solve new problems relating to the content and principles just studied

_____ *j.* Allowing learners to check own learning by completing self-check tests; by getting correct answers learner sees positive progress

_____ *k.* Dividing content for a topic into small sections with participation activity for each section before learner starts next section

_____ *l.* Showing a film to a class as introduction for a new topic

_____ *m.* Following Gagné's structure of content for designing activities

2. Which teaching/learning pattern is *most appropriate* for each situation?

_____ *a.* The learner group is very diverse, with great variety in subject background.

_____ *b.* After learners have studied a topic, they must demonstrate their ability to apply the practices learned through role playing.

_____ *c.* Topic requires frequent updating as new content becomes available and revisions are necessary.

_____ *d.* Learners are to be oriented to procedures for activities at the beginning of a new program.

_____ *e.* You want learners to have the opportunity of hearing and then questioning two experts on a special topic.

_____ *f.* Program will be available at different locations; qualified subject experts are not available at most locations.

3. Which self-paced learning activity would you choose for each of the following?

_____ **a.** A number of learners in an advanced class lack suitable background in some basic concepts in the subject. The instructor would like these learners to learn the essential concepts on their own.

_____ **b.** In this course, the instructor feels that much of the information learners need to learn can be acquired through self-paced learning, especially if he can direct the learners in a pleasant, informal way as they study in the department's learning lab. He also wants to meet with groups of learners weekly and periodically has an activity for the total class.

_____ **c.** An instructor wants to treat the entire course content, based on a new textbook, in a self-paced format, permitting each student to progress at his or her own pace through a study of the text in order to reach a satisfactory level of achievement.

_____ **d.** A teacher is planning to develop a number of self-study packages that will supplement required course content. The subjects to be treated will require many pictures and diagrams in color. The teacher will provide explanations on tape to accompany visuals. About 300 students will use the materials in a learning center.

_____ **e.** The responsibility is on the learner to select a topic, complete the research, and present a report to the instructor.

_____ **f.** The professor would like to conduct her class with emphasis on discussions, problem-solving situations, and applications of content rather than to present lectures. She has assigned chapters in the textbook and wants students to study on their own, thus being prepared to participate in class activities.

_____ **g.** A new piece of laboratory equipment has been purchased. Each person is to learn how to operate the equipment when ready to use it and also to review the procedures if the equipment is used infrequently.

_____ **h.** For relicensing, certain technicians need to update their knowledge. The material requires explanation, simple diagrams, and the opportunity to apply many new concepts. The format must be simple, low cost, and allow the person to study at home. The total package must be self-contained and presented in an interesting fashion.

_____ **i.** For a new course, separate study units for each topic are being developed. They require use of a variety of resources providing alternatives for studying the content and are used separately from the study units.

4. Which interaction activity would you choose for each of the following?

_____ *a.* As part of their self-paced learning, each learner has completed a module which introduces the basic terminology used in conducting research on health-related topics. The instructor now wants learners to see the practical applications of names and expressions they have learned. They will form into small groups and be competitive in this activity.

_____ *b.* Learners have been studying the topic of genetic engineering. Some learners have interviewed researchers in the field and others have talked with religious leaders. Learners are ready to share their information and individual viewpoints about the topic.

_____ *c.* The learners are divided into teams. They are to review and analyze how a number of major ecological projects to preserve wildlife have been organized and carried out in different places around the world. Each group makes a report, evaluating and criticizing the data and results found.

_____ *d.* College students will be examining the problem of local airport expansion and its impact on surrounding home owners who are against the expansion. The class is to make recommendations for a solution.

_____ *e.* Four experts on aspects of community recreation services for the elderly will visit a class on *leisure and recreation.* The instructor would like each person to express views before the class and follow with discussion.

_____ *f.* Trainees in a management skills workshop are to experience some of the situations they most likely will face when they fill a position having leadership responsibilities. The experience is to be as realistic and spontaneous as possible.

_____ *g.* As the culminating activity, while attending a training course on fire safety procedures, it is necessary for the trainee to experience and react to a number of situations that are as realistic as possible.

5. Classify each of the following as:
   (1) Teacher activity
   (2) Student activity
   (3) Combination of both teacher *and* student activity
   ____ *a.* Teacher uses chalkboard to describe how a geometric shape is formed.
   ____ *b.* Each trainee practices the operation of equipment.
   ____ *c.* As a class, learners view a 20-minute film.
   ____ *d.* As learners engage in role playing, the instructor raises questions to help the group interpret the actions dramatized.
   ____ *e.* The instructor projects a number of overhead transparencies as learners take notes.
   ____ *f.* Learners cooperate to develop their project materials.

C. Application

    1. Sky Diving

    Specify the teaching/learning pattern and activities for each objective or set of related objectives.

_____

_____

_____

_____

_____

    2. Your Subject

    Specify the teaching/learning pattern and activities for each objective or set of related objectives.

_____

_____

_____

_____

_____

REFERENCES

Conditions and Principles for Learning

DeCecco, John P., and William R. Crawford. *The Psychology of Learning and Instruction,* 2d ed. (Englewood Cliffs, NJ: Prentice-Hall, 1974).

Gagné, Robert M. *The Conditions of Learning,* 3d ed. (New York: Holt, Rinehart, and Winston, 1977).

Huckabay, Loucine M. Daderian. *Conditions of Learning and Instruction in Nursing* (St. Louis: C. V. Mosby, 1980).

Klausmeier, Herbert J., and William Goodwin. *Learning and Human Abilities: Educational Psychology,* 4th ed. (New York: Harper and Row, 1975).

Levin, Tamar, and Ruth Long. *Effective Instruction* (Alexandria, VA: Association for Supervision and Curriculum Development, 1981).

Travers, Robert M. W., ed. *Second Handbook of Research on Teaching* (Chicago, Rand McNally, 1974).

Presentation

Bligh, Donald. *What's the Use of Lectures* (Devon, United Kingdom: Briar House, Clyst Honiton, Exeter EX5 2LZ, 1971).

Brock, Stephen C. *Aspects of Lecturing* (Manhattan, KS: Center for Faculty Evaluation and Development in Higher Education, 1977).

Kemp, Jerrold E., and Ron J. McBeath. *Preparing Lectures* (San Jose, CA: Faculty and Instructional Development Office, San Jose State University, 1981).

Osterman, Dean N. *Feedback Lecture: The Process and Components* (Corvallis, OR: Oregon State University, 1980).

Self-paced Learning

Bell, Normal T., and Allan J. Abedor. *Developing Audio-Visual Instructional Modules for Vocational and Technical Training* (Englewood Cliffs, NJ: Educational Technology Publications, 1977).

Bullock, Donald H. *Programmed Instruction,* The Instructional Design Library Series, vol. 14 (Englewood Cliffs, NJ: Educational Technology Publications, 1978).

Esbensen, Thorwald. *Student Contracts,* The Instructional Design Library Series, vol. 17 (Englewood Cliffs, NJ: Educational Technology Publications, 1978).

Gale, Fred L. *Determining the Requirements for the Design of Learner-Based Instruction (Columbus, OH: Charles E. Merrill, 1975).*

Holt, H.O., and F.L. Stevenson. "A Model Delivery System for Individualized Instruction," *NSPI Journal,* 14 (March 1980), 3–6.

Johnson, Stuart R., and Rita B. Johnson. *Developing Individualized Instructional Materials* (Palo Alto, CA: Westinghouse Learning, 1970).

Keller, Fred S., and J. Gilmour Sherman. *The PSI Handbook: Essays on Personalized Instruction.* Lawrence, KS: International Society for Individualized Instruction, 1982.

Kemp, Jerrold E. *Planning and Preparing Eight Types of Self-Paced Programs* (San Jose, CA: Faculty and Instructional Development Office, San Jose State University, 1980).

————, and Ron J. McBeath. *Types of Self-Paced Learning Programs* (San Jose, CA: Faculty and Instructional Development Office, San Jose State University, 1980).

Klingstedt, Joe L. "Contracting for Individualization: Let's Take a Fresh Look," *Educational Technology,* 23 (March 1983), 27–30.

Knowles, Malcolm S. *Self-Directed Learning: A Guide for Learners and Teachers* (Piscataway, NJ: New Century, 1975).

Langdon, Danny G. *The Adjunct Study Guide,* The Instructional Design Library Series, vol. 1 (Englewood Cliffs, NJ: Educational Technology Publications, 1978).

Langdon, Danny G. *The Audio-Workbook,* The Instructional Design Library Series, vol. 5 (Englewood Cliffs, NJ: Educational Technology Publications, 1978).

Langdon, Danny G. *Interactive Instructional Designs for Individualized Learning* (Englewood Cliffs, NJ: Educational Technology Publications, 1973).

Lineberry, Claude S., and Donald H. Bullock. *Job Aids,* The Instructional Design Library Series, vol. 24 (Englewood Cliffs, NJ: Educational Technology Publications, 1980).

Postlethwait, Samuel N., et al. *Exploring Teaching Alternatives* (Minneapolis: Burgess, 1977).

Rahmlow, Harold F. *The Teaching–Learning Unit,* The Instructional Design Library Series, vol. 18 (Englewood Cliffs, NJ: Educational Technology Publications, 1978).

Russell, James D. *The Audio-Tutorial System,* The Instructional Design Library Series, vol. 3 (Englewood Cliffs, NJ: Educational Technology Publications, 1978).

Russell, James D., and Kathleen A. Johanningsmeier. *Improving Competence Through Modular Instruction* (Dubuque, IA: Kendall-Hunt, 1981).

Sherman, J. Gilmour, and Robert S. Ruskin. *The Personalized System of Instruction,* The Instructional Design Library Series, vol. 13 (Englewood Cliffs, NJ: Educational Technology Publications, 1978).

Stolovitch, Harold D. *Audiovisual Training Modules,* The Instructional Design Library Series, vol. 4 (Englewood Cliffs, NJ: Educational Technology Publications, 1978).

Wydra, Frank T. *Learner Controlled Instruction,* The Instructional Design Library Series, vol. 26 (Englewood Cliffs, NJ: Educational Technology Publications, 1980).

Small-Group Interaction

Ames, Russell. "Designing Small Group Instruction," *NSPI Journal,* 16 (May 1977), 5–8.

Hyman, R.T. *Improving Discussion Leadership* (New York: Teacher's College, 1980).

Kelly, Helen. "Case Method Training: What It is, How it Works," *Training/HRD,* 20 (February 1983), 46–49.

McBeath, Ron J., and Janice M. Lane. *Conducting Discussions* (San Jose, CA: Faculty and Instructional Development Office, San Jose State University, 1981).

McKnight, Philip. *On Guiding (Not Leading) Discussions* (Manhattan, KS: Center for Faculty Evaluation and Development in Higher Education, 1978).

Thiagarajan, Sivasailam, and Harold D. Stolovitch. *Instructional Simulation Games,* The Instructional Design Library Series, vol. 12 (Englewood Cliffs, NJ: Educational Technology Publications, 1978).

Wales, Charles, and Robert A. Stager. *The Guided Design Approach,* The Instructional Design Library Series, vol. 9 (Englewood Cliffs, NJ: Educational Technology Publications, 1978).

Wohiking, Wallace, and Patricia J. Hill. *Role Playing,* The Instructional Design Library Series, vol. 32 (Englewood Cliffs, NJ: Educational Technology Publications, 1980).

chapter 9

Instructional Resources

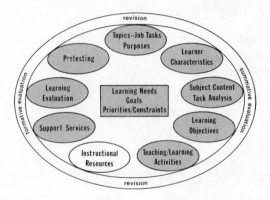

"Which is the best kind of AV media to use for these objectives?"

"Should I standardize on one resource or use a variety of them in this unit?"

"Are certain media forms more adaptable to one teaching/learning pattern than are other types?"

"Are slides preferred to filmstrips for viewing still pictures?"

"Isn't cost the most important factor when selecting media?"

"Do we have a training aid that can combine still and motion pictures in a single format?"

Most successful teaching/learning activities rely on the use of appropriate instructional resources. An overhead projector with transparencies may be important to the instructor who delivers a lecture. A manual correlated with an audiocassette recording may be essential for the learner who studies in a self-paced learning program. Printed handouts and simulated episodes on video-tape often are necessary with a small group for a problem-solving activity. In each instance, the resources used make substantial contribution to carrying out the activities and accomplishing the objectives they were selected to serve.

If resources are carefully selected and prepared, they can fulfill one or more of the following instructional purposes:

- Motivate learners by capturing their attention and stimulating interest in a subject.
- Involve learners vicariously but meaningfully in learning experiences.
- Contribute to the formation of attitudes and the development of appreciations.
- Explain and illustrate subject content and performance skills.
- Provide opportunities for self-analysis of individual performance and behavior.

RESOURCES AND THEIR FEATURES

The resources available for instruction can be grouped into a number of categories. The most useful ones for education and training, with a brief overview of their main features, are described below:

Real Things

- Guest speakers—Qualified persons can motivate as well as inform a group of students.
- Objects and devices—Seeing and manipulating real things are actions directly beneficial for learning.
- Models and mock-ups—Tangible simulations can substitute for real items which are too big, too small, or too complex to be made available in the classroom or learning lab; nonessential elements can be omitted; models are frequently smaller than the original, and mock-ups are often larger and greatly simplified; each permits learning an operation through careful study of the way it functions.

Nonprojected Materials (Two-dimensional)

- Printed paper copies—Most common resource for use by learners; includes single sheets and bound pages to serve almost any instructional purpose
- Chalkboard and flipchart—Useful for displaying lists as outlines or summaries to accompany verbal presentation; may be used to communicate words, symbols, and drawings
- Diagrams, charts, and graphs—Present information and illustrations in graphic forms; especially useful for communicating quantitative data and simplifying complex relationships; inexpensive and flexible to use
- Photographs—Inaccessible objects, situations, or procedures can be represented as realistic pictures for close-up, detailed study
- Job aids—Consist of a procedure list for performing a specific task; often in the form of a booklet including directions and line drawings or photographs; used at a worksite for reference

Audio Recordings

- Audiocassette recording—Easy-to-use media form for presenting verbal information; most appropriate for self-paced learning applications; can serve as alternate source of learning for individuals with low reading ability
- Disc recording—Limited to commercial products; because of potential damage, materials to be used are often transferred (with copyright permission) to tape

Projected Still Pictures

- Slides—Colorful, realistic reproductions of original subjects; may contain verbal, graphic, and photographic forms of information; useful for group presentations to support a lecture or for individual study; relatively inexpensive to prepare and use; can be rearranged and updated easily
- Filmstrips—Similar to slides, but images always in same order for use; cannot be rearranged or revised; inexpensive when a number of copies are required
- Overhead transparencies—Easy to use for presenting verbal and graphic information to groups; simple methods available for making black-and-white and color transparencies; various techniques can be used for systematically disclosing information on a transparency to hold audience interest
- Computer programs—Display information and instructions on video screen; interactive, self-pacing with assured learning through careful application of learning principles; require skill for program preparation; numerous programs available for drill, acquisition of information, concept development, simulation, and gaming exercises

Projected Motion Pictures

- Films—Widely used commercial medium when motion (regular speed, slowed down, or speeded up), relationships, and dramatizations are to be shown; being replaced by videorecordings in many instructional programs
- Videorecordings—Preferred medium for producing motion pictures with visual and audio elements recorded in synchronization; permits results to be viewed immediately; can store and transmit other media forms (slides, transparencies, films, etc.); tape editing and duplication widely used; suitable for both group and individual uses

Combinations of Media

- Printed paper/audiotape—Combines audio narration with printed information in any verbal, graphic or photographic form as an inexpensive, easy-to-use, self-paced learning resource

- Slides/audiotape—Combines narration, music, and sound effects synchronized with slides; may be shown to groups or used for individual study
- Filmstrip/audiotape—Combines narration, music, and sound effects synchronized with each frame; may be shown to groups or used for individual study
- Microfiche/audiotape—Combines narration, music, and sound effects with each frame and is manually changed by signal for individual study
- Multi-images/audiotape—Consists of two or more slide images projected simultaneously on adjacent screens with synchronous sound for group viewing; may include brief motion picture sequences; useful as motivational introduction or orientation to a topic
- Interactive computer/videotape or videodisc—Provides most sophisticated method of instruction as computer program controls display of verbal information and still or motion picture sequences; allows for flexible branching patterns of information and response sequences; preparation requires programming skill and careful planning of video materials

The above descriptions provide minimum information about the resources you may have available from which selections can be made. Become familiar with each type you might use, and especially those types with which you have had little or no experience. See the references in the bibliography, talk with persons who have used the ones unfamiliar to you, and, if possible, use them yourself in a learning activity. Then you will be better prepared to judge the suitability for use of each resource.

MEDIA SELECTION

For years, educational researchers have been pondering such questions as: "Is there a medium or combination of media that would be best for teaching a particular subject?" and, "Can media be classified according to their effectiveness for teaching certain kinds of facts, concepts, principles, or other generalizations?" No simple answers have been forthcoming.

Much of the research in learning with audiovisual materials has been inconclusive, or even contradictory. What has resulted is evidence that many learning experiences might be accomplished equally well by any of a number of media. On the other hand, it has also been shown that a medium that is well adapted for one instructional function may be unsatisfactory for a different purpose, within the same instructional sequence. This suggests that a variety of materials may have to be selected for a given program, with each one doing specifically what it can best do at a specific point in the learning sequence.

There are three procedures which are generally used for selecting resources in an instructional program:

1. Selection on the basis of what is readily available. ("The department purchased video equipment, so that's what I must use.")

2. Selection on the basis of what the instructor is most familiar with or most comfortable in using. ("I like filmstrips; therefore I usually use them in each unit I teach.")

3. Selection on a more objective basis whereby some guidelines can be followed so that selection can be justified in a nonsubjective manner. ("We chose the slide/tape format as best fulfilling the criteria established for making media decisions.")

If there are limitations or constraints with equipment, services, or facilities, then possibly the first procedure described above is the only one that could be used. But do note that there are simple resources, like printed paper worksheets or study guides and audiotape, that might be considered even though a major media resource (video, for example) had been given primary attention within an organization.

It should be possible to broaden a person's sights if the second procedure has been followed. Frequently we can demonstrate possibilities and advantages for using alternative resources.

The third procedure above is the one, it is hoped, you will consider employing. It can provide a basis for making logical, educated guesses that will lead to practical resource decisions.

Here is a media selection procedure based on the specific features, sometimes called "attributes," of the various resources. The important attributes are the following:

- Situation for use—Large-group presentation, small-group interaction situation, or for self-paced learning
- Treatment required of subject—Real or symbolic/verbal
- Pictorial representation—Photographic or graphic
- Factor of size—Nonprojected or projected
- Factor of color—Black-and-white or full color
- Factor of movement—Still or motion
- Factor of language—Oral sound or printed words
- Sound/picture relationship—Silent picture or picture with sound

By considering as many of these features as you feel to be important in terms of the learning objectives or requirements of subject content, you do have a basis for selecting media. The best way to do this is to ask a series of questions like the following:

1. "Will the material be presented to a group or will it be used for self-paced learning?" Some resources, like overhead transparencies, are best used for presentations. Others, like materials on paper, are more suitable for self-paced learning. Most can be adapted to either group or individual uses.

2. "Does the content require graphic treatment (design, artwork, lettering, coloring), photography, or a combination of graphics and photography?" Graphics (diagrams, artwork, cartoons, charts) can clarify and simplify complex concepts, but for some needs the truer reality of a

photographic form (photographs, slides, film or videorecording) may be necessary.

3. "Should visuals be prepared in the form of still pictures or as a motion picture (film or videotape)?" A motion picture is a "transient" medium, requiring learners to grasp the message as each concept or bit of information in the film is being presented. A still picture is a "persistent" medium, allowing a learner to study the message at length. These differences may be important when selecting the visual medium unless an overriding need for motion is critical to the treatment of the subject.

4. "Should the visual materials be accompanied by recorded sound?" When used with visuals, sound on tape or film can direct attention, explain details, raise questions, provide answers, and make transitions from one picture or idea to the next one. On the other hand, some subjects can be treated visually so that they have suitable impact without verbal explanations. If necessary, explanatory information can be put on paper to accompany silent visuals.

The above questions illustrate the type of reasoning that can lead to a media decision. If all the features previously listed are considered, a flow diagram for each of the three teaching/learning patterns (presentation, group interaction, and self-paced learning) can be developed. See the media selection diagrams following on page 139. In using a diagram, start with one or a group of related learning objectives and subject content for which you want to select a medium. Decide on an answer for the question or questions at the first level, near the top of the diagram. A "yes" answer to a question will lead you to the next lower level. Answer the questions on that level. Your decision at each level eventually leads to a group of related media from which a final choice can be made. Although each of us might answer a question differently and end at a different place in a diagram, the decision would be acceptable as long as you can justify the answer to each question as you proceed.

FINAL MEDIA DECISION

As the three diagrams (Figures 9.1, 9.2, 9.3) indicate, often your answers lead to a group of related resources near the bottom—for example, to still pictures such as the box containing photographs, slides, filmstrips in Figure 2. Each of these is a still picture form, any one of which may be acceptable as appropriate for accomplishing the topic objectives. The final choice, from among these three still picture resources, should be based on the most practical form to use, considering the relative merits of a number of empirical factors that result from asking the following questions:

- Does the needed material already exist in suitable form and quality?
- What would be the cost of purchase or preparation?
- What are the reproduction or duplicating costs, if any?
- How much time will be required to locate or prepare the material?

MEDIA SELECTION DIAGRAMS

Based on learning objectives and subject content, what attributes are required in the resources?

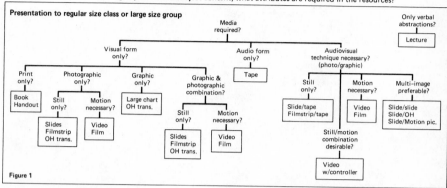

Figure 1

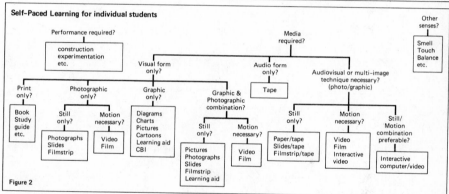

Figure 2

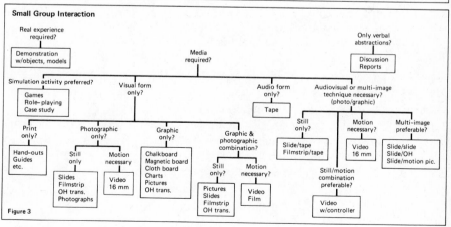

Figure 3

Figure 9.1

Table 9.1 FACTORS TO CONSIDER IN MAKING FINAL MEDIA
            DECISION

Factor	Alternative Materials		
	Photographs	Slides	Filmstrips
Commercially available			
Preparation costs			
Reproduction costs			
Time to prepare			
Skills/Services required			
Viewing and handling			
Maintenance and storage			
Students' preference			
Instructor's preference			

- What are the production requirements for equipment, facilities, and technical skills?
- Is one medium more suitable than the others because of ease of viewing or handling by learners?
- Will there be any problems regarding equipment, facilities, supervision, and scheduling for use?
- Will there be problems in the maintenance and storage of the materials for future use?
- Do you have evidence that learners may prefer to use one kind of material over the other ones?
- Does the instructor have a preference for use?

In order to answer some of these questions, the assistance or opinions of qualified media specialists may be desirable. You will find that some materials will rate high on one criterion, moderate on a second, and possibly low on a third. Prepare a table or *matrix* like the one illustrated in Table 9.1.[1] Mark the appropriate boxes. You will quickly see how each medium rates with respect to the criteria you wish to use. By following this procedure, you will have an objective basis on which to make the final media decision.

SUMMARY

One or more resources are required to support the teaching/learning activities that have been chosen to carry out the instruction. Resources can be selected

[1]Also see cost factors relating to types of media in Chapter 10.

from specific items within six categories. A selection procedure has been described in this chapter which can assist you to make the most appropriate choice for your situation.

REVIEW AND APPLICATIONS*

A. Recall

   1. What are three reasons for which instructional resources may be used to support instructional activities?

     a. _____
       _____
       _____

     b. _____
       _____
       _____

     c. _____
       _____
       _____

   2. Complete the following outline, which is a listing of resources under the various headings included in this chapter.

     a. Real things
       (1) Guest speakers
       (2) _____
       (3) _____
     b. _____
       (1) _____
       (2) Disc recordings
     c. _____
       (1) Diagrams, charts, graphs
       (2) Job aids
       (3) _____
       (4) _____
       (5) _____
     d. Projected still pictures
       (1) _____
       (2) _____
       (3) overhead transparencies
       (4) _____
     e. Combinations of media
       (1) _____
       (2) _____
       (3) Filmstrip/audiotape
       (4) Multi-images/audiotape
       (5) _____
     f. _____
       (1) Films
       (2) _____

*See answers on page 265.

3. Mark *true* or *false* for each statement about an instructional resource.

_____ *a.* To study the way something functions it is preferable to use real objects.

_____ *b.* A model is often smaller than a real thing while a mock-up is larger with parts eliminated for simplicity.

_____ *c.* The most widely used form of nonprojected material for self-paced learning is the photograph.

_____ *d.* A job aid is a listing of procedures for doing a specific task.

_____ *e.* The most widely used audio material is a recording on audiocassette tape.

_____ *f.* An advantage of filmstrips over slides is their flexibility for use and ease of replacing individual pictures.

_____ *g.* Of the forms of projected still pictures listed on page 135, the only one that is solely for use in making presentations to classes is the overhead transparency.

_____ *h.* Film continues to be the primary motion picture medium used for instruction.

_____ *i.* The simplest form of combination media is the multi-image/audiotape.

_____ *j.* The type of combination media that allows for a variable sequencing order for viewing information, including still and motion picture sequences is the computer/videotape or videodisc.

_____ *k.* An effective way to introduce a new topic, with the plan to build interest, is with a multi-image/audiotape presentation.

4. Which of the following "attributes" of media are helpful in the selection process?

_____ *a.* Black-and-white or color

_____ *b.* Still or motion

_____ *c.* Instructor or learner preference

_____ *d.* Photographic or graphic

_____ *e.* Preparation or purchase

_____ *f.* Silent or sound

_____ *g.* Symbolic/verbal or real

5. When using a media selection diagram, to what group of media does each set of questions lead?

a. *Presentation*
Media required?   _____
Visual form only?   _____
Graphic and photographic combination? _____
Still only?   _____
Which media?   _____

b. *Self-Paced Learning*
Media required?   _____
Audiovisual technique necessary?   _____
Motion necessary?   _____
Which media?   _____

c. *Small-Group Interaction*
Media required?   _____
Audiovisual technique necessary?   _____
Still only?   _____
Which media?   _____

6. Which factors are useful for making a final media decision?
     _____ *a.* Purchase cost
     _____ *b.* Preparation time
     _____ *c.* Instructor preference
     _____ *d.* Length of material
     _____ *e.* Maintenance requirements
     _____ *f.* Handling by learners
     _____ *g.* Proven to be a better way of learning
B. Comprehension
   1. Use the media selection diagrams (Figures 9.1, 9.2, 9.3) on page 139 to choose a single type or group of audiovisual materials to accomplish each of the following. First, indicate those questions in the appropriate diagram you would answer *positively,* then list your media choice.
     a. To illustrate to a government class the sequence of steps followed as a legislative bill becomes a law.
        (1) Questions: _____
        _____
        _____
        (2) Media choice: _____
        _____
        _____

     b. For individual students in a sewing class to learn the technique for putting a zipper in a skirt.
        (1) Questions: _____
        _____
        _____
        (2) Media choice: _____
        _____
        _____

     c. For groups of students learning to become community health nurses to overcome communication problems when working with clients from various ethnic minority groups.
        (1) Questions: _____
        _____
        _____
        (2) Media choice: _____
        _____
        _____

     d. An overview presentation on the services of a major charity organization for showing at large fund-raising meetings.
        (1) Questions: _____
        _____
        _____
        (2) Media choice: _____
        _____
        _____

   e. To review how to make adjustments to a plastic molding machine right at the technician's station.

      (1) Questions: _____

         _____

         _____

      (2) Media choice: _____

         _____

         _____

   f. For Savings and Loan Association employees to study procedures for handling new types of savings accounts during their free working time.

      (1) Questions: _____

         _____

      (2) Media choice: _____

         _____

         _____

2. Consider the following objectives or general purposes and descriptions of specific situations including instructional needs. Do two things with each one: (1) Indicate the teaching/learning pattern you would choose to serve each one; and (2) note what medium or media combination you would use.

   a. *Terminal objective:* To operate woodshop equipment (table saw, drill press, etc.). Instruct 20 students in specific procedures for using equipment safely.

      (1) Pattern: _____

         _____

         _____

      (2) Medium: _____

         _____

         _____

   b. *Learning objective:* To compare art forms found in Nature with similar forms in man-made structures. Part of a college humanities course for 200 students.

      (1) Pattern: _____

         _____

         _____

      (2) Medium: _____

         _____

   c. *General purpose:* To prepare students for studying a new course. Inform 60 high school students of schedules, location of materials, and assignments for self-paced learning. Then to present materials that will motivate and interest students in the course.

      (1) Pattern: _____

         _____

         _____

      (2) Medium: _____

         _____

   d. *Terminal objective:* To complete recertification as a radiation therapist. Required program for updating skills for technicians at hospitals within the state. As a therapist's license expires, the person must become informed of latest law changes and new procedures in treatment.

(1) Pattern: _____

_____

(2) Medium: _____

_____

e. *Terminal objective:* To practice supervisory duties. In groups of 8, give to new supervisors in an industrial company experiences in directing employees in their work, in maintaining good relations, and otherwise dealing with people.
(1) Pattern: _____

_____

(2) Medium: _____

_____

C. Applications
1. *Sky Diving*
Specify instructional resources for the activities previously chosen.

_____

_____

_____

2. *Your Subject*
Indicate the instructional resources to be used.

_____

_____

_____

REFERENCES

Anderson, Ronald. *Selecting and Developing Media for Instruction,* 2d ed. (New York: Von Nostrand, 1983).

Brown, James W., Richard B. Lewis, and Fred F. Harcleroad. *AV Instruction: Technology, Media and Methods* (New York: McGraw-Hill, 1983).

Fleming, Malcolm L., and W. Howard Levie. *Instructional Message Design* (Englewood Cliffs, NJ: Educational Technology Publications, 1978).

Heinich, Robert, Michael Molinda, and James Russell. *Instructional Media and the New Technologies of Instruction* (New York: Wiley, 1982).

Kemp, Jerrold E. *Planning and Producing Instructional Media,* 5th ed. (New York: Harper & Row, 1985).

Levie, W. Howard. "Models for Media Selection," *NSPI Journal,* 16 (September, 1977), 4–7.

Reiser, Robert A., and Robert M. Gagné. *Selecting Media for Instruction* (Englewood Cliffs, NJ: Educational Technology Publications, 1983).

Spangenberg, Ronald W., Vair Riback, and Harold L. Moon. *The State of Knowledge Pertaining to Selection of Cost-Effective Training Methods and Media* (Alexandria, VA: Human Resources Research Organization, June, 1973).

chapter 10

Support Services

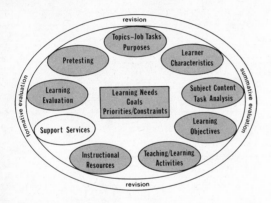

"Are sufficient funds available to purchase the materials we need?"

"Where do we find a room that can be adapted for a learning lab?"

"How do I schedule staff help for preparing materials?"

"Do we have enough equipment for learner use in the program we've planned?"

A point is reached during instructional planning when it becomes necessary to consider requirements for implementing the new program. You should be able to specify the requirements and be aware of the constraints or limitations which may need to be faced realistically.

During the learning needs assessment study (Chapter 3), when a new program or course is initially being considered, often the planning team is informed of the constraints within which the program can be developed. These may include:

- Monetary limitations (a budget, or the lack of one!)
- The time when the program must be ready for use (next year, next semester, next month, tomorrow!)
- The equipment on hand that should be used ("Last year we purchased filmstrip viewers . . . use them!")

- The size of an available room ("Only ten study stations can be put in that room!")

In other situations, necessary support must be carefully specified and justified as teaching/learning activities and resources are decided upon. Now you should consider needs relative to the following interrelated areas of instructional support:

- Budgetary matters
- Facilities
- Materials
- Equipment
- Personnel services
- Time frame for completing phases of the planning and development

Teachers and planning teams frequently neglect to request these necessary services—certain equipment, a particular room, a sum of money, or specific professional or technical assistance—until the time when they are needed for use. This procedure is not suitable in the instructional design process. If certain support, like funds or facilities, is not available, the successful completion and implementation of a newly planned program can be severely limited.

BUDGET

All new programs require funds to get started. Any institution or organization interested in supporting innovation in its instructional program must provide money for development and operation or implementation. Financial support may be necessary for any or all of the following during each of these two phases:

During Development

- Professional planning time
- Clerical support time
- Construction or renovation of required facilities
- Purchase of equipment, its installation, and check for operation
- Purchase or preparation of instructional materials, including professional search and planning time, inhouse technical and production staff time, or outside vendor services, raw materials, and duplicating multiple copies
- Development of testing instruments for evaluation of learning and for evaluation of the program
- Costs of consultative services
- Costs for tryouts, including personnel time and consumable materials
- Time for planning any necessary revisions, materials needed, and preparation
- Time for training instructors and staff for implementation phase

- Administration time for coordination and supervision
- Administrative costs (travel, telephone, overhead)

During Implementation or Program Operation

- Faculty and staff salaries
- Replacement of consumable and damaged materials
- Servicing and maintenance of equipment
- Depreciation of equipment
- Overhead charges for facilities and services
- Updating the program periodically (time and materials)

Further attention is given to financial matters as part of program cost measures in Chapter 16.

FACILITIES

Facilities to carry out an instructional program may require any of the following:

- Room for presentation to groups of average size (20 to 40), or to large groups (100 or more), requiring chalkboards, audiovisual projection, and sound amplification.
- Self-paced learning study stations (carrels or open tables) of a suitable size to hold necessary equipment and study materials for learner use.
- Small-group meeting rooms with informal arrangements of furniture for teacher–learner or learner–learner interaction, equipped with chalkboards and provision for audiovisual projection.
- A resource center where materials and equipment are gathered, organized, and made available to instructors and learners.
- Staff meeting room and workroom

When deciding on facilities for a learning center to serve a self-paced learning program, consider the following four questions:

- How many learners are expected in the program?
- How many hours will the average learner spend in the learning center?
- How many stations or carrels will be required or how many pieces or sets of equipment will be needed?
- How many hours will the center be open weekly (possibly with supervision)?

If you know or can decide on answers for any three of these questions, you can calculate the fourth. For example:

100 learners

4 hours—average study time per learner in a week

10 stations, fully equipped, to be provided

Question: How many hours should the center be open weekly?

$$100 \times 4 = 400 \text{ student hours per week}$$
$$400 \div 10 = 40 \text{ hours of use per week}$$

Thus, this learning center should be available a minimum of 40 hours per week. This assumes continuous, full use of each station. A factor of 10 to 20 percent should be added to allow flexibility for repeated use by some learners, equipment failure, variations in learner schedules, and other unforeseen needs. So, in this problem, 45 to 48 hours of operation should be provided. If the hours of operation become too great, then the number of stations might be increased.

As the need for specific facilities becomes obvious, consider which existing rooms can be used without modification, which ones require minor or major adaptations, and where new construction is essential. Many ideas for adapting present facilities can be obtained by visiting locations that have similar programs in operation. It may also be necessary to consult with qualified experts who know about space needs for various activities, availability of special equipment, electrical requirements, and other technical matters.

MATERIALS

Once resources to support activities have been decided (Chapter 9), it is necessary to locate and acquire specific commercial items or to prepare materials. Reference librarians or film library specialists can assist with catalogs and other sources of available audiovisual materials.

If materials are to be prepared, then a planning and production sequence for audiovisual and video items should be followed. This includes outlining content (from subject content or task analysis lists), as related to the learning objectives, and developing a storyboard and/or script. Then arrange for or carry out the production—preparing graphics, taking pictures, making slides, videotaping, audio recording, editing, and so forth.[1] Once the original material is completed and accepted, necessary duplicate copies should be made.

Other required materials, including printed items such as information sheets, study guides, worksheets, and workbooks, need to be written and prepared in sufficient copies for the number of learners to be served.

EQUIPMENT

When you are deciding upon the kinds of materials to use in a program, consideration should be given to the equipment required for using the materials. Is sufficient equipment already available, or must it be obtained? Although decisions about equipment usually depend on your choice of materials, there are instances when the kind of equipment available may

[1] For specific details and guidance in all audiovisual planning and production steps see Kemp, *Planning and Producing Instructional Media.*

influence the type of material to be used. For example, still pictures in the form of slides might be preferred for self-paced learning, but because filmstrip viewers are available, or are much less expensive in quantity and easier to use than are slide units, it may be preferable to prepare filmstrips rather than slides.

Here again, expert help may be advisable. Because such a wide variety of equipment is available for both group presentations and individual use, knowing what to choose without having an extensive background and up-to-date experience can be difficult. Find out which kinds of equipment have proved to be durable and easy to use and which cause the least damage to the materials. However, do not leave the final decision on equipment to consultants. Those persons to be involved in a new program should themselves carefully examine and try out whatever equipment is recommended. Have learners work with the equipment also, before you make a final decision.

Sometimes we are impressed with highly sophisticated, complex equipment that apparently can do many things, some of which may not be needed. Often, less complex and less costly equipment can serve equally well. The cost of maintenance and the replacement of parts must also be taken into consideration. This is particularly true with respect to video and computer equipment. Be practical in requesting what you will need, but be reasonable in terms of the funds that are available, the complexity of the equipment, and the eventual cost of upkeep.[2]

PERSONNEL CAPABILITIES

Professional and technical skills in at least 11 different areas are essential for planning an instructional design, developing the resources, and implementing and testing a program. Very likely some members of a planning team will either have a number of these skills to a degree or be able to acquire them. The services of persons with special skills can be called upon as needed.

The responsibilities of the various members of a planning team are indicated below.

Instructor or Teacher

The instructor or teacher knows the characteristics of the learners for whom the instruction is to be designed. He or she must be well informed in the subject area and, therefore, be able to specify the necessary learning objectives while recommending instructional methods. The teacher should be experienced in using various media for presentations. When the new program is being carried out, the teacher or teaching team has the major responsibility for its success. Rather than being a lecturer or solely a disseminator of information, the instructor or the team now plays an active part in:

[2]The most complete source listing of audiovisual equipment is *The Audio-Visual Equipment Directory.*

- Motivating people to learn
- Guiding the learning experiences of individual learners and groups of learners
- Monitoring learner progress
- Diagnosing difficulties and providing corrective measures
- Recognizing good performance and offering encouragement
- Supervising the work of assistants or aides

Instructional Designer

The person who holds the assignment of instructional designer must have had teaching experience and a background in educational philosophy, learning psychology and instructional methods. This person must be experienced with the instructional design process and know about teaching/learning methods and instructional resources of all types. He or she must be able to guide the planning process, work with all personnel, and coordinate the program with administrators. The designer must supervise the scheduled completion of materials, assist in evaluating the tryouts, and help put the program into operation.

Some educators believe instructional designers should be competent in the subject area in which they work. Others feel the designer should have experience in teaching but not necessarily in the content area being planned. Without being involved in the teaching role or in the subject of the course, the designer may guide the planning and view the objectives, content, methods, resources, and procedures of evaluation in a fresh, unbiased way. Chapter 14 gives further attention to the role of the instructional designer.

Subject Matter Expert

The subject matter expert (SME) (a role usually filled by the teacher or teaching team) must be competent in the subject. Such a person would suggest content topics, recommend the sequence for presenting them, and select activities based on the course objectives. This expert must be able to check the accuracy of the subject content selected and of the treatment of content in instructional materials chosen or produced for the program. He or she must be well aware of the relationship of this subject to other subjects in the curriculum or training program. The role requires a person who has a fresh, broad, and imaginative view of the subject and its applications. Further attention is given to this role in Chapter 14.

Learning Theorist

The learning theorist must have a background in learning psychology. This person's role is to guide the sequence of learning experiences. Suggestions how to utilize the conditions and principles of learning (as presented in Chapter 8), so as to make learning as interesting and effective as possible, are another responsibility of the learning theorist. With suitable qualifications, the instructor, the instructional designer, or the evaluator might fill this role.

Evaluation Specialist

The role of the evaluator is to assist the professional staff in developing testing instruments to: pretest learners' previous learning levels; measure cognitive, psychomotor, and performance accomplishments as the instructional program proceeds; and test learning at the end of course units. The evaluator will assist in formative testing during program tryouts and in applying the findings for improving the program. He or she may be asked to develop attitudinal and rating scales and to design summative evaluation measures to determine the effectiveness and efficiency of the program. It is strongly recommended that the evaluator be someone from "outside"—having no connection with the program—so the analysis and resulting recommendations will be as objective as possible.

Administrator

The program administrator, a role often filled by the instructional designer, supplies administrative leadership and usually arranges schedules, personnel assignments, equipment and budget allocations, and requests facilities as the program moves from planning into development and implementation. Managing the "politics" associated with introducing any new program in an organization (including obtaining permissions or clearances to do things, being alert to human conflicts, and supporting staff actions) should be an additional responsibility of the administrator.

Media Specialist

The media specialist must know the advantages and limitations of all kinds of instructional media. This specialist helps select appropriate materials and equipment for each set of objectives. He or she plans, supervises, or carries out the production of all instructional materials made locally, including print, graphic, photographic, audio, and video forms. The media specialist also supervises the adaptation of facilities needed in connection with the use of the media and must be able to instruct teachers and learners how to use the materials and equipment.

Librarian

The librarian must have a broad knowledge of what may be available in order to suggest commercial print and nonprint materials for teaching/learning activities. The librarian is responsible for locating needed materials as well as for providing the services for using them during implementation of the program.

Media Technician

The media technician's job is to prepare instructional materials, package items needed for the program, and install as well as maintain equipment.

Aides

Aides (sometimes called tutors, proctors, or facilitators) assist teachers and others on the staff with semi-instructional and housekeeping tasks. These may include—preparing simple materials, supervising laboratory and learner-group activities, handling and distributing materials and equipment, providing remedial or special assistance to learners, and administering and grading tests. Aides may be graduate students in the subject field, undergraduates or former trainees who have previously completed the new program, or paid or volunteer assistants.

Secretary

The secretary's duty is to handle all office and clerical work, including typing, correspondence, filing, ordering materials, preparing reports, duplicating and labeling materials, and assisting the instructional designer, instructor, and administrator.

Learners

Increasingly, learners are participating in activities that affect them. Many learners are intellectually mature and articulate. Their reactions and suggestions to proposed instructional plans can be beneficial. Select two or three learners who have already studied the subject, and ask them to participate in review sessions. They can react to activities and evaluate unit materials.

The Planning Team

The initial planning team should be small. It may consist of one or more teachers who have subject content capabilities, an instructional designer who has media specialist capabilities, and an evaluation expert who has learning theory capabilities. It is possible that a team of two may possess all the necessary skills. Persons with other abilities should be brought into the program as their services are required.

TIME AND SCHEDULES

Next to personnel, the allocation of time is the most difficult category of support service to deal with during the development of any new program. Finding time to work on the many aspects of a project may be formidable. Often the idea of a new program will not be accepted by the administration until some preliminary planning has been completed and a detailed proposal presented. The time for this preliminary work may have to be borrowed from time that would have been spent on other activities. A real dedication is often required to complete the initial planning.

When a design project is approved, time is required for professional planning, for staff and clerical assistance in locating and preparing materials, for support services to adapt facilities and install equipment, and for numerous other things. After the planning is completed, schedules must be set for trying out the program. During the same period, time must be scheduled for staff orientation and training, as necessary. Finally, work schedules must be drawn up for instructors, aides, and learners in order to put the instructional program into operation.

In a self-paced learning program learners must be helped to assume responsibilities for completing their assignments within a given time period. In scheduling learner time, be alert to the tendency that some will procrastinate on their responsibilities. Therefore, set deadlines for learners to complete work and take tests.

COORDINATING WITH OTHER ACTIVITIES

Too often a new instructional program in an institution or organization is treated as if it occupies a special world of its own. It may be given preference over regular classes in using facilities, and its participants may seem to have special privileges that other teachers and learners know little about and may resent. Coordinating and communicating with others in the building or in the organization can develop understanding and thus maintain good feelings. Therefore, it is a good plan to explain a new program to all members of a faculty or department, and to keep them advised of progress. Inform them of any activities that may interest them professionally or that may have some influence on them or on their learners.

SUMMARY

Once the actual instruction—teaching/learning activities and resources—has been planned, then attention should be given to any of a number of services necessary to support the instruction. Six specific areas are outlined in this chapter: budget, facilities, materials, equipment, support personnel, and time schedules. Without taking them into consideration, the successful development and implementation of the program can be jeopardized.

REVIEW AND APPLICATIONS*

A. Recall

    1. What are the *six* areas necessary for support of instruction?

        a. _____

        b. _____

*See answers on page 267.

c. _____

d. _____

e. _____

f. _____

2. In the chapter, budgeting is organized under two phases. Relate the following items to the proper budget phase.

____ *a.* Servicing equipment

____ *b.* Adapting facilities

____ *c.* Preparing instructional materials

____ *d.* Salaries of program-use personnel

____ *e.* Cost for tryout evaluation

____ *f.* Updating materials

____ *g.* Planning team activities

____ *h.* Replacing damaged materials

____ *i.* Designing evaluation instruments

____ *j.* Purchasing equipment

____ *k.* Revising materials after tryout

____ *l.* Depreciating equipment

3. What are the three kinds of facilities that may be required in an instructional program?

a. _____

b. _____

c. _____

4. How many learners might be served in a learning lab that has 12 stations available for 20 hours a week and requires about 3 hours use per learner for study each week? _____

5. The subject of Chapter 9 is *instructional resources.* In this chapter, one of the support areas is *materials.* How do you differentiate between these two related elements and give attention to each one during planning?

_____

_____

_____

6. If audiovisual materials such as a slide/tape program or a videotape recording is to be produced, the production staff should be responsible for obtaining approval from subject specialist and audiovisual designer at what *four* stages during the media development and production process?

a. _____

_____

_____

b. _____

_____

_____

c. _____

_____

_____

d. _____

_____

_____

7. If you wanted information about available sources and prices of specific models of a certain kind of audiovisual equipment, where would you look for this information?

_____

_____

_____

8. Of the eleven categories of personnel described in this chapter, which one is referred to by each of the following?
   - _____ *a.* Supervises the adaptation of facilities for using media in the program
   - _____ *b.* Able to specify the necessary learning objectives
   - _____ *c.* Competent in the content of the subject being planned
   - _____ *d.* Guides the planning process
   - _____ *e.* Knows the group for whom instruction is planned
   - _____ *f.* Plans and carries out production of AV materials
   - _____ *g.* Checks accuracy of content treatment in materials
   - _____ *h.* Conducts summative evaluation of program
   - _____ *i.* Helps the instructor with special assistance for learners
   - _____ *j.* Coordinates the program with administrators
   - _____ *k.* Installs and maintains equipment
   - _____ *l.* Locates available commercial materials for possible use in program
   - _____ *m.* Major responsibility for carrying out the new program
   - _____ *n.* Assists in developing tests

9. List four instances during the instructional design process when *time* should be an important consideration.
   a. _____

   _____

   _____

   b. _____

   _____

   _____

   c. _____

   _____

   _____

   d. _____

   _____

   _____

10. What is a major problem that may be faced when learners are given the freedom to set their own pace in learning?

_____

_____

_____

B. Comprehension

This is a practical problem for determining costs and making equipment selection.

Situation: A company has recently been awarded a large contract for providing special services on a project. In 3 months about 250 unskilled people will be employed. They will be hired in small numbers over a period of time. Each person must be carefully oriented to the company, the project, and their responsibilities.

Terminal Learning Objective: Prepare new employees to fulfill their role in the company and in the project.

Student Group: As each unskilled person is employed, he or she will complete an orientation program. Up to 25 trainees may go through the program each day. Therefore, 5 study stations will be necessary.

To serve the objective, it is decided that some form of still picture medium would be most suitable along with recorded narration and print material for trainee use in a learning center. It is anticipated this part of the orientation would take 1 to 1½ hours for each individual.

Your job: 1. What medium would you recommend for the orientation program? What is your justification for selection?
2. What are the costs of producing training materials?
3. What type of equipment would you select for use and what is the cost?
4. What sum of money should be budgeted for the project?
5. What facilities, with what use, and requiring what supervision, are needed?

This information is available to you:

a. Planning, storyboard, and script (length 20 minutes) has all been prepared about the company and the project relating to the objective. The visuals include some slides already on file, pictures to be taken of company activities, diagrams to be drawn and photographed, narration to be refined and recorded, and a booklet containing information and participation questions. All materials must be ready for use in 6 weeks.

b. The breakdown of required materials is:
Total number of scenes—63
Slides readily available—18
Slides to be shot on location—26
Studio and copystand work—8
Art work for slides—11

c. Cost for services:
Photography—$20/hr
   0.5 hour per slide on location
   15 minutes per slide in studio and on copystand
Graphics—$20/hr
   2 hours average time for art work (diagrams, titles, etc.)
   15 hours to prepare art work for booklet
Audio recording—$25/hr
   4 hours to prepare 20 minute recording with music and sound effects

d. Cost for materials:
$1 per slide on location
$0.50 per slide in studio and on copystand
$2 per visual for graphics
$10 for audiotape
$15 for print booklet

e. Final materials:
$0.50 duplicating slides
$3 per frame for master filmstrip
$0.05 per frame for duplicates

$3 each audiocassette
$1 each box for filmstrip and audiocassette
$7.50 per minute for converting slide/tape program to videotape
$15 each videocassette
$2 each printed booklet

f. Equipment for use:
$500 for 35mm synchronized sound/slide unit
$5 Carousel slide tray
$250 35mm synchronized sound filmstrip unit
$1200 video playback unit and receiver

Based on the above information, answer the five questions above under the heading *Your job.*

_____
_____
_____
_____
_____
_____
_____
_____
_____
_____

C. Applications
1. *Sky Diving*
What support services are necessary for the activities and resources selected to accomplish the objectives? Indicate them under the six categories that are presented in this chapter.

_____
_____
_____
_____
_____
_____

2. *Your Subject*
List necessary support services.

_____
_____
_____
_____
_____
_____

REFERENCES

The Audio-Visual Equipment Directory (Fairfax, VA: NAVA/ICIA, annual).
Gelbach, Deborah L. "Designing the Training Room of Your Dreams," *Training/HRD,* 19 (December 1982), 16–21.

Goff, Myron R. "Carrels for Self-paced Instruction," *NSPI Journal,* 14 (March 1980), 16–19, 34.

Kemp, Jerrold E. *Planning and Producing Instructional Media,* 5th ed. (New York: Harper & Row, 1985).

Knirk, Frederick G. *Designing Productive Learning Environments* (Englewood Cliffs, NJ: Educational Technology Publications, 1979).

Liebbe, Jake A. "Guideline Recommendations for the Design of Training Facilities," *NSPI Journal,* 14 (March 1980), 21–22.

chapter *11*

Evaluating Learning

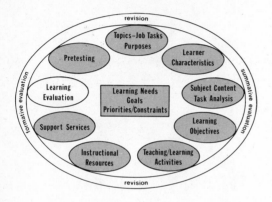

"The questions on this test don't relate to the objectives the instructor gave us at the beginning of the unit. Shouldn't they?"

"If *all* students satisfactorily accomplish *all* the objectives I set for a topic, shouldn't they *all* receive a grade of A?"

"Should each student's learning be evaluated relative to that of other students in a class, or should their learning be judged against a specific standard I set?"

"When a major activity in a unit is completed, can the results be judged as evaluation for the objective?"

"What are some ways to measure the accomplishment of performance skills besides observing a person at work on a job?"

"How can I determine whether an attitudinal objective is being satisfied?"

Evaluating learning is the last of the four essential elements in the instructional design process as reflected by the above questions. After examining the learners, you identified the learning objectives to be accomplished. Then, you selected instructional procedures to accomplish the objectives. Now finally, you must develop the testing instruments and materials to measure the degree to which learners have acquired the knowledge, can perform the skills, and exhibit changes in attitude as required by the objectives.

RELATIONSHIP BETWEEN EVALUATION AND LEARNING OBJECTIVES

There must be a direct relationship between learning objectives and test items. Some authorities even suggest that as soon as a subject content list and the details of a task analysis are first completed, you should immediately write examination questions relating to the content. In turn, the questions can be reworded as learning objectives. This may seem to be a backwards way of planning, but it points up the importance of directly relating evaluation to learning objectives.

It is customary to derive test items from the objectives, with subject content or task items being used for details. Once you are satisfied with the extent and completeness of the learning objectives, you are ready to develop ways for evaluating them. The result becomes the *posttest*—a measurement of learning when study of a topic or unit is concluded.

The verb component of the learning objective indicates the form that a test item should take. Here are some examples:

To *identify* or *recognize*—Choosing an answer in an objective-type test item (see types below)

To *list* or *label*—Writing a word or brief statement

To *state* or *describe*—Writing or speaking a short or lengthy answer

To *solve* or *calculate*—Writing or choosing a solution or numerical answer

To *compare* or *differentiate*—Writing about a relationship or choosing an answer which shows a relationship

To *operate* or *construct*—Rating the quality of performance or product against criteria

To *formulate* or *organize*—Writing a plan or choosing an order of items relative to a plan

To *predict* or *judge*—Writing a description of what is expected to happen, or choosing from alternative decisions

While there will be some variation in interpretation of the meaning of a verb for evaluation purposes, these examples illustrate the close relationship that is necessary between a learning objective and a test item. In the testing and measurement area this relationship is an indication of the *validity* of a test question.

A learner should anticipate being tested in the same type of behavior as indicated by the objective. Thus the verb in an objective alerts the learner to the emphasis necessary when studying the content.

TESTING WITH PAPER AND PENCIL

Most cognitive-domain objectives are evaluated by tests prepared on paper. The tests can be of various types and are grouped into two categories—*objective* and *written-answer* forms. Some learning objectives might preferably be measured by one type of test rather than another. Therefore, you should become familiar with the various considerations that can influence your choice. The discussion that follows indicates features of each of the commonly used types of tests. For help with the details in formulating properly stated test questions, see the references for this chapter.

Objective-type Tests

Persons scoring test items in this category can easily agree on the correct answer. Hence the term "objective" test. This category includes questions for which the student must recognize and select an answer from two or more alternatives, or respond to prepared statements. No writing, other than marking an answer, is required. Objective-type tests are of three major types.

Multiple-choice Items   Multiple-choice is the most useful and versatile type of objective testing. It consists of a *stem* which is a question or an incomplete statement. The possible answers are called *options* or *alternatives.* They may number from three to five, with one of them being the correct or best reply.

All levels of the Bloom cognitive-domain taxonomy can be tested with multiple-choice questions. This type of objective test is of particular value when judging the more complex aspects of cognitive learning, including discriminatory thinking by learners. Guessing is greatly reduced because there are three to five alternative answers from which to choose (as compared to the 50 percent chance for guessing the correct answer in true–false questions). Ambiguity, which can frustrate learners if a test question is not carefully written, can be more easily avoided than in composing the brief statements in true–false and short-answer test questions.

Here are examples of multiple-choice questions on various levels of the Bloom taxonomy:

1. *Knowledge:* How does cardiovascular death rank as a killer in the United States? (a) first, (b) second, (c) fifth, (d) tenth.

2. *Comprehension:* When the temperature of a moving air mass is lower than that of the surface over which it is passing, transfer of heat takes place vertically. This principle results in which designation for the air mass? (a) k, (b) w, (c) A, (d) P.

3. *Application:* An operator can be expected to drill 6 holes a minute with a drill press. The amount of time required to drill 750 holes is (a) 3 hours 14 minutes, (b) 2 hours 30 minutes, (c) 2 hours 5 minutes, (d) 1 hour 46 minutes.

4. *Analysis:* Examine the sample photographic print. What should you do to correct the condition shown? (a) use another negative; (b) expose paper for a longer time; (c) develop paper for a longer time; (d) use a stronger developer.

5. *Evaluation:* You note while checking your patient 6 hours after delivery that the fundus is approximately 3 cm above the umbilicus and on the right side. You suspect (a) nothing is wrong because the fundus should be there; (b) a distended bladder; (c) hypertrophy of the uterus; (d) postpartum hemorrhage.

True–False Items   True–false test questions are presented as statements to which the learner indicates truth or falsity. Variations may take the form of "right–wrong," "correct–incorrect," "yes–no," "fact–opinion," and "agree–disagree." Only content material which lends itself to these *either-or* answers should be written as true–false items. The elements of content that can be tested are fairly narrow, often limited to the recall of factual information or the identification of statements or principles.

Because they seem easy to write, true–false items are very popular. Unless thought and care are applied when constructing an item, to be certain that the statement is entirely true or entirely false, learners can misinterpret the intended meaning. This can lead to confusion and potential arguments.

Here are examples of questions to be answered as either *true* or *false*:

1. An individual with "Type A" behavior pattern is at risk for coronary artery disease.

2. A colder mean yearly temperature is found at the North Pole than at the South Pole.

3. An isosceles triangle has three equal sides.

4. The "separate but equal" doctrine was rejected by the Supreme Court in the *Plessy v. Ferguson* decision.

Matching Items   Matching items is a special multiple-choice form. It requires the learner to identify the relationship between entries in a list of *premises* forming one column, with *alternative* responses in a second column. A matching test can be used when a series of homogeneous facts are to be related on recall, comprehension, or application levels. Matching items are most suitable for testing knowledge of associations such as: definitions and terms, events and dates, achievements and people, descriptions or applications and principles, functions and parts, or classifications and structures.

With a matching test, a large amount of material can be condensed to fit in less space on a page than is required for a multiple-choice treatment of the same content. By careful selection of terms, chances for guessing correct associations can virtually be eliminated.

Here are examples of matching tests:

A. In column I are descriptions of geographic characteristics of wind belts.
    For each statement, find the appropriate wind belt in column II. Answers
    may be used more than once.

Column I	Column II
1. Region of high pressure, calm, and light, baffling winds	a. Doldrums
	b. Horse latitudes
2. The belt of calm air nearest the equator	c. Polar easterlies
	d. Prevailing westerlies
3. A wind belt in the northern hemisphere	e. Prevailing easterlies
4. Most of the U.S. is found in this belt	

B. Select a lettering device in column II to carry out the task in column I.
    Answers may be used only once.

Column I	Column II
1. Making a thermal transparency quickly	a. Soft lead pencil
	b. Broad-tip felt pen
2. Preparing a transparency directly on clear acetate	c. Fine-tip felt pen
	d. Mechanical pressure
3. Quick lettering for a paste-up sheet	e. Dry transfer
4. Producing colored lettering for a large poster	f . Photocomposing
	g. Hard-lead pencil
5. Preparing titles, without equipment, to be photographed as slides	

Written-Answer Tests

The major limitation of objective-type tests is that learners are not required to
plan answers and express them in their own words. These shortcomings are
overcome by using written-answer tests. They may range from the requirements
for a one-word response to a lengthy reply for a complex question. An
important value for using written-answer tests is that high-level cognitive
objectives can more satisfactorily be evaluated.

Short-Answer Items   The short-answer type of question requires a learner to
write a single word, a few words, or a brief sentence in response to an
incomplete statement or a question. The terms "fill-in," "completion," or
"restricted-response" also apply to this type of answer-generating question.

   As a category of tests, these items fall between objective types and full-
scale essay questions. The answers required are often very specific—a certain
word, phrase, number, or symbol. Since the expected answers are specific,
scoring can be objective. For other questions, learners may have greater

freedom of choosing words in responses. Numerical problems also fall into this category.

Most short-answer items are limited to testing the recall of facts (knowledge level) and comprehension or application of specific information. A large amount of content in a unit can be treated by a series of short-answer items. But remember that while one mind (the instructor's) designs test questions, there will be many minds (the learners') to interpret and analyze each question. It is therefore important to direct learner thinking to the acceptable answer by the careful phrasing of a question.

Here are examples of short-answer test questions:

1. Turbidity is a term which describes water that is _____.
2. Air is never injected into an ampule because _____
   _____
3. What is the formula for finding total resistance in a series circuit containing four resistors?
4. What are the duties, in order of their importance, of an air traffic control supervisor?

Essay Items   Essay questions are most useful for testing higher levels of cognitive learning. In particular, learning objectives on levels of analysis, synthesis, and evaluation can be measured when learners are required to organize and express their thoughts within a structured framework, describe relationships, and defend positions in writing.

There are both important advantages and limitations to essay tests. Among the advantages are these:

- They are relatively easy to construct, taking less time than does the design of a comparable objective-type test.
- They require learners to express themselves in writing, a verbal skill to which more attention needs to be given.
- They can supplement an objective test as a final measurement for a unit or topic, requiring learners to relate and summarize components of the unit.
- By reading responses to an essay question, an instructor becomes aware of a learner's approach to problem solving.

Disadvantages of essay tests include:

- Only a limited number of concepts or principles relating to a topic can be tested.
- Because it is considered easy to write an essay test, questions asked can be broad and ambiguous, making the scoring difficult and unreliable.
- Because of this subjective nature of essay-test grading, some learners having good literary skills, can impress an instructor with their writing, even though their knowledge of the subject may be limited.
- Time required for different learners to complete an essay test will vary greatly.

- Much time and care must be taken when grading so as to be as objective as possible and avoid making personal judgments about individual learners.

Here are examples of essay questions:

1. Prepare a hypothetical route weather forecast from your station to a location 500 miles away. Assume that a winter cold front exists at the beginning of the forecast period halfway between the two locations, with squall lines and icing conditions below 12,000 feet MSL. Make reference to the general situation, sky conditions and cloud base, visibility, precipitation, freezing level, winds aloft, and other factors you deem important. (*20 points*)

2. In your judgment, what will be the most difficult change human society will have to adapt to in the 21st century? Support your position with reference to at least three utopian objectives and their significance for the future. (*15 minutes*)

EVALUATING PERFORMANCE

By using a performance test you are able to determine how well a trainee or learner can carry out a particular task or a group of related tasks. Attention has already been given to the means for measuring cognitive knowledge required for a task (identifying equipment parts, their functions, and similar pertinent knowledge). Now the degree of skill acquired needs to be determined. The kinds of learning that can be evaluated, as related to psychomotor behavior, include:

- Physical skills—using machines and tools, operating procedures, doing construction work
- Mental skills—trouble-shooting, problem-solving behavior, human relations skills

The standards of performance are judged according to the requirements of the learning objectives and should be the same as those covered during instruction. Prior to this testing phase, the learner should have had sufficient opportunities to practice and apply the skills to be able to demonstrate the learning. If so, he or she should be prepared to complete the test successfully.

Preliminary Considerations

When preparing to evaluate performance, answers to the following questions should be sought.

Will process, product *or* both *be evaluated?* When a learner performs a task, the confidence, care, and accuracy with which the procedures are carried out usually are important. This is a measurement of the **process** portion of the task, which may include elements such as: following a proper sequence of actions or steps; performing detailed manipulations; using tools or instruments properly; and working within a specified time period.

Product evaluation focuses primarily on the end result or outcome of the effort. Attention is on the quality and possibly quantity of a product or on the final action that results from applying the process.

The evaluation of most tasks includes both process and product components.

What constraints or limitations should be recognized when planning a performance evaluation? The conditions under which a task is normally performed should be considered before developing the test. Such elements as size and complexity of the task, cost for materials or services required, human safety factors, and time needed for testing can help to influence whether a realistic or a simulated testing situation should be used. Other matters that need attention when deciding on the method of testing include: the required place for testing; necessary or specialized equipment, instruments, tools, and supplies needed; and the required involvement of other persons, in addition to the learner to be tested.

Will the testing conditions be simulated or realistic? By considering the various factors indicated in the answer to the previous question, you can be prepared to decide whether the test can be conducted under realistic conditions or, if this is impractical, whether it can be handled in some abbreviated or simulated fashion. The simulation should be as joblike as possible in order to serve as a valid measure of performance.

When deciding whether to test under realistic or simulated conditions, consideration should be given to recording the performance on videotape. With this procedure, evaluation of a performance can take place at a convenient time later on and may involve the learner in the review.

Developing the Test

Once you have established parameters for the test, review the learning objectives and details of the task to be evaluated. Then follow this procedure for designing the test:

1. Write down the steps or specific procedures of the task that comprise the criteria to be judged. Establish the proficiency level that will be accepted (as indicated by the objective).
2. Plan how the performance will take place, including its location and the application of the procedure.
3. List the equipment, tools, materials, and printed resources to be made available.
4. Write the instructions that direct the actions of the learners during the test.

Design the Measuring Instruments

When evaluating the *process* component of performance, the test requires that the instructor or other qualified judge observe learner actions and rate them in terms of the necessary criteria. The ratings are commonly made using one of the following instruments. There are advantages and disadvantages of each type for various situations.

Checklists   A checklist can be used to determine whether sequential steps in a procedure or other actions are successfully performed. The evaluator indicates "yes–no" or "done–not done" for each element. A checklist does not allow the action to be assessed for quality of performance.

Rating Scales   With a rating scale, special value can be assigned to each element of a performance. Only behaviors which can be observed and rated objectively should be included in a rating scale.

A numerical scale is commonly used. It consists of standards from low to high, such as these:

0	1	2
unacceptable	acceptable with corrections	acceptable

1	2	3	4
poor	fair	good	excellent

Although descriptive terms are often used, they are more suitable for norm-referenced tests than for individualized performance tests (see page 173). Learners should not be judged in comparison with each other, but according to the acceptable standards for performance. Here is an example of a descriptive rating scale:

1	2	3	4	5
unsatisfactory	below average	average	above average	superior

An important limitation for using rating scales can be any personal bias an evaluator may have in giving preference to one learner over another for any of a number of reasons. Also, careful attention is required to discriminate each level of performance from the others on a scale. It is for this latter reason that most rating scales are limited to three to five levels. Training of evaluators may be necessary to standardize their measurements.

Anecdotal Records   An anecdotal record is an open-ended instrument for evaluating performance in a narrative fashion. An outline-type form containing behaviors to be observed is prepared. In addition to a description of performance, interpretations of what was done along with recommendations for improvement, can be included in such a record. The written record should be made while observing the performance, or brief notes should be taken and then expanded on the record form immediately after the evaluation session.

Descriptive evaluation is time-consuming and often impractical with large numbers of learners. As with rating scales, a degree of subjectivity can easily, and often unknowingly find its way into an evaluation report. But when carefully prepared, with reference to a number of tasks over a period of time, valuable cumulative data on the performance of an individual can be gathered.

Rating Products

In addition to evaluating the process component of a skill, a rating form should be used to judge the quality (and quantity) of a resulting product. Such factors as these may be included:

- General appearance of product
- Accuracy of product details (shape, dimensions, finish)
- Relation among components or parts (size, fit, finish, color)
- Quantity of products produced during a time period

Here are examples of a checklist and rating scale for process and product evaluation:

CHECKLIST FOR TASK: DRY MOUNT A PICTURE

Skill	Performed Yes/No
1. Plug in press	_____
2. Set press at 225°	_____
3. Plug in tacking iron	_____
4. Set tacking iron on *high*	_____
5. Wait for press to reach temperature before use	_____
6. Dry picture in press	_____
7. Dry cardboard in press	_____
8. Tack dry mount tissue to back of picture	_____
9. Trim picture and tissue together	_____
10. Align picture on cardboard	_____
11. Tack tissue under picture in two corners	_____
12. Seal picture to cardboard in press for 10 seconds	_____
13. Remove and immediately cool mounting under weight	_____

Final Product	Low		High	
1. General appearance (alignment, adhesion to surface, absence of tick marks)	0	1	2	3
2. Care with detail (trimming and visible tissue)	0	1	2	3

RATING SCALE FOR TASK: ASSISTING A PATIENT TO WALK

Procedure	Rating	Necessary Corrections
1. Wash hands	0 1 2 3	
2. Identify patient	0 1 2 3	
3. Explain procedure	0 1 2 3	
4. Enlist cooperation	0 1 2 3	
5. Position bed	0 1 2 3	
6. Assist patient to a dangling-feet position	0 1 2 3	
7. Assist patient to dress	0 1 2 3	
8. Help patient to stand	0 1 2 3	
9. Assist patient to walk	0 1 2 3	
10. Assist patient to return to bed	0 1 2 3	
11. Provide for patient's comfort	0 1 2 3	
12. Report and record	0 1 2 3	
Summary rating	0 1 2 3	

Prior to Using the Test

Before the measuring instrument is to be used, it should be tried out with a sampling of two to three persons from the potential learner group or equivalent. This trial allows checking for: (1) the learner's clear understanding of the testing procedure; (2) the effectiveness of each part of the instrument; and (3) the required length of the testing period for each learner. Also, if more than a single evaluator will be used, the procedure must be standardized so that each person making a judgment would grade similar performances equally.

EVALUATING OBJECTIVES IN THE AFFECTIVE DOMAIN

Just as it was a demanding task to write affective-domain objectives that stated expected attitude changes, so much planning and thought is required to assess the degree to which learners accomplish these objectives. The feelings, values, and beliefs of individuals are very private matters that cannot be measured directly. Attitudes can be inferred only through a person's words and actions, as described on page 86.

The problem of evaluating affective objectives is further compounded for two other important reasons. First, a response expressed by a learner in an attitudinal survey may be stated so as to please or to be socially acceptable, regardless of the individual's actual feelings. Therefore, it might be difficult to assess true sentiments. Second, outcomes of the most important objectives in a course may not become evident until some time after the program is completed, thus making it impossible to measure an attitude at the end of the study time for a unit or the course.

In spite of these limitations, there can be benefits from attempting to determine whether attitudinal objectives are satisfied, at least to a degree, at the conclusion of a unit or portions of an instructional program. The common methods for gathering data include the following (see examples that follow):

Questionnaire

This may take either of two forms. First, as open-ended questions to which the learner writes answers. Second, as closed-item questions having a number of fixed responses from which the learner chooses the most (or possibly least) appealing answer. A variation of this latter type consists of a lengthy list of alternatives from which the learner checks interesting or important choices, or rates the alternatives with a series of numbers.

The decision to use either an open-ended or closed-item questionnaire (or some combination of the two) may depend on the time available to tabulate the replies. The open-ended type provides data which are time consuming to summarize, but which may be of more value. Closed-item questions are quicker to process, but may limit the learner's opportunity to provide useful information.

Rating Scale   A rating scale for use in an attitudinal evaluation process, is a modification of the questionnaire on which the learner replies to a statement by selecting a point along a scale. The scale may be comprised of two points (yes/ no), three points (yes/no opinion/ disagree), or up to five points (very often/ quite often/ sometimes/ hardly ever/ never).

Observation   Observation is a direct technique for assessing behavior associated with attitudes and interactions among individuals. It is often carried out by the instructor while learners are at work in their normal study or activity area. The instrument for recording what is observed can be a simple questionnaire, a rating scale, or an open-ended form on which descriptions and comments are made as in an anecdotal record.

Interview   An interview is a face-to-face meeting in which the learner is asked specific questions by an interviewer. The questions can be in a fixed sequence or unstructured, the latter form giving the interviewer the opportunity to probe more deeply in order to clarify the meanings of the learner's responses. This method takes a greater amount of time than do the previously described techniques. Also, for objectivity, the interviewer should be a person not affiliated with the instructional program.

For further descriptions, including benefits and limitations of these various instruments, and for guidance in designing any of them, see the references for this chapter.

Here are examples of questionnaires, rating scales, and an interview guide:

Questionnaire (open-ended)

1. What is your general reaction to this topic, the content treated, the way it was taught, your participation, etc?

2. In your opinion, what was the greatest *strength* or *advantage* to you as a learner of the approach used to teach the unit you have just completed?

Questionnaire (closed-item)

1. Learner interest
   a. I feel this topic challenged me intellectually.
   b. I was generally attentive in class.
   c. I was not stimulated very often.
   d. I do not feel the topic was worthwhile.

2. Topic organization
   a. I could see how the concepts on this topic were interrelated.
   b. The instructor attempted to cover only the minimum amount of material.
   c. I didn't know where the instructor was heading most of the time.

Rating scale

1. Did you have any difficulty or trouble in obtaining and operating the equipment?
   ____No   ____Yes   Comment:

2. How do you rate the self-study activity as a learning experience?

0	1	2	3	4
Waste of time	Slightly useful	Satisfactory	Good	Excellent

3. The format used in this experimental unit was probably
   ____more   ____less   ____about equally demanding in terms of study time and energy as compared with a conventional unit.

4. Indicate your feeling about the overall value of the unit just completed in terms of your job:

Little or no value	1	2	3	4	5	Great value

Interview guide

1. What is your reaction to the value of the unit you have just completed?

2. How would you rate the amount of assistance that the instructor and the assistants provided you outside of the discussion sessions?
   ____None   ____Low   ____Some   ____Sufficient
   ____Excellent

3. Do you feel the criteria adapted by your instructor for assigning letter grades in this unit were fair to you? If not, why not?

4. What suggestions do you have for improving the activities you completed for this topic?

STANDARDS OF ACHIEVEMENT

Two standards of achievement can be applied when interpreting test scores and assigning grades for the evaluation of learning. These standards are designated as **relative** or **absolute.** An understanding of the meeting of each standard, as well as its particular implications within the instructional design process, is important as you develop this evaluation component of an instructional program.

Relative Standard

In most conventional educational programs the performance of one learner is compared to that of other learners in the class. A test based on relative standards will indicate that one learner has learned more or less than have other learners. This results in a relative rating of each learner within the group. The rating does *not* necessarily signify the level of proficiency of any learner in the group with respect to a specific standard of accomplishment as contained in the learning objective.

For example, assume the highest score on a test given to a class is 73 (out of a total of 85 possible points) and the individual levels of accomplishment range down to 44. The instructor would assign grades, starting with the 73 score at the top of the *A* level. In this procedure, it is common to have about 7.5 percent of the learners receive a grade of *A,* 17.5 percent a *B,* 50 percent a *C,* 17.5 percent a *D,* and 7.5 percent an *F* (see Figure 11.1).

This is called a *normal distribution* and is known as "grading on the normal curve." Grades are assigned in a *relative* or *normative* fashion. The term *norm-referenced testing* is used to describe this method of reporting achievement. It cannot be assumed that the achievement of a learner who received the *A* grade in this class is comparable to the achievement of another learner who received the *A* grade in the same course when conducted at another time.

Norm-referenced testing procedures are of value when data have been gathered on a general question about large numbers of individuals, for example, the height of all ten-year-old girls in the United States. The distribution of height for this population will form a normal distribution—a

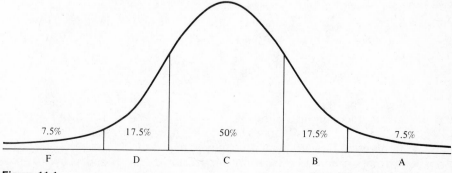

Figure 11.1

few very tall, many average, and a few very short. The same result can be obtained if a carefully designed multiple-choice test in algebra is administered to all ninth-grade students in a state. Because of the range in abilities (and the variety of objectives tested) there will be a normal distribution of scores.

Such standardized testing procedures are important in comparing the overall accomplishments of a class with respect to established local, state, or national norms. But this method does not fit a plan in which we strive to make instruction and resulting learning effective and successful for the great *majority* of learners in a class or training program.

Absolute Standards

As the result of planning within an instructional design, we intend to have as many learners as possible reach a satisfactory level of achievement. Therefore, we need to measure learning outcomes against a specific standard, rather than against a relative standard. The specific standard is the *criterion* specified by the learning objectives. The term *criterion-referenced testing* is applied to the measurement of how well *each* learner attains the required level of comprehension and competence specified for *each* objective pursued. This degree of achievement is independent of the performance of other students.

The terms *competency-based instruction* and *performance-based instruction* are used interchangeably with *criterion-referenced instruction* to identify a program that provides experiences intended to bring most learners to a satisfactory level of proficiency in learning or in performing a task that will be measured by the testing instruments.

When criteria are set and learners successfully meet them, the concept of *mastery learning* is realized. This goal is in part the justification for giving increased attention to self-paced learning methods and providing more than one opportunity for a learner to restudy, self-test, and then be retested to measure learning until the mastery level is attained.

There is concern about the emphasis on mastery learning in some programs. While it is successful when high level competencies are required, for example in the training of medical surgeons or airline pilots, some people fear that with conventional letter grading (A–B–C–D–F) each learner satisfying the requirements should receive a grade of *A* and that this will lead to "grade inflation" and a lowering of academic standards. Ideally, in a well-designed and properly executed instructional program, each learner could attain mastery of each topic and receive the *A* grade. This might be expected to happen only when a combination of the following conditions is satisfied:

- The learner group has been carefully selected with each individual having outstanding abilities.
- Each learner is highly motivated to learn.
- Preparation of learners in prerequisite requirements has been excellent.
- Instruction has been carefully prepared, pretested, and proven to be effective.

On the other hand, mastery can be accepted as attainment of *minimum* or *essential* knowledge and skills at a reasonable competency level (for example, an 80 percent performance standard). This may guarantee a *B* or *C* grade (or possibly a *P* for "pass," or credit). Then to reach a higher level, or an *A* grade, additional accomplishment may be required, such as correctly answering nine or all ten items, rather than the required eight out of the ten, on a posttest, or achieving optional objectives and engaging in additional activities. If a number of performance levels above the acceptable minimum are set, each learner could be permitted to choose a goal on the basis of his or her capabilities, background, and motivation. This procedure is similar to the *contract concept* used in some educational programs.

In comparing the norm-referenced and criterion-referenced testing and grading methods, two final matters should be emphasized. First, in the norm-referenced approach, tests are constructed so that expected learner attainment levels are purposefully spread out to achieve high, average, and low scores. To do this, test items are written and analyzed so that easier and more difficult ones are added, revised, or dropped until, through trial testing, a normal distribution results. In the criterion-referenced method test items are included as relevant to the required standards. The results clearly indicate what a learner has learned and can do.

Second, guiding and assessing learners to help them accomplish their objectives is a normal procedure in criterion-referenced measurement and mastery learning. This fosters cooperation among learners. The norm-referenced approach, on the other hand, emphasized competition with resulting discrimination among learners based on achievement levels.

VALIDITY AND RELIABILITY OF TESTS

There are two important features that tests must fulfill in order for them properly to accomplish the job for which they are intended. These are *validity* and *reliability*.

Validity

Attention was previously given to validity when the necessity for a direct relationship between learning objectives and evaluation items was indicated. Thus, a test requires that the learner demonstrate the knowledge and skills essential to satisfying the learning objectives for the topic. A test is valid when it specifically measures what was supposedly learned in terms of the subject content or task as specified by the learning objectives for the unit or topic.

On page 91 the benefits of developing a specification table that relates objectives to learning levels were described. One way of ensuring a high degree of test validity is to devise a second table of specifications which relates test items to objectives. Such a table can serve two purposes. First, to verify that outcomes at the higher learning levels (application, analysis, synthesis, and evaluation) do receive adequate attention. Second, to show the number of

Table 11.1 SPECIFICATIONS RELATING NUMBER OF TEST ITEMS TO LEARNING OBJECTIVES ON COGNITIVE LEVELS

Topic: Community Services for the Elderly

Objectives	Knowledge	Comprehension	Application	Analysis	Synthesis	Evaluation
1. Recognize misconceptions and superstitions about the elderly	3					
2. Differentiate between facts and opinions about physical and social behaviors of the elderly		2				
3. Describe attitudes toward the elderly as practiced by various ethnic groups		2				
4. Locate information relative to community programs for the elderly		4				
5. Classify community organizations according to types of services offered for the elderly				2		
6. Develop a plan for judging the value of individual community programs for the elderly					3	
7. Assess the merits of a community program for the elderly						2
8. Given a hypothetical or real situation, analyze the needs of a senior citizen and recommend one or more community programs			4			

questions needed for measuring single learning objectives or groups of related objectives. These numbers reflect the relative importance of each objective or the proportion of emphasis given during instruction.

Table 11.1 indicates the nature and number of test questions for learning objectives in a knowledge-based unit. Table 11.2 is for a psychomotor task. By designing such tables, you can be reasonably certain you will test for all learning objectives and give each objective the proper amount of attention.

Reliability

Reliability refers to the ability of a test to produce consistent results whenever used. If comparable learners, with similar preparation, were to take the same test, or an equal form of the test, there would be little variation in the scores. Certain procedures can affect the reliability of a test. First, the more questions used on a test, relating to an objective, the more reliable the test. If only one question is asked about a major objective or an extensive content area, it can be difficult to ascertain whether a learner has acquired the knowledge or was lucky by guessing the answer. See the previous procedure for developing a specification table relating the number of test questions to the objectives.

Second, the administration of the test should be standardized. If more than one person directs testing, similar instructions must be given to each group of learners or individuals who take the test over a period of time. Third, everyone should be tested under the same conditions so that distractions do not contribute to discrepencies in the scores. Fourth, the length of testing time is an important factor; it should be the same for all learners. Fifth, and possibly the most important factor which can affect test reliability, is the method of scoring a test. This is most important when marking an essay test or judging performance on a rating scale. Even though attempts are made to standardize the methods of scoring employed by different persons, criteria can be viewed in different ways and variations are unavoidable. The less subjective the scoring, the more reliable will be the test results.

PHASES IN EVALUATION OF LEARNING

At various points during the period of an instructional program determining learning levels and performance abilities of the learner can be important both to the instructor and to the learner. In addition to the usual evaluation of learning during and at the end of instructional units, there are at least three other times when evaluation should take place.[1]

Student Self-evaluation

As indicated on page 103, an important principle that contributes to successful learning is to provide feedback to a learner on how well he or she is learning as

---

[1]For an example of how to score essay questions objectively, see Simas and Seyer, *Constructing and Scoring Essay Tests.*

Table 11.2 SPECIFICATIONS RELATING NUMBERS OF TEST ITEMS TO LEARNING OBJECTIVES ON COGNITIVE LEVELS AND FOR PSYCHOMOTOR PERFORMANCE

Task: Measuring Electrical Values in Series Circuits

Objectives	Knowledge	Comprehension	Application	Psychomotor
1. List symbols used for components in an electrical circuit	2			
2. Recognize the makeup of a complete series circuit		3		
3. Identify a series circuit in a schematic diagram		1		
4. Assemble a series circuit on a board using component parts			2	2
5. Set up and adjust a multimeter for measuring each of three electrical values				1
6. Measure and calculate voltage, current flow, and resistance in a series circuit			3	3

instruction takes place. This can be accomplished by administering short tests at the end of a set of learning activities or at the conclusion of a unit. Allow the learner to check answers. The results will inform the learner as to whether the material studied has been learned satisfactorily, or whether further study may be needed.

By completing such self-check tests, a learner can evaluate progress, recognize difficulties or confusion in understanding, and review material prior to taking the instructor's test covering the same objectives. This procedure can better ensure learner preparation for and success with the posttest for the unit.

Formative Evaluation

Self-evaluation is as important to the student as formative evaluation is to the instructor or planning team, who want to know how well the program is serving the objectives as it progresses. The process called *formative evaluation* takes place during development and tryouts. It is useful for determining weaknesses in the instructional plan so that they can be eliminated before full-scale use. Test results, reactions from learners, observations of learners at work, and suggestions from colleagues may indicate deficiencies in the learning sequence, in procedures, or in materials. For example, the pace of instruction may be too rapid, or too slow, or a learner may find a sequence uninteresting, confusing, or too difficult.

Formative evaluation also allows the instructor to determine whether, at any point in the instructional sequence, too much previous learner knowledge has been assumed or whether the emphasis is on subject matter that learners already know, and so it does not require them to pay much attention.

The procedure of formative, or trial testing and revision (and possibly retesting and further revision, if necessary) is important to the success of a plan. It should relate not only to the suitability of objectives, subject content, learning methods, and materials, but also to the roles of personnel, the use of facilities and equipment, schedules, and other factors that all together affect the optimum performance for achievement of the objectives. Recall the outer ring around the various elements in the instructional design diagram on page 11. This indicates the possible need for changes in what has been planned as the result of formative evaluation. Remember, the planning process is highly interactive. Each element has effects on other elements. A careful evaluation can reveal shortcomings in one part of a plan that require modifications elsewhere.

Sometimes a new program must be implemented without testing the procedures and materials in advance because there is no time or money for doing so. In such a case, to determine whether revisions are necessary, the instructor or members of the planning team must rely on their observations of learner performances during the first period when the program is in actual use.

Questions that might be used to gather data during formative evaluation are suggested on page 180.

1. In terms of the objectives for the unit or module, is learning at an acceptable level? What weaknesses are noted?
2. Are learners able to use the knowledge or perform the skills at an acceptable level? Where are any weaknesses?
3. How long a time period did the instruction and learning require? Was this acceptable?
4. Did the activities seem appropriate and manageable to the instructor and learners?
5. Were the materials convenient and easy to locate, handle, use, and file?
6. What were the learners' reactions to the method of study, to the activities, to the materials used, to the evaluation methods?
7. Do the self-evaluation tests and the posttest satisfactorily measure the learning objectives?
8. What revisions in the program seem necessary (content, format, and so on)?

Summative Evaluation

The summative evaluation is directed toward measuring the degree to which the major outcomes are attained by the end of the course, during regular use. Summative evaluation includes the results of both the unit posttests and the final examination for the course. Summative evaluation may also mean following up learners after the program is completed to determine if and how they are using or applying the knowledge, skills, and attitudes learned. Summative evaluation receives full attention in Chapter 16.

In both formative and summative evaluations of new full-course programs, engaging the services of a competent outside evaluator is recommended. The evaluator will know how to devise instruments for measuring learners' attitudes and instructors' reactions, and how to analyze the data on learning for each objective.

SUMMARY

Through evaluation, success in learning can be determined. When developing tests, give attention to the following:

1. Relate test items directly to learning objectives.
2. Use an objective-type test when you want learners to recognize or select an answer.
3. Use written-answer tests when you want learners to plan answers and express them in their own words. Grading is much more difficult, but higher learning levels can be tested.
4. Evaluate performance in terms of either process or product, or both. Select from three instruments to measure performance.
5. Plan to gather evidence relating to feelings, values, and beliefs affected through the instructional program. Recognize that affective objectives can only be measured indirectly. Use one or more of four methods for gathering attitudinal data.

6. Early in planning, decide on the standard that will be used for measuring learning—relative among learners in the class, or against an absolute standard as specified in the learning objectives.
7. Give attention to both the validity and reliability of test items to be certain they properly fulfill their functions.
8. Provide opportunities for learners to evaluate their own learning prior to the testing by the instructor.
9. Consider a formative evaluation to judge the success of program components as they are prepared. This can determine if any revision is needed to ensure better success of the program when implemented.
10. Plan for a summative evaluation to determine the success at the conclusion of instruction during regular use.

REVIEW AND APPLICATIONS*

A. Recall
  1. Fill in the blanks in the following outline. On levels (a) and (b), list the broad categories of paper and pencil tests. Below each category, list the most commonly used types. Each line should get an entry.

  a. _____

      (1) _____

      (2) _____

  b. _____

      (1) _____

      (2) _____

      (3) _____

  2. Which statements are *true* about paper and pencil tests?

  _____ *a.* A test item consisting of a *stem* with *alternatives* is an example of a matching test item.

  _____ *b.* Essay tests are *both* easier to write and to grade than are objective-type tests.

  _____ *c.* Among the forms of objective tests, the multiple choice is the best type for measuring higher level objectives.

  _____ *d.* A major limitation of true–false items is the high possibility of correctly guessing an answer.

  _____ *e.* A limitation of essay testing is that a small amount of content can be tested by a question.

  _____ *f.* Two testing forms that can treat a large amount of subject content are short-answer items and a matching test.

  _____ *g.* Questions requiring numerical answers are classified as objective tests.

  _____ *h.* Knowledge of associations can satisfactorily be tested with a matching test.

  3. Which statements are *true* concerning performance testing?

  _____ *a.* The instruments used in performance testing include anecdotal records, rating scales, and checklists.

  _____ *b.* Immediately after developing the test consider any constraints that need attention when using the test.

  _____ *c.* This is a good procedure for developing a performance test: List steps to be performed; decide how performance will take place; list things needed during testing; list instructions that direct the learner.

*See answers on page 269.

_____ **d.** Performance tests are designed primarily to measure physical skills.

_____ **e.** A checklist consists of a series of descriptive words from which those that are appropriate to a learner's performance are checked.

_____ **f.** Sufficient practice should be provided for learners before testing takes place.

_____ **g.** Testing the *process* of a skill is more important than evaluating the resulting *product.*

_____ **h.** Applying a rating scale is the most useful way to evaluate a product.

_____ **i.** A rating scale differs from a checklist in that the former includes a number of levels for judging each component of a skill while the latter does not have any levels.

_____ **j.** Before using a performance test it is only necessary to make certain all evaluators agree to grade performances in the same way.

_____ **k.** The most time-consuming way to evaluate performance is to use a checklist.

_____ **l.** It is possible to simulate a performance and judge it in relation to a real situation.

4. Relate the following to the components of performance testing:
   a. Process testing
   b. Product testing
   _____ **(1)** Working within required time period
   _____ **(2)** Quality of actions
   _____ **(3)** Number of items resulting
   _____ **(4)** Using tools correctly
   _____ **(5)** Quality of the units prepared
   _____ **(6)** The sequence of actions

5. What are *two* limitations which can make the satisfactory evaluation of affective domain objectives difficult?

   a. _____

   _____

   _____

   b. _____

   _____

   _____

6. What are the *four* categories of instruments or methods that may be used to collect information about attitudes?

   a. _____

   _____

   _____

   b. _____

   _____

   _____

   c. _____

   _____

   _____

   d. _____

   _____

   _____

7. The testing method in which each learner's performance is compared with that of all others in the class is called _____.

8. The testing method in which each learner's performance is compared to a standard set by the instructor is called _____ .

9. Other terms that may be used to answer question 8 are:

_____

_____

_____

10. Which statements are *true* with respect to *mastery learning*?
    ____ *a.* Measures learning relative to other students
    ____ *b.* Makes use of competency-based instruction
    ____ *c.* Is competition-based, rather than cooperation-based
    ____ *d.* Similar to a "contract" method of instruction
    ____ *e.* Requires learners to reach at least a minimum level of accomplishment
    ____ *f.* Final grading is often higher than in a conventional program
    ____ *g.* A single opportunity for taking unit tests is allowed
    ____ *h.* It is important to include a performance standard in objectives

11. Answer each item as *true* or *false*.
    ____ *a.* When a test item is compatible with its objective we have an example of item *validity*.
    ____ *b.* The more important objectives may require just a single good testing item for satisfactory measurement of learning.
    ____ *c.* Reliability of a test can be affected by variations in scoring by different persons doing the grading.
    ____ *d.* Test questions that correctly measure learner competencies indicate that the questions are *valid* ones.
    ____ *e.* Each objective in a unit should be tested in one form or another.
    ____ *f.* Consistently correct responses to test questions by comparably capable learners is an indication that the questions are *reliable*.
    ____ *g.* A specification table is helpful to insure reliability of a test.
    ____ *h.* A specification table may be used to relate form of test questions (multiple choice, essay, etc.) to the learning objectives.

12. In this chapter it was indicated that there are *four* points at which evaluation should be given attention. What are they?

    a. _____

    _____

    _____

    b. _____

    _____

    _____

    c. _____

    _____

    _____

    d. _____

    _____

    _____

13. Alongside each of the evaluations you listed in reply to question 12, write the correct letters of the following that apply. It may be necessary to use the same letter with more than one evaluation method.
    a. To discover whether equipment and materials are convenient to use
    b. Completed periodically while studying a unit
    c. A unit posttest

    d. Employed during program tryout
    e. Course final exam
    f. To determine how well former learners perform on the job
    g. Learner checks own answers

B. Comprehension

   1. Select the most appropriate testing method (more than one if necessary) for each stated learning objective:

     a. To describe the four major concepts of Jeffersonian democracy.

     ____ *(1)* Complete short-answer questions on Jeffersonian democracy.
     ____ *(2)* Select correct concepts from a list.
     ____ *(3)* Write an essay on the concepts.
     ____ *(4)* Answer True–False questions about the concepts.

     b. To apply principles of weather forecasting for a 5-day period based on the first day's weather map data.

     ____ *(1)* Ask learners to name some principles for forecasting.
     ____ *(2)* Ask learners to mark on a map anticipated daily weather conditions for 5 future days.
     ____ *(3)* Tell learners what the weather conditions are daily and have them indicate the principles that apply.
     ____ *(4)* Ask learners to explain the data marked on the first day's weather map.

     c. To practice the accepted roles of courtesy and fair play.

     ____ *(1)* During class, a difficult social situation is described. Ask learners to indicate the course of action to take.
     ____ *(2)* Observe each learner in the classroom and during activity periods, making notes of behavior at intervals. Use the notes to evaluate each learner.
     ____ *(3)* During a group game, the instructor deliberately breaks the rules. Observe and record what learners do.
     ____ *(4)* Simulate a social situation in the classroom. Evaluate reactions on a five-point scale.

     d. To compute the dollar cost of using credit in making a time purchase.

     ____ *(1)* Solve credit problems.
     ____ *(2)* Write the formula for solving credit problems.
     ____ *(3)* Explain in a paragraph how to handle a credit problem.
     ____ *(4)* Choose correctly solved credit problems from a list of possible solutions.

     e. To identify the seven general paper forms frequently completed by a health worker.

     ____ *(1)* Compare types of general and special forms.
     ____ *(2)* Indicate seven general forms used in health work.
     ____ *(3)* Choose the form when shown a picture of each kind of general form.
     ____ *(4)* Select the general forms from a list of many kinds of forms.

   2. Which method of paper and pencil testing would you select for each of the following?

     _____ *a.* To relate a number of events to the correct date for each one.
     _____ _____ *b.* To recall factual information by completing a statement.

_____ *c.* To discriminate among various kinds of action that might be taken by choosing the best one to solve a problem situation.

_____ *d.* To explain a position in answer to a problem that is presented.

_____ *e.* To decide whether a rule or law is stated properly.

3. A group of young people is being trained in camping skills. You have the responsibility to evaluate each person's ability to *build and maintain a fire* at a campsite.

   a. Is there a *process* component? If so, what is it?

   b. Is there a *product* component? If so, what is it?

   c. Do any constraints or limitations need attention?

   d. Will performance be simulated or realistic?

   e. What necessary evaluation instruments might be used?

4. Five types of data-gathering instruments and methods are described in the text for evaluating affective-domain objectives. For which item is each of the following an example?

   _____ *a.* good .... bad

   _____ *b.* Learner cleans up work station at end of period.

   _____ *c.* During the group activity period there were a number of opportunities for learners to offer direction. Each time John seemed to take leadership and the others accepted his suggestions.

   _____ *d.* Tell me whether the time devoted to the Heat Energy unit was sufficient or not.

   _____ *e.* At this stage of the course, how would you talk to your friends about this course: (1) encourage them to take it; (2) warn them to stay away from it; (3) not say much at all?

5. Mark items as *N* for norm-referenced measurements, or *C* for criterion-referenced measurements.

   ____ *a.* Learner spells correctly 90 percent of the words.

   ____ *b.* Learner demonstrates three applications of the scientific principle as required by the objective.

   ____ *c.* Learner scores at the 84th percentile on unit test.

   ____ *d.* Learner analyzes quality of products produced as specified according to the standards established by instructor.

   ____ *e.* Learner rates third from the top with respect to the total class for her project report.

   ____ *f.* Test is based on a general description of subject content, such as "to understand logic circuits."

   ____ *g.* Eliminate the test question on measuring blood pressure because all previous learners answered it correctly.

   ____ *h.* Most trainees were wrong in answering the set of questions on reading metric scales; therefore improve the instruction relating to these objectives.

6. Which situations relate to *reliability* and which to *validity* of test questions?

   ____ *a.* You are careful to give the same instructions to each group of learners prior to their starting the test.

_____ *b.* A performance test is carefully designed to measure a set of psychomotor objectives for a topic.

_____ *c.* You decide to use four questions for the terminal objective and only two questions for each of the supporting objectives.

_____ *d.* During formative analysis testing, the questions for an important learning objective are answered differently by each learner.

_____ *e.* An instructor checks the test items in order to be certain that each objective for the unit has been addressed on the test.

7. Mark each question as applicable to *formative* (*F*), *summative* (*S*), evaluation or both (F/S).

_____ *a.* What are learners' reactions to the method of study and use of materials?

_____ *b.* Is there suitable use of the skills learned after a period of time?

_____ *c.* How long does the learning activity take?

_____ *d.* Are there deficiencies in learning activities that should be improved?

_____ *e.* Do materials hold up after repeated uses?

_____ *f.* Are objectives being satisfactorily accomplished?

_____ *g.* What are learners' attitudes toward the program?

_____ *h.* Do test questions satisfactorily measure all learning objectives?

_____ *i.* How do the results of this class compare with those of previous classes?

C. Applications

1. *Sky Diving*
   a. Develop necessary paper and pencil and performance tests to:
   (1) Measure learning.
   (2) Allow learners to self-check their own knowledge and skills.
   b. Describe how you would carry out formative evaluation.

2. *Your Subject*
   a. Develop necessary paper and pencil and performance tests to:
   (1) Measure learning.
   (2) Allow learners to self-check their own knowledge and skills.
   b. Describe how you would carry out formative evaluation.

REFERENCES

General

Bloom, Benjamin S., George F. Madaus, and J. Thomas Hastings. *Evaluation to Improve Learning* (New York: McGraw-Hill, 1981).

———. *Handbook on Formative and Summative Evaluation of Student Learning* (New York: McGraw-Hill, 1971).

Mager, Robert F. *Measuring Instructional Intent or Got a Match?* (Belmont, CA: Pitman, 1973).

Popham, W. James. *Evaluating Instruction* (Englewood Cliffs, NJ: Prentice-Hall, 1973).

Written Tests

Denova, Charles C. *Test Construction for Training Evaluation* (New York: Van Nostrand Reinhold, 1979).

Gronlund, Norman E. *Preparing Criterion-Referenced Tests for Classroom Instruction* (New York: Macmillan, 1973).

Hively, Wells, ed. *Domain-Referenced Testing* (Englewood Cliffs, NJ: Educational Technology Publications, 1974).

Kryspin, William J., and John F. Feldhusen. *Developing Classroom Tests.* (Minneapolis: Burgess, 1974).

McBeath, Ron J. ed. *Faculty Development Materials* (San Jose, CA: Faculty and Instructional Development Office, San Jose State University, 1981).

Simas, Robert. *Constructing Multiple Choice Test Items,* Faculty Development Materials (San Jose, CA: Faculty and Instructional Development Office, San Jose State University, 1981).

————, Jerrold E. Kemp, and Jeanne Lassen. *Constructing True/False Test Items,* Faculty Development Materials (San Jose, CA: Faculty and Instructional Development Office, San Jose State University, 1981).

Smith, Carole R. *Constructing Matching Test Items,* Faculty Development Materials (San Jose, CA: Faculty and Instructional Development Office, San Jose State University, 1981).

————, and Philip C. Seyer. *Constructing and Scoring Essay Tests,* Faculty Development Materials (San Jose, CA: Faculty and Instructional Development Office, San Jose State University, 1981).

Performance Testing

McBeath, Ron J., and Jeanne Lassen. *Performance Testing* (San Jose: CA: Faculty and Instructional Development Office, San Jose State University, 1981).

Affective Objectives

Henerson, Marlene E., Lynn Lyons Morris, and Carol Taylor Fitz-Gibbon. *How to Measure Attitudes* (Beverly Hills, CA: Sage, 1978).

Seyer, Philip C., and Carole R. Smith. *Developing Opinion, Interest, and Attitude Questionnaires* (San Jose, CA: Faculty and Instructional Development Office, San Jose State University, 1981).

Standards of Achievement

Block, James H. *Mastery Learning: Theory and Practice* (New York: Holt, Rinehart, and Winston, 1971).

Bloom, Benjamin S. *Human Characteristics and School Learning* (New York: McGraw-Hill, 1976).

Horton, Lowell. *Mastery Learning* (Fastback 154) (Bloomington, IN: Phi Delta Kappa Educational Foundation, 1981).

Nagel, Thomas S., and Paul T. Richman. *Competency-Based Instruction* (Columbus, OH: Charles E. Merrill, 1972).

Formative Evaluation

Dick, Walter. "Formative Evaluation," in *Instructional Design: Principles and Applications,* Leslie J. Briggs, ed. (Englewood Cliffs, NJ: Educational Technology Publications, 1977), 311–333.

Lawson, T.E. *Formative Instructional Product Evaluation: Instruments and Strategies* (Englewood Cliffs, NJ: Educational Technology Publications, 1974).

chapter 12

Pretesting

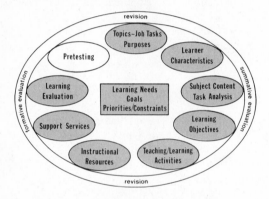

"How well-prepared are learners to undertake study in this course or topic?"

"Are some learners already competent in all or parts of the course or topic?"

"What are values to both learners and the instructor for pretesting?"

Remember when you might have become interested in participating in some form of strenuous athletics? What was it advisable that you do before "going out for the team" or starting a serious jogging program? You were told to have a physical examination to be sure that your body was prepared for the rigorous exercise it would perform.

A similar practice is important in the instructional process. It is advisable to determine the level of preparation that learners must have for the course or program they are about to undertake. This is the *pretesting* element of the instructional design process.

In the sequence of elements in the instructional design process we are treating this topic last. Even though in actual use with learners this is probably the first phase of the instructional program to which they are exposed, you can best design the pretest after most other elements have been developed—especially the subject content, the learning objectives, and the tests to evaluate learning.

In Chapter 5, the close relationship between information about learners and pretesting was pointed out. As a result of studying Chapter 5, you should be aware of the value of gathering these data about learners: their academic status, personal and social characteristics, and learning styles. Now we are interested in information on two additional matters directly relating to the course or topic: (1) the learner's preparation to study the course or topic, and (2) competencies the learner may already have with some of the learning objectives for the course or topic.

TESTING FOR PREREQUISITES

A *prerequisite* test determines whether learners have the appropriate preparation for starting a course or studying a topic. For example:

> Can junior high school students perform basic arithmetic at a level that qualifies them to start learning algebra?
>
> Is an apprentice entering a furniture manufacturing training program competent in using such machines as a table saw, a sander, or a jointer?
>
> Does a nursing student have adequate knowledge about anatomy and physiology to study a module on cardiogenic shock (a heart ailment)?

Refer to the listing of subject content for the topic or the analysis of the task to be taught (Chapter 6). Enumerate the required competencies that a learner should have *before* starting this phase of the program. From the list, develop appropriate methods to gather information about necessary prerequisite knowledge and abilities:

- Paper and pencil tests (sometimes standardized tests in fundamental areas like reading, writing, mathematics, chemistry, or physics) can be used.
- Observations of performance and rating of competencies exhibited by learners.
- Use of a questionnaire to determine learner background, training, and experiences.
- Review of learner's previous or related work.
- Talk with supervisors or other persons with whom the learner has worked.

The results of this prerequisite testing will indicate which learners are fully prepared to start studying the topic, which ones need some remedial work, and which are not ready and should therefore start at a lower level.

Do not assume that grades in previous or related courses necessarily indicate the degree of readiness for a learner to be successful in a program. The objectives of courses taken elsewhere may be quite different from what you interpret them to be by reading the titles or descriptions of those courses. Do your own prerequisite evaluation of each learner's preparation.

TESTING FOR TOPIC CONTENT AND SKILLS

A second reason for pretesting is to determine which, if any, of the learning objectives for the topic or task learners may already have achieved. If learners have no acquaintance with a topic, this part of pretesting may be of little value. You may feel it unnecessary or even inappropriate to formally pretest learners under these conditions.

Since the accomplishment of learning objectives is measured by the evaluation test for each objective, some authorities recommend using the actual evaluation test (or a modified form of it) for both pretesting and final evaluation (the *posttest*). In this case, the amount of learning is determined from the gain in scores between pre- and posttests. If you find that the final examination is too detailed for use as a pretest, select the most important or representative test items to use in the pretest. Do not test only the easiest (often knowledge level) or the most difficult (higher cognitive levels) objectives. Maintain a fair balance.

To determine learners' previous experience with a topic, instead of a formal test, you might use a pretopic questionnaire, or even an informal, oral questioning of the class—"How many of you have ever used an ohmeter?" Have learners reply with a show of hands. For mature learners, a questionnaire, in which each learner indicates his or her level of skill or knowledge for all items to be studied, will go further than the few questions of a pretest.

When developing your pretest, make use of the details about testing methods and test forms discussed in Chapter 11. Finally, provide learners with information on the results of this pretest. You may not want to return the actual test papers to learners because of the need to reuse questions for the final examination.

BENEFITS OF PRETESTING

For the more traditional group-instruction situation, in which learners move together through all teacher-controlled activities, pretesting may be of limited value. The instructor may find there exists a range of preparation within the group. Not much can be done to provide for the differences among learners other than to recommend some remedial work while the instruction moves ahead as planned. If some learners show by the pretest that they already are competent with some of the content to be treated in the lecture and other class activities, they most often still have to sit through the regular instruction. Some adjustments in assignments could be made by a concerned instructor, but only infrequently is this done.

If you plan to individualize or provide for self-paced learning, then pretesting will be important for the following reasons:

- It determines learners' readiness for the program by alerting each of them to what they do and do not know about the topic.
- It indicates both to learners and instructor the point at which to start the program, or to complete remedial (or lower level) course work before starting the program.
- It may motivate learners to study the topic because as they read pretest questions or otherwise experience what they will be learning, their curiosity and interest may be aroused.
- It informs learners of what will be treated during study of the topic, so that they may be aware of what will be required of them.
- It indicates the style and methods of testing that will be used by the instructor in the final examination since there is a close relationship between the pre- and posttests.
- It enables the instructor to organize and schedule learners so as not to waste their time on things they already know, and thus plan for maximum efficiency in terms of use of learners' and instructor's time.
- It provides base data for determining learner growth in learning by comparing scores on pre- and posttests.
- It provides information useful to the instructor in modifying parts of the course or program (adding or eliminating objectives and/or activities) so the program can be started at the point of learner readiness; if this is inappropriate, it allows for revision of the program the next time it is to be conducted.

When you pretest, be sure learners understand the purpose. Taking any test is a traumatic experience for many learners, and when they must reply to questions, problems, or situations with which they have little, if any, knowledge or experience, they may exhibit considerable frustration. Tell them clearly the purpose for the pretest and that it in no way counts toward grades.

SUMMARY

A pretest determines how well prepared a learner is to start an instructional program or a specific unit. This procedure includes the measurement of necessary background knowledge and skills (prerequisites) and any competence the learner has with learning objectives for the course or unit.

REVIEW AND APPLICATIONS*

A. Recall
  1. Why is this element of the instructional design process given attention so late in the planning sequence?

  _____

  _____

  _____

  2. The information about learner competencies obtained through pretesting is closely related to information from what other element of the planning process?

  _____

  _____

  _____

*See answers on page 272.

3. Is pretesting more useful in planning for group instruction or in designing a self-paced learning program?

_____

_____

_____

4. What are the two purposes of pretesting?

a. _____

_____

_____

b. _____

_____

_____

5. In addition to paper and pencil tests, what other techniques might be used to gather information on learner prerequisite knowledge and skills?

_____

_____

_____

6. What are three aspects of the relationship between a pretest and a posttest for the same topic?

a. _____

_____

_____

b. _____

_____

_____

c. _____

_____

_____

7. Should a pretest and a posttest be exactly the same? Explain.

_____

_____

_____

8. When might you decide *not* to use a pretest?

_____

_____

_____

9. State two benefits of pretesting for the learner and two benefits for the instructor.
   a. Student:
      (1) _____

_____

_____

      (2) _____

_____

_____

   b. Instructor:
      (1) _____

_____

_____

      (2) _____

_____

_____

B. Comprehension

Which of the following items may be used for determining *prerequisite* ability and which are for *pretesting the topic*?

_____ *a.* Reading level competency

_____ *b.* Competency with some objectives of the topic

_____ *c.* Success with the posttest of the previous, related topic

_____ *d.* Ability to perform the skills that are to be taught

_____ *e.* Understanding concepts basic in the subject field

_____ *f.* Essential skills in math computations

_____ *g.* Ability to express thoughts in writing

_____ *h.* Successful completion of other courses or units

_____ *i.* Through experience, proven knowledge of topic content

C. Applications

1. *Sky Diving*

   a. Would you use a pretest? _____

   b. If so, of what does it consist?

   _____

   _____

   _____

   _____

   _____

2. *Your Subject*

   Design a pretest, if one is appropriate.

chapter *13*

The Mechanics of Planning

"While planning, frequently I find it necessary to make changes in one element or another. Writing on paper certainly limits my flexibility."

"The lists of items and their relationships on this sheet of paper are difficult to follow. After working a while, the paper looks like a mess."

"It's hard to share and discuss the details of my instructional design with colleagues when each of us must look at our own paper copy."

"It's not easy to be creative as well as systematic when carrying out this complex process of planning on paper. Isn't there a better way to handle the planning process?"

These statements and the final question indicate that how you handle "the mechanics of planning" can have an important bearing on the success of any instructional design project.

Planning for instruction is a complex process that requires keeping many separate elements in mind and continually reevaluating the relationship of each part of the plan to the whole, because each element can affect the development of the others. You will find that insights gained in later planning steps often lead to revisions of earlier ones. Therefore, as you proceed through the sequence of elements, you will find that changes, deletions, reordering items, and additions will be necessary; thus, keeping an open mind is essential throughout the planning process.

It is usual to put thoughts, plans, and procedures on paper. However, a sheet of paper is a very limiting medium for use in instructional planning. Lists on paper are static, making changes or additions difficult.

194

USING CARDS FOR PLANNING

A more flexible procedure is to make all notations on 3 × 5 inch cards. Cards of this size are large enough for most entries and are easy to handle. On the cards, list details for each element in the plan. Write *only* one item—an objective, an element of content, an activity, an evaluation item, and so forth—on each card. Do *not* start by working on paper and then, when you have worded the item in its best form, transfer the material to a card. Place a stack of cards in front of you and go to work. Don't worry about the number of cards you use (or throw away). They are inexpensive in terms of their value in the organization of ideas and the use of planning time. Write large, with a fine-tipped felt pen so that entries can be easily seen when the cards are displayed.

If possible, use cards of different colors for the various planning elements (at least five colors are available at most office supply stores), or stripe the upper edge of white cards with felt pens of various colors. For elements that are closely related, such as learning objectives/evaluation/pretest, use cards of the same color. For the other elements use cards of different colors if possible.

The cards can be a highly visible planning tool. They enable you and other planners to identify the various elements of the instructional design plan and see their relationships at a glance.

By using cards, rearrangement, additions, and deletion of items is easy. This provides the flexibility you need in planning. As was mentioned earlier, while you work on one element of the design plan, ideas may come to mind that will be useful at a later stage. When this happens, jot down the idea on a card and set it aside until you are ready to use it.

The cards should be displayed (as described below) so you can see the sequence developing and also so that other persons can examine your plan. **Vertically**, a series of learning objectives should be developed in a sequential order—from simple to complex, from supporting objectives to the terminal objective, or other use as described on page 88. **Horizontally**, you can observe how an objective is handled in terms of subject content, activities, resources, necessary support services, evaluation, and pretest.

This use of cards for planning can be related to the flow charting procedure as described in Chapter 6, page 68. To visualize this analysis, show each information, action, or decision function that comprises the skill, on a card, in sequence.

USING A PLANNING BOARD

One way to display the cards is to lay them out on a table, although loose cards can easily get out of order. Another technique is to tack the cards to a corkboard wall or hold them in place on a magnetic board with small magnets. With any of these methods, moving cards, making changes, and adding new cards within a sequence is cumbersome.

The best way to display cards is to use some type of strips stapled to a portable board or to a wall as a *planning board.* The cards are held firmly in the strips (which function as pockets), but they can be slipped in and out easily. Write design plan elements as headings on individual cards of appropriate color. Arrange these cards horizontally across the board, and as the planning proceeds, place cards relating to each element vertically under the appropriate heading. Then it is easy to shift, add, and remove cards until the best sequence is developed. With this arrangement, seeing the development of the plan as it takes shape is possible. When it is completed, the whole plan, displayed in this way, can be viewed by one person or by a small group of individuals.

Establish a numbering system for your cards so it is easy to relate items both vertically and horizontally. This can be important if the cards are displayed, removed, and then reset at another time. A numbering system can also be valuable when the planning is completed and a typist is to transfer all the information to paper in an arrangement comparable to that displayed on the planning board. See the illustrations starting on the following page.

If possible, allow the cards to remain on display for members of the planning team to study the arrangements during meetings and at leisure. Planning for instruction, like many other creative activities, requires a kind of gestation period for ideas to settle in and to mature. Therefore, any opportunities for people to look at, study, and think about the entries on the cards and their arrangements, may result in worthwhile suggestions for bettering the program. This method of displaying your plans also enables consultants, administrators, and other interested persons to see and grasp the intent, extent, and details of the program quickly, even though they themselves have not been involved in the day-to-day planning.

Once the information on the cards reaches final form, using the numbering system, the total plan can be transferred to paper and duplicated.

Cards are also useful for planning the specific details of the learning activities and audiovisual resources. For example, if the decision has been made to use a slide/tape program for instruction relating to one or a series of learning objectives and associated subject content, make a sketch of each scene along with notations for the narration on a card. You can also use cards to diagram the content of a set of transparencies or outline the questions for a worksheet. The layout of these cards on the planning board can be studied and evaluated before production or preparation is started. This is the *storyboard* technique commonly used in planning a slide/tape program, a motion picture, a video recording, and other audiovisual materials.[1]

MAKING A PLANNING BOARD

A planning board is easy to construct. It consists of strips that are stapled to a sturdy board. The board can be made from a heavy gauge cardboard (14 ply or

[1]For procedures on planning for the production of audiovisual materials, see Jerrold E. Kemp, *Planning and Producing Instructional Media* (New York: Harper and Row, 1985).

Figure 13.1 A planning board consisting of clear plastic strips stapled to a wall surface.

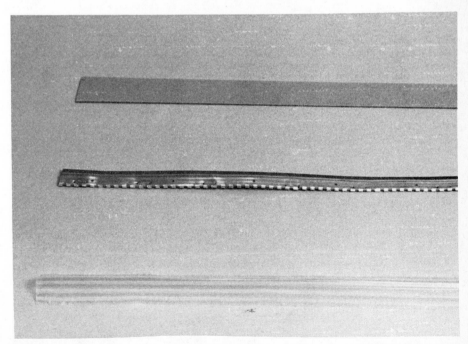

Figure 13.2 Materials which may be used for strips—cardboard, weatherstripping, carpet runner.

Figure 13.3 Stapling a plastic carpet-runner strip to make a planning board.

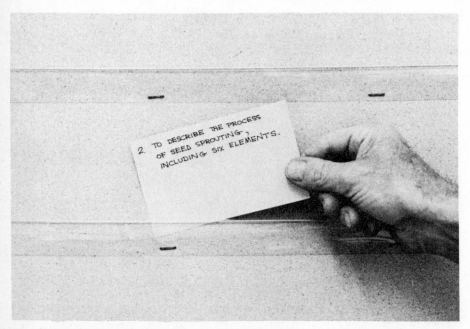

Figure 13.4 A planning card being placed behind a strip.

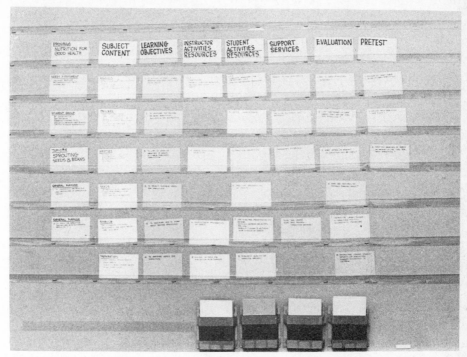

Figure 13.5 A complete instructional design plan displayed on a planning board.

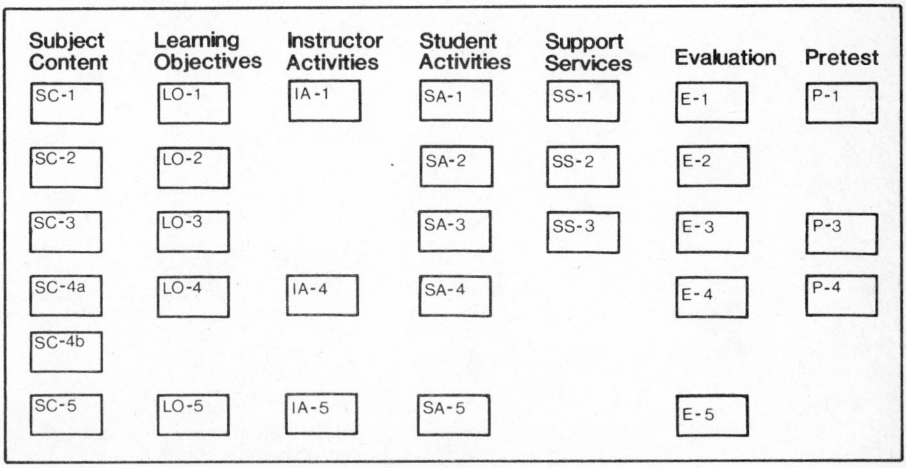

Subject Content	Learning Objectives	Instructor Activities	Student Activities	Support Services	Evaluation	Pretest
SC-1	LO-1	IA-1	SA-1	SS-1	E-1	P-1
SC-2	LO-2		SA-2	SS-2	E-2	
SC-3	LO-3		SA-3	SS-3	E-3	P-3
SC-4a	LO-4	IA-4	SA-4		E-4	P-4
SC-4b						
SC-5	LO-5	IA-5	SA-5		E-5	

Figure 13.6 A numbering system used on planning cards.

199

Topic #4	Learning Objectives	Subject Content
Sprouting Seeds & Beans	1. To explain at least three reasons why seed sprouting is of value.	Nutritional value - protein, vitamins Taste Uses in cooking dishes Inexpensive Minimum preparation time
General Purpose		
To understand the principle and procedure of sprouting seeds.	2. To describe the process of seed sprouting, including 6 elements.	Seed absorbs water Seed coating softens Root tip grows through covering Growth as a plant - root, stem, leaves Daylight vs darkness
	3. To list at least 6 varieties of seeds suitable for easy sprouting.	Soybeans Lentils Mung beans Peas Alfalfa seeds Wheat Chia seeds
	4. To select suitable seeds for sprouting.	Untreated with chemicals Viable for sprouting Good color Not cracked or broken
	5. To describe how to store seeds before sprouting.	Dry in sealed container Refrigerate for long period Label and date
	6. To prepare seeds for sprouting.	Use good, whole seeds Wash seeds Place in bowl of warm water Soak overnight
	7. Given the necessary equipment and materials, to apply at least three methods of sprouting for two kinds of seeds.	Jar Flower pot Paper towel Sprinkle Commercial products
	8. To evaluate the results of sprouting according to stated criteria.	Growth amount Aroma Flavor Color Crispness

Instructor Activities Resources	Student Activities Resources	Support Services
1, 2, 3 Orientation Present video on reasons, process, variety of seeds	1, 2, 3 Complete worksheet Discuss information	Video projector Videocassette - "Introduction to Seed Sprouting" Variety of storage containers
	3. Identify sample seeds	Variety of seeds
4. Demonstrate seed selection	4. Practice selection	
	5. Examine storage method samples	Variety of storage containers
6. Demonstrate preparation of seeds	6. Practice preparation of seeds	Preparation materials
	7. View slide/tape presentation on methods Restudy methods selected for use Carryout sprouting - 3 methods with 2 kinds of seeds	Slide/tapeviewer Program - "Sprouting Methods" Sprouting equipment and materials
8. Explain criteria for evaluation of samples	8. Evaluate quality of sprouts grown	

Evaluation	Pretest
1. Describe at least three values of seed sprouting.	1. Why is seed sprouting important?
2. How does seed sprouting take place?	
3. What six varieties of seeds or beans can be used for easy sprouting?	2. List names of some seeds that can be used for sprouting.
4. From the sample of seeds, choose those suitable for use in sprouting.	
5. How would you store seeds before use?	
6. Describe, in as few words as possible, how seeds are prepared for sprouting.	
7. (Instructor judges success in sprouting activity according to procedure).	3. What method (or methods) of sprouting can be used?
8. (Instructor judges student results of evaluating samples according to criteria)	4. What are features of properly sprouted seeds?

Figure 13.7 Final copy on paper of an instructional design plan taken from planning cards.

Figure 13.8 Storyboard sketches as guides for preparing visual materials.

Figure 13.9 A planning board with a carrying handle.

Figure 13.10   A planning board designed to be folded.

thicker) or one-quarter inch plywood. A 22 × 44 inch sheet of display cardboard or a 4 × 4 foot piece of plywood (half of a 4′ × 8′ sheet) makes a planning board of suitable size. You will want space for at least six horizontal strips to hold six rows of cards in six to seven columns. Various materials can be used for the strips:

- Cardboard strips cut about 1 inch wide. Attach the strips to the backing board with heavy-duty staples. Place the staples 3 to 4 inches apart. With this spacing, 3 × 5 inch cards on display cannot slip down, which could be a likely occurrence since flat cardboard exerts little pressure to hold a card in place.
- Heavy clear plastic used in the same way as the cardboard strips. Clear plastic is preferable to cardboard since writing placed low on a card can more readily be seen.
- Lightweight clear acetate cut into 2-inch strips, folded over, and then stapled. The pressure of the fold holds cards somewhat more firmly than does single thickness material.
- Weatherstripping material which consists of rubber edging set in an aluminum frame. The metal part has holes for small nails; therefore attaching the stripping to plywood is easy. The rubber edge will hold cards securely.
- Plastic carpet or stair-runner material which has a ribbed finish that presses firmly against a card. With the ribbing running lengthwise, cut the plastic into strips 2 inches wide; fold over and staple to the backing

board. (Note: Clear, plastic carpet-runner material may be found in hardware supply stores.)

Other suggestions when making a planning board include:

- Allow 5 to 6 inches between strips for ease of inserting and removing cards.
- Use a heavy-duty stapling gun to attach strips to the board. Then on the back, bend the staple tips that protrude; with a hammer tap each tip so it is tight to the back of the board.
- A portable board is easy to carry if a handle is provided at the top. This can be made by punching two spaced holes, threading strong twine through them, and tying the ends.
- A planning board that folds into a small size for storage and transport in a suitcase can be made by cutting a prepared board into sections. Sufficient space between adjacent sections is left to allow for both the thickness of the backing and of the strips when folded over. Attach sections together, on the back, with wide cloth tape.

The matter of giving attention to the mechanics of planning, as described in this chapter, including the use of cards and making a planning board, may seem to be of minor importance to such an intellectual process as instructional design planning. But as the process itself indicates, *all* aspects of planning need careful attention. Therefore, consideration of such details as those presented here can contribute significantly to the acceptance and eventual success of such a new practice as systematic instructional design planning.

REVIEW AND APPLICATIONS*

A. Recall

1. What is a major reason for using cards instead of paper to list items while planning?

_____

_____

_____

2. What are two advantages for displaying cards on a planning board?

a. _____

_____

_____

b. _____

_____

_____

3. What three materials might be used as strips for a planning board? Indicate advantages or limitations.

a. _____

_____

_____

b. _____

_____

_____

c. _____

_____

_____

4. In what three forms might a planning board be prepared?

a. _____

_____

_____

_____

b. _____

_____

_____

c. _____

_____

_____

B. Applications

1. Prepare a planning board of your own, according to the instructions in this chapter.

2. *Sky Diving*

Obtain index cards (multiple color if possible) or use cut pieces of paper. Transfer your planning work to cards and display them on a board.

3. *Your Subject*

Transfer the information to cards. Display them on a board.

chapter 14

Role of the Instructional Designer

"What personal traits and behavior patterns are important to be successful as an instructional designer?"

"What educational background is desirable for an instructional designer?"

"What specific experience should a person have had to be successful as an instructional designer?"

"What are some pros and cons for an instructional designer to be competent in the subject matter of a planning project?"

"What procedures can be used to ensure a satisfactory working relationship between an instructional designer and the instructor or client?"

"What responsibilities does the instructor or client share in the design process?"

"How does an instructional designer work with media personnel and other support staff?"

"What are the instructional designer's responsibilities for administering or managing a project?"

As you are well aware, the instructional designer (also called an *instructional developer, performance technologist,* or *learning system specialist*) fills a key role in implementing the instructional design process. This includes both managerial and operational functions. Furthermore, this process may require the coordinated efforts of a number of people as the instructional designer guides the planning. Therefore, as the planning process takes place, recognizing the relationships and responsibilities of various personnel is important.

In Chapter 10, Support Services, the qualifications required for a person filling the instructional designer role were mentioned. Here we will consider the competencies and responsibilities in greater detail.

PREPARATION FOR THE ROLE

When a person attempts to qualify for any role, be it in a job-related area or for a special activity, preparation can take place through training and/or experience. To specify which elements of competency can be attributable to formal or informal education and which to experience is difficult. However, some arbitrary groupings are made in the following discussion. Relate them to your own situation.

In addition to training and experience, another contribution may affect a person's ability to become a competent instructional designer. That contribution includes the personal attributes and characteristics of behavior of the individual.

Personal Attributes

Not everyone can become an instructional designer. Just as the work of a medical doctor or that of an airline pilot requires that a person possess certain personal traits and act in certain ways, so there are personality factors and behavior patterns which can indicate whether or not an individual could engage successfully in instructional development work.

First and foremost, instructional design is an intellectual activity. The designer must be mentally alert and should enjoy the challenges that require the application of careful thought processes. This means being inquisitive and able to employ both logical thought and creative abilities. Also, having the talent to analyze a complex topic and then to identify the pertinent elements is useful. While mental skills may be improved to some degree through study and practice, a person must already possess an inherent aptitude for this form of high-level mental activity.

Personality can affect the ability of a person to relate to other individuals and to be able to work cooperatively with them. The designer must like working with other people and experience a sense of satisfaction from helping them solve their instructional problems.

Here are other personal attributes that are important in the successful practice of instructional design work:

- Willingness to assume responsibilities and make decisions
- Enthusiasm, with a sense of commitment to one's work
- Patience, combined with the ability to avoid frustration
- Persistence in staying with a difficult problem
- Interest in handling many details and organizing them into meaningful patterns
- Tact in dealing with other persons

- Integrity and honesty
- The maturity to put up with resistance, resentment, and even obstructionism
- Good sense of timing, to know when to act and when to remain silent
- Willingness to innovate and try new things
- Willingness to admit mistakes and ability to say, "I don't know."

In terms of the attributes and critera presented in this section, how do you rate yourself as being prepared for the instructional designer role? For help in answering this question, see the self-evaluation activity in the Review and Applications section at the end of the chapter.

Education and Training

While studying the content of this book, you no doubt realize that more knowledge is necessary than solely a well-rounded general education and information about the instructional design process. Before attempting to design instruction in any subject, a sound base in educational theory is also necessary.

This includes having understandings from psychology, with particular attention to learning and perception principles, human development, and adult learning theory. The elements that comprise the communication process need attention. You must also become aware of the way the process can take place among people with different ethnic and experiential backgrounds and interests. Information and skills relative to instructional media need to be acquired—the characteristics of the media types available and the prevailing practices in planning, production, and utilization of them. Competency in writing skills should be developed by completing a course in technical writing, if necessary.

Skills in evaluation techniques need to be acquired so that the instructional designer may assess learning and performances, and may provide advice and assistance on test and questionnaire construction, analysis of exam results, and measurement of program outcomes. Other subject matter needing attention relates to organization management, budgeting, and administrative practices. Courses and special seminars can acquaint the beginning designer with principles and procedures relative to these last important areas.

Experience

Being directly involved, for a number of years, as a teacher in an instructional program is the best way to learn about the teaching/learning process. This is essential experience for an instructional designer. It is difficult to help other persons plan for teaching without having been involved in the process yourself.

As you probably recognize, the instructional design process is actually a problem-solving procedure. Silber indicates that in order for an instructional designer to reach proficiency, learning an internal problem-solving strategy in addition to specific instructional design skills is of primary importance.[1] He

[1] Kenneth Silber, "Applying Piaget's Stages of Intellectual Development."

suggests that the cognitive strategy procedure as applied by Gagné, along with Piaget's formal operational thought, and Guilford's structure of intellect model might serve as the basis for teaching problem-solving skills. But unfortunately, Silber finds that there is little evidence that problem-solving skills can be formally taught to adults.

The alternative is to take advantage of many opportunities to practice solving problems so that, through experience, a degree of proficiency can be attained. By developing the habit of facing problems in one's personal as well as professional life and applying a scientific mindset—identifying the problem, gathering information, formulating a solution, testing the solution, and so forth—a person can gain competency in analyzing and solving problems. Such experiences can contribute to preparation for becoming a competent instructional designer.

Subject Matter Competency

Many people expressing different points of view have questioned whether or not an instructional designer needs to have studied in the subject field for which he or she has been engaged to assist in instructional planning.[2] Some believe that the designer should be fully competent in the subject content and skills for the topics being planned in order to communicate with the instructor and content specialists on their own terms. This might save planning time and might avoid errors. On the other hand, an instructional designer who is competent in the subject area being planned could threaten the instructor or subject specialist.

In many situations, the designer is *not* also the subject expert. Often, in educational institutions or business organizations, instruction must be planned for a wide variety of either academic areas, job classifications, or special tasks. Therefore, the instructional designer must be prepared to work in content areas with which he or she may have had no previous knowledge. Can the designer meet the need?

The answer is a strong YES. This conclusion can be supported for two important reasons. First, most subject disciplines have a similar content structure. The same components of *facts, concepts,* and *principles* (page 61) can be found in every subject—from electronics to philosophy. By asking the proper questions, the designer can draw from the subject expert the information and skill sequences that are necessary for logically developing the components of the instructional design process.

Second, the other reason why a designer can work in unfamiliar areas is that he or she quickly becomes sufficiently familiar with the content and skills

---

[2]Barry Bratton, "Training the Instructional Development Specialist." Ruth Bollettino, "Why the Training Consultant Need Not Be a Subject Matter Specialist." Mary DeWeaver, "Why Does the Client Want a Subject Matter Expert?" Marc Rosenberg, "The Cross-Training of Subject Matter Experts and Instructional Technologists."

of a topic. Through conversations with the content specialist, reading and viewing audiovisual materials on the subject, then conducting a needs assessment and performing a task analysis, the designer acquires necessary insights and understandings. This accomplishment can be compared to that of a book editor who rewrites and clarifies a manuscript without being an expert in the subject matter as is the author.

Another justification for not requiring the instructional designer to be competent in the subject area is that as the planning proceeds, the content, learning objectives, and activities being selected and organized need to be considered from the learner's viewpoint. Thus, to help in revising sequences, and to improve many aspects of the instructional plan, "how" and "why" questions can be asked for clarification.

WORKING WITH THE INSTRUCTOR OR CLIENT

Most instructional design projects are initiated by an instructor, a teaching team, or a management person who recognizes a need to revise a course, initiate a new program, or otherwise change present instructional practice. In a business or industrial training environment the person who may be responsible for the project, or may serve as subject specialist to work with the instructional designer, is often called "the client."

If the instructional designer is also an expert in the subject content and the skills to be taught, then he or she could successfully carry out much of the planning alone. More often, as indicated in the previous section, the designer must work with an instructor, client, or planning team to implement the instructional design process. Because of different perceptions of what needs to be done by the individuals involved, and the expectations of how best to achieve the desired end product, careful attention should be given to this working relationship. The manner in which this association takes place can directly affect the success of a project.

There may be one of three approaches to this relationship between instructor (client) and instructional designer:

- *Designer directed*—The instructional designer is in charge and tells the client what to do and when to do it. Most, if not all, decisions are made by the designer. Input by the client is given only on request.
- *Client directed*—The client takes most responsibility, asking the designer for assistance as needed. Most decisions are made by the client. The designer serves more as a technician to do things as requested than as a professional colleague exercising some initiative.
- *Cooperative*—A joint endeavor in which each person participates and shares responsibilities on an equal footing in keeping with each one's knowledge and abilities. Mutual respect is established and the project proceeds as participants harmoniously work together.

While there are instances in which either of the first two models may be applied, the procedure that is supported here follows the third description. In this framework, the following discussion will consider the role of the instructional designer while *cooperating* with the instructor or client as instructional planning is initiated and carried out. Guidelines will be offered as suggestions for behavior and action during planning. References are appended if the reader would like to explore this topic further.

Initiating a Project

Prepare for the first meeting by becoming familiar with background information about the project through reading the proposal, a report, or a memo that may serve as the basis for the project. Also talk informally with persons who may have information relative to the need for the project.

Then, at the first meeting get to know the instructor, client, or members of the planning group with whom you will be working. Since first impressions are very important, establish rapport by giving attention to:

- Knowing the names of those who are in attendance
- Meeting in a suitable, informal environment
- Avoiding disturbances (telephone calls) and possible distractions
- Employing personal behavior techniques that are commonly used in counseling—low key, pleasant attitude, positive body language, active listening, careful questioning, and so forth
- Exploring the purposes for the project; encourage the instructor or client to describe the situation, needs, expectations, and desired outcomes
- Finding out who, besides those present, will need to review and possibly approve the output as work is performed
- Defining constraints, including time, personnel, space, and budget limitations
- Finally, agreeing on responsibilities, methodology to be followed, and initial tasks to be performed by each person; then setting a schedule for completion of project phases, and times for meetings

By applying these suggestions, each person present can become acquainted with the others, and you can successfully establish full support for participation. Now you are ready to start collecting and organizing information for design decisions.

Carrying Out the Planning

The client, as subject specialist, is best qualified to converse and write about his or her subject for colleagues already acquainted with the subject. Such a person will use subject-based terminology and make assumptions about what others already know about a topic. For the planning discussions, time may be required to make the instructor or client aware of the need to explain technical language and substitute it with easily understood phrases.

On the other hand, the instructional designer must realize that the instructor or client does not know the design process and should not employ specialized terminology; the designer should use easily understood expressions until the client is receptive to such expressions. Here are some examples:

- In place of *task analysis,* talk about "steps" or "the sequence for performing a job or part of a job."
- In place of *learning outcomes,* speak of "the results of accomplishing learning objectives."
- In place of *cognitive strategies,* refer to "teaching and learning methods."
- In place of *formative evaluation,* explain that "in order to judge whether revision may be necessary, parts of the program should be tested with learners or trainees while it is under development, and then, before full-scale use, it should be field-tested when it is complete."

Here are important suggestions to use when engaging in the planning process with an instructor, client, or team:

- Help the instructor or client to be specific with information by rephrasing what is said and by continually asking questions of the instructor or client for clarification, and by giving direction for selecting and sequencing material.
- Encourage the instructor or client to offer new ideas and to clarify explanations; illustrate by showing examples of what other persons have done in new instructional ways.
- Revise the organization of subject content, as developed by the instructor or subject expert, if necessary into logical sequences as the instructional design is planned. This matter must be approached carefully because the instructor may become angry if someone outside the field questions the subject organization and thus, indirectly, the instructor's knowledge.
- Be alert to the possibility that initially an instructor may be more interested in making a media decision (for example, using video or an audio-tutorial application) rather than in working on solving an instructional problem.
- Give particular attention to helping the instructor or client include learning objectives and activities that serve the higher levels of Bloom's cognitive domain.
- Planning with a team of subject specialists may cause disagreements and misunderstandings. Some of these may be caused by discrepancies found in different approaches taken by individuals to a subject. You can help them to resolve such differences objectively by asking clarifying questions and pointing out similarities of positions and facts.
- Periodically summarize to show a structure or pattern that is developing and to indicate the progress being made.
- By questioning, obtain reactions from those involved in planning so as to judge the acceptance or suitability of the planning elements being considered.

- Recognize the effort and work being performed by the instructor or client by acknowledging accomplishments and giving praise or encouragement.
- Consider obtaining reactions from a small number of learners or trainees as the proposed learning activities and materials, especially for a self-paced learning program, are developed. Through the learner responses, you can judge the activities and materials for appropriateness, ease of use, and contributions to the learning process.
- At agreed checkpoints during planning, be sure that necessary approval is obtained from other persons concerned.

Here are some additional, second-level suggestions for the designer:

- Be punctual at meetings.
- Keep a planning meeting reasonably brief. A person's attention span and ability to concentrate drop off after about two hours. It is preferable to have shorter, more frequent meetings.
- Be flexible in using the instructional design process model that you have learned from reading this book. Adjust your procedure to the nature of the problem and to the personalities of those with whom you are working.
- When conflicts arise, be patient and control your emotions. Turn the participants away from the dispute by reviewing a recent sequence of work or moving to another section of unfinished planning.
- Recognize your own potential limitations and ask for help when necessary.
- Keep careful notes of happenings during a meeting—content decisions made, assignments accepted, and dates when the next section of work is due.
- Duplicate and distribute the minutes as soon as possible after the meeting, as a reminder of what was accomplished and what was agreed is to be done next, and by when.
- Complete your own work, as agreed, for each meeting.

There are also some *don'ts* to which the instructional designer should be alert:

- Do not present large amounts of information, or lengthy explanations or procedures, or theoretical background information all at one time. Explain what you feel is needed at the time. Offer it at a pace that seems appropriate to the situation and the persons involved.
- Do not push an instructor or subject expert to state learning objectives exactly early in planning. If difficulty in expressing an objective arises, it may be both more productive and personally acceptable to move ahead in planning. The wording will clarify itself in time.
- Do not appear threatening or too assertive by having the only *right* answer—"This *is* how we should do it!"—when a problem or disagreement arises.

- Avoid openly criticizing the instructor or client either directly or with colleagues. If a problem arises, give it attention before it becomes too serious by initiating an informal conversation on the subject. If a problem persists, speaking with the person's immediate supervisor may be necessary.

Concluding the Planning

When all necessary elements of the instructional design plan have received adequate attention and the instructor or client accepts the details, you are ready to conclude the planning and take the next steps in course development. First, make certain, if required, that necessary approval is obtained from persons other than the planning team.

Then, arrange for necessary support services such as preparation of materials, acquisition of commercial materials and equipment, adaptation of facilities, and orientation for instructional personnel and aides. (See Chapter 10.)

Next, review or revise plans to carry out a formative evaluation of the new program when planning of sections or the entire program is completed. (See Chapter 11 for suggestions about formative evaluation procedures.)

Finally, when the program is implemented, initiate plans to design instruments for evaluating the learning benefits, costs, effectiveness, and opinions toward the new program. This is the summative evaluation procedure, considered in Chapter 16.

RESPONSIBILITIES OF THE INSTRUCTOR OR CLIENT

While attention has been given primarily to the responsibilities of the instructional designer and to his or her relations with the instructor or client, this person shares the responsibility for the success of the project. Therefore, the behavior and actions of the instructor or client are important to the designer. Help the instructor or client to modify initial assumptions and attitudes as necessary. Some desirable characteristics and behaviors of instructors and clients that are important include:

- Being open-minded and not defensive when one's beliefs, ideas, or position are not readily accepted
- Recognizing that there might be more than one way of answering a question or solving a problem
- Realizing that there may be errors in subject content that one knows, as revealed in publications, or as pointed out by colleagues
- Being willing to learn new things and to try them out
- Taking responsibilities commensurate with one's position, knowledge, and abilities
- Providing resources needed for planning

- Performing required work by the time agreed
- Showing enthusiasm and expressing a positive attitude about the project when conversing with colleagues and learners

It is not always easy to help a person change well-established beliefs or personal behaviors when new approaches are needed. By being aware of these matters and recognizing their importance to successful instrumental planning, the instructional designer should attempt to assist the instructor or client to make adjustments both for individual growth and for the benefit of the project.

WORKING WITH SUPPORT STAFF

Many instructional design projects result in the development of instructional units that may include a range of activities and the use of numerous audiovisual materials. The services of various support personnel may be required for preparing materials, locating commercial items, making materials available to learners for use, selecting and installing equipment, adapting facilities, or filling other needs. It is the responsibility of the instructional designer to involve the necessary support personnel and coordinate the preparatory work.

Here are suggestions for ways to fulfill this responsibility:

- As planning progresses, involve staff members at appropriate times. For example, inform production staff (graphic artist, photographer, video producer, audio recording specialist, computer programmer) about materials to be prepared, how they relate within the instructional plan, and the date required for completion.
- In detail, go over the work to be done with those to be responsible for the work.
- Set deadlines and require progress reports.
- Review the results with the instructor or client when materials are in the preliminary stage, and again when they are in final form for use.
- Permit staff to see the materials as they are being used.
- Share evaluation reports with support staff; commend them for successes; examine shortcomings with them.

WORKING WITH AN EVALUATOR

The instructional designer engages in planning with the instructor, client, or planning team. If the services of an evaluator will be required, it probably will be the responsibility of the designer to bring this person into planning meetings at suitable times. The evaluator would be responsible for developing tests and other measurement instruments. Sometimes an "outside" evaluator is employed to measure the outcomes of a program when it is fully implemented (summative evaluation). In order to be as objective as possible, such a person should have had no previous contact with the project and may need a limited orientation to the program.

ADMINISTRATIVE RESPONSIBILITIES

Many of the responsibilities that an instructional designer has for managing a project have been identified throughout this chapter. The following list may serve as a summary:

- Establish and maintain communication (in person and on paper) with everyone involved in the project relative to project objectives, responsibilities, progress, and difficulties encountered.
- Gain agreement on a time schedule for planning and executing work; attempt to stay within the schedule; modify the schedule only with the concurrence of the other persons.
- Coordinate required work and services with support staff and other agencies; check for completion of assigned tasks within the time frame.
- Periodically evaluate progress, informing participants and reporting to administrators.
- Analyze, with staff, results of formative evaluation; arrange for revisions and retesting as necessary.
- Maintain records of time being devoted to the project by staff and expenses incurred; relate costs to actual budgeted amounts.
- Arrange for summative evaluation of the project when implementation takes place.
- Continue interest in the program when it is in full operation; check on: on-going levels of learner performance; maintenance and replacement of equipment and materials; continued suitability of other support services; and attitudes or opinions of succeeding groups of learners and staff, relative to quality and value of the program.

REVIEW AND APPLICATIONS*

A. Recall
  1. Which statements are *true* concerning the instructional designer? For those you believe to be *false,* indicate why this is so.
  _____ *a.* Most instructors have the qualifications for becoming instructional designers.
  _____ *b.* Instructional design work requires both creative abilities and logical thought processes.
  _____ *c.* The ability to organize ideas as broad generalities is important.
  _____ *d.* Such a person enjoys helping other people rather than working alone.
  _____ *e.* Such a person is motivated to reach closure quickly on a problem and move to the next matter.
  _____ *f.* Such a person is not willing to admit mistakes.
  _____ *g.* Such a person has a sense of commitment when working on a project.
  _____ *h.* In addition to having a good general education and knowledge about the I.D. process, training in areas of psychology and communication skills will satisfactorily qualify someone to be an instructional designer.
  _____ *i.* The most important experience is to have been a teacher.
  _____ *j.* Problem-solving skills, so important to the instructional designer, generally cannot be taught to an adult.

*See answers on page 273.

     _____ *k.* A good way to learn problem-solving skills is to work on solving problems.

     _____ *l.* It is necessary for the instructional designer to be competent in the subject area under planning so that a technical conversation with the subject specialist can take place.

     _____ *m.* An argument supporting the position that the instructional designer can work in an unfamiliar subject field is that most disciplines have a similar cognitive structure.

2. Which statements are *true* as the designer works with the instructor or client? For those that are *false,* indicate why this is so.

     _____ *a.* The designer-directed approach is the one recommended in this book.

     _____ *b.* When starting a new project, plan to obtain background information at the first planning meeting.

     _____ *c.* Define constraints and responsibilities early in planning.

     _____ *d.* Make certain that no one besides those on the planning team will have to review and approve plans as they are developed.

     _____ *e.* Techniques used in personnel counseling are valuable when working with a client.

     _____ *f.* Early in planning, explain to the client the technical expressions you will be using during conversations.

     _____ *g.* As necessary, rephrase what the instructor says for clarification.

     _____ *h.* Use examples to clarify explanations and to encourage new ideas.

     _____ *i.* If an instructor is more interested in deciding on a type of media to use for teaching a lesson, rather than to examine the elements of planning, this procedure should be encouraged.

     _____ *j.* Help to resolve differences among members of the planning team by raising questions that clarify points of view and pointing out similarities of positions.

     _____ *k.* Indicate progress in planning by periodically summarizing what has been done.

     _____ *l.* Only recognize the efforts of a client through praise *after* all planning is completed.

     _____ *m.* The best way to obtain reactions to what is being planned is to obtain approval from supervisors and other administrators.

     _____ *n.* A planning meeting is most effective if it is limited to a time period of under 2 hours.

     _____ *o.* Do not necessarily treat all elements of the I.D. plan nor follow the sequence as presented in this book.

     _____ *p.* Distribute a summary report of one meeting at the beginning of the next meeting.

     _____ *q.* Limit any tendency to make long explanations of theoretical justification for an action or decision.

     _____ *r.* Make sure the planning group understands that you are the final authority for any decision when a disagreement arises.

     _____ *s.* If you must criticize an instructor, let the person's supervisor know about it *before* talking with the instructor.

3. When planning has been completed, what matters then need attention? Check all that apply.

_____ *a.* Obtain necessary approvals of the planning

_____ *b.* Arrange for preparation of materials

_____ *c.* Announce the immediate availability of the program for use

_____ *d.* Plan to orient teaching aides to the program

_____ *e.* Make plans for formative evaluation procedure

_____ *f.* Initiate plans for summative evaluation

4. Which of the following are desirable behaviors and responsibilities that can be expected of the client or instructor? Check all that apply.

_____ *a.* Complete required work on time.

_____ *b.* Be enthusiastic about the project when talking with others.

_____ *c.* Be prepared to strongly defend your own opinion, in keeping with your professional position.

_____ *d.* Be willing to take responsibilities in keeping with your abilities.

_____ *e.* Recognize that discrepencies in subject content may appear and should be resolved.

5. Which statements are *true* when the instructional designer follows up planning with support staff? For those you mark *false,* indicate why this is so.

_____ *a.* Set deadlines for work to be completed.

_____ *b.* Wait until planning is completed before contacting support staff about work on a project.

_____ *c.* Review preliminary production work with instructor or client.

_____ *d.* Inform support staff how successful the materials are during use.

6. Which are administrative responsibilities of the instructional designer in connection with a project? Check all that apply.

_____ *a.* Maintains a schedule of work to be performed

_____ *b.* Coordinates activities among those involved in the project

_____ *c.* Establishes open communication among everyone in the project

_____ *d.* Evaluates progress

_____ *e.* Arranges for formative evaluation of the program

_____ *f.* Conducts summative evaluation of the program

_____ *g.* Maintains records (time, budget, expenses, etc.)

_____ *h.* Terminates contact with the project once the program is implemented

7. In this review, we have given attention to all aspects of the role of the instructional designer with the exception of the relationship with one other professional position. Who is this other individual with whom the instructional designer might work? What is this other person's role and its relationship to the instructional designer?

_____

_____

_____

B. Application

How do you rate yourself as an instructional designer? Judge your competencies and behavior patterns on the following criteria. Mark each item. Then add up the points. Classify yourself as follows:

140 to 160 points	Super instructional designer
120 to 139	Above-average instructional designer
95 to 119	Average instructional designer
65 to 94	Below-average instructional designer
32 to 65	Poor instructional designer

Personal attributes:	Low				High
1. Able to think in careful, logical ways	1	2	3	4	5
2. Ability to think creatively	1	2	3	4	5
3. Ability to analyze complex subjects	1	2	3	4	5
4. Satisfaction in working with people	1	2	3	4	5
5. Able to ask probing questions	1	2	3	4	5
6. Good listener	1	2	3	4	5
7. Willing to assume responsibilities	1	2	3	4	5
8. Able to make decisions	1	2	3	4	5
9. Flexible and willing to change	1	2	3	4	5
10. Shows enthusiasm	1	2	3	4	5
11. Exhibits patience	1	2	3	4	5
12. Exhibits persistence	1	2	3	4	5
13. Can be tactful	1	2	3	4	5
14. Has integrity and honesty	1	2	3	4	5
15. Able to put up with resistance and resentment	1	2	3	4	5
16. Knows when to speak and when to remain silent	1	2	3	4	5
17. Willing to try new things	1	2	3	4	5
18. Willing to admit mistakes	1	2	3	4	5
19. Able to recognize own limitations (admit you may not know something)	1	2	3	4	5
20. Has positive self-image	1	2	3	4	5

Training:	Low				High
1. Rounded general education	1	2	3	4	5
2. Background in psychology	1	2	3	4	5
3. Knowledgeable in adult learning theory	1	2	3	4	5
4. Aware of elements in communication process	1	2	3	4	5
5. Knowledgeable about most educational media and their use	1	2	3	4	5
6. Experienced in the production of media	1	2	3	4	5
7. Knowledgeable with testing and evaluation techniques	1	2	3	4	5
8. Understands organizational management	1	2	3	4	5
9. Competent with instructional design process	1	2	3	4	5

Experience:					
1. Teaching	1	2	3	4	5
2. Problem-solving skills	1	2	3	4	5
3. Subject area (fill in)					
_____	1	2	3	4	5
_____	1	2	3	4	5
_____	1	2	3	4	5
4. Other pertinent experience (fill in)					
_____	1	2	3	4	5
_____	1	2	3	4	5

Total points per column
Grand total

How might you proceed to improve any competencies or behaviors on which you rate low (scale values 1 or 2)?

_____

_____

_____

REFERENCES

Bell, Chip R., and Leonard Nadler, eds. _The Client-Consultant Handbook_ (Houston, TX: Gulf, 1979).

Bollettino, Ruth. "Why the Training Consultant Need Not Be a Subject Matter Specialist," _NSPI Journal,_ 19 (June 1980), 28–33.

Bratton, Barry. "The Instructional Development Specialist as Consultant," _Journal of Instructional Development,_ 3 (Winter 1979–80), 2–8.

———. "Training the Instructional Development Specialist to Work in Unfamiliar Content Areas," _Journal of Instructional Development,_ 4 (Spring 1981), 21–23.

Brown, Jerry L. "I.D. Managers' Do's and Don'ts," _NSPI Journal,_ 19 (December 1980), 17–18.

"Competencies for Instructional Development Specialists," _Instructional Innovator,_ 25 (December 1980), 27–30.

"Consultant-Client Relationship," _NSPI Journal,_ 17 (November 1980), whole issue.

DeWeaver, Mary. "Why Does the Client Want a Subject Matter Expert?" _NSPI Journal,_ 19 (November 1980), 44.

Haney, John, Phil Lange, and John Barson. "The Heuristic Dimension of Instructional Development," _AV Communication Review,_ 16 (Winter 1968), 358–371.

Rosenberg, Marc. "The Cross-Training of Subject Matter Experts and Instructional Technologists," _NSPI Journal,_ 20 (February 1981), 16–17, 33.

Silber, Kenneth. "Applying Piaget's Stages of Intellectual Development and Guilford's Structure of Intellect Model in Training Instructional Developers," _Journal of Instructional Development,_ 4 (Spring 1981), 33–40.

Wallington, Clinton J. "Generic Skills of an Instructional Developer," _Journal of Instructional Development,_ 4 (Spring 1981), 28–32.

chapter 15

Managing Instructional Development Services

"Where should an instructional development service be located within the structure of an organization?"

"What size staff may be necessary to carry on instructional design projects?

"Are special facilities required to support instructional development services?"

"In what ways can the activities of instructional development services be financed?"

"What policies need attention as guidelines for instructional design activities?"

If instructional development activities in an organization are to require more than only casual attention, then a plan for supporting and managing the services should be considered, as indicated by the above questions. As with any important program, attention should be given to the purposes to be served and services to be provided, placement of the program within the organization, staffing required, facilities needed, budgetary support necessary, and the operational policies for carrying out the activities. The instructional designer should become aware of these requirements for satisfactorily managing the instructional development services to be performed.

PURPOSES AND SERVICES

The fundamental assumption upon which instructional development services must be based is that teaching and learning can be improved through the application of a systematic planning process. It follows that a person who is skilled in applying an instructional design procedure can work with subject matter specialists to design effective instruction.

Some requests for help in instructional planning may be received which do *not* require instructional solutions but rather indicate changes in operating procedures or possibly attention to personnel problems. Other requests may reflect an instructional need, which is limited, for example, to the preparation of certain visual materials and does not require consideration of other instructional design elements. Careful attention to a learning needs assessment (Chapter 3) can indicate whether education or training may be an appropriate way to handle a problem.

There is increasing conviction that systematic planning should be employed in situations which indicate the desirability of more effective, efficient, and cost-saving learning procedures. Because of four important factors—(1) growth and changes in subject content and skills that must be learned, (2) the changing nature of learners and trainees, (3) increased knowledge about how learning best takes place, and (4) the availability of new technological instructional resources—the services of an instructional development office or department can prove essential to designing a successful training program.

PLACEMENT WITHIN AN ORGANIZATION

Within a school or college program, instructional development services should be placed administratively as close as possible to the chief academic officer (often the curriculum director or academic vice-president). This arrangement is desirable because service should be available to any academic area, and therefore the director of instructional development would need authority to work with and attain the cooperation of any office or agency within the institution.

Because in nonacademic organizations the main function of an instructional development service is to improve training, it is usually located in the training department. Consequently, the individual in charge of instructional development would be responsible to the director of training.

In all situations there is a direct working relationship between instructional development services and audiovisual media services. If a separate testing or evaluation office exists, it should have close ties with instructional development. All these services should report to the same administrator so that project activities can easily involve each service in a cooperative fashion.

STAFFING

The permanent staff for instructional development services should be a small one. An administrator (labeled as a manager, director, or coordinator) and a secretary are essential. One or more instructional designers handle projects. In a small operation, part of a designer's time could be devoted to management responsibilities.

One designer can coordinate no more than about three major projects simultaneously. Many more short-term projects can be developed during a period of time. Depending on the extent of services, a full- or part-time evaluator may be on the staff. In some situations a contract is drawn up with an evaluator from outside the organization.

Subject specialists or clients are usually not permanently assigned to an instructional development office. Since each project requires its own subject specialist or client, such people would be drawn from appropriate teaching or operational departments in an organization or institution. If necessary for administrative or budgetary purposes, subject experts can be assigned temporarily to the instructional development services.

FACILITIES

In addition to an office for the administrator, instructional designer, and secretary, one or more conference-type planning rooms are necessary. A conference room should be furnished with a table for seating at least six people. One wall should contain a large planning board on which cards can be displayed during planning sessions (Chapter 13). For viewing audiovisual and video materials, provision for a screen and the use of projectors are essential. Try to create an informal, welcoming atmosphere in the conference room.

BUDGETARY SUPPORT

There are three ways to provide financial support for instructional development activities. First, by means of a suitable sum of money being budgeted for the services from the institution or organization. Allocations are made to fund personnel time and developmental costs for projects that are commissioned or selected through a competition or by request. Second, an academic department or a division of an organization assigns funds from its own budget to cover the costs for a project it has requested be carried out in conjunction with instructional development services. Third, funding from outside the institution is obtained as a grant specifically to support a project. This latter method usually requires the submission of a written proposal that is evaluated according to certain criteria, often in competition with other proposals.

Funding is used in part to pay for the time personnel are assigned to the project. This may include time spent by the instructional designer, the subject specialist, the evaluator, and the support staff. Also, costs are covered for such expenses as those incurred for developing or purchasing materials and equipment, adapting facilities, or meeting overhead charges and other requirements. See page 233 for further information about program cost factors.

OPERATING POLICIES

While the details for initiating and managing an instructional development project receive attention elsewhere (page 215), some general policies need identification as part of management functions.

Any project that is accepted for planning should be part of an overall strategy for improving instructional effectiveness, making better use of personnel, and controlling instructional costs. For example, a decision may recommend a gradual shift of part or all of a training program from conventional classroom instruction to self-paced learning and small-group interaction activities. First, the new method has to be proven feasible in terms of identified needs. This can be done by supporting the planning and field testing of one or more experimental courses. Then, if results are acceptable, sequences of courses would be selected for revision.

Sometimes provision for incentives or rewards is advisable or even necessary for the instructors or content specialists who participate in an instructional development project. In a business organization such inducements may not be of serious concern because employees are rarely free to reject a directive for participating in a project. With success of the project, they may be rewarded with a promotion or a raise in salary.

In an academic institution participation is much more voluntary. Therefore it is advisable to recognize, encourage, and reward participation in acceptable ways. These may include:

- Free or specially assigned time to participate in the project as opposed to required overtime for the work to be done
- Extra monetary payment for time devoted to the project (during vacation or summer period, or as overtime)
- Recognition of success in project work through acclaim by colleagues
- Opportunities to report on project procedures and results through presentations at meetings and acceptance of articles written for professional journals
- Opportunities to follow up with additional projects or other desirable activities
- Recognition by receiving a tenured appointment and/or promotion in professional rank

Another area for management decision relates to the ownership of materials and programs developed during a project. In a commercial organization, program resources usually remain the property of the company. They may even be marketed to other organizations for use in their training programs. The persons involved in the planning and development may have their names appended to printed, audiovisual, and video materials.

An academic institution may establish a policy that allows the institution to hold title to all program components of a project funded by the institution. On the other hand, a different policy may allow an agreement to be made between the institution and faculty members to share royalties on the sale of ber can utilize experience gained in developing instructional materials for a project and redesign them completely outside of the institution. The instructor can then contract with a publisher, or other distributor, to handle sales.

If an institution receives money for sale of materials resulting from instructional development projects, such funds could justifiably be returned to the instructional development office to support further projects. This could prove to be a sizeable source of income.

REPORTING ON SERVICES

Any new endeavor like instructional development services must be accountable for proving its value within an institution or organization. Therefore, careful and detailed records should be kept on planning, progress, personnel time required, costs incurred, and benefits derived. This documentation will be important when reports are prepared and results need to be publicized. Keeping people in the institution or organization informed about instructional development activities, progress, and successes, can be essential for continued support and for requested increases in personnel and funding for projects.

In addition to separate reports on individual projects and annual reports of all yearly activities, consider a cumulative report for a longer period, perhaps 5 years. This can illustrate the ongoing, overall benefits to an organization that supports strong instructional development services.

REVIEW AND APPLICATIONS*

A. Recall
  1. What do you see as the strongest justification for establishing an instructional development services department within an organization or institution?

  _____

  _____

  _____

  2. Where should instructional development services be placed within an organization?
  a. School or college _____

  _____

  _____

  b. Business company or governmental agency _____

  _____

  _____

  3. Which statements are *true* concerning instructional development services?
  _____ *a.* Subject specialists in various areas should be permanent members of instructional development services.
  _____ *b.* The only necessary facility is an office.
  _____ *c.* Permanent staff should consist of a manager/designer and secretary.
  _____ *d.* One instructional designer can handle up to three major projects at one time.

*See answers page 275.

_____ *e.* Support staff such as technicians and media producers are other persons who may be required to be members of the instructional development services.

_____ *f.* Field testing to try out new instructional approaches should be a part of the development process.

_____ *g.* Profits derived from materials developed as part of an instructional design project should be shared between the organization and the instructor engaged in the project.

_____ *h.* It is usually a waste of effort to issue periodic reports on I.D. activities.

4. What three ways can I.D.S. be supported financially?

a. _____
_____
_____

b. _____
_____
_____

c. _____
_____
_____

5. What are three ways that instructors in an academic institution can be rewarded for engaging in I.D. projects?

a. _____
_____
_____

b. _____
_____
_____

c. _____
_____
_____

B. Application

Consider an instructional development situation—one in which you are presently involved, one you might or would hope to be involved with in the future, or dream about one.

a. Where would you like to see the services located within the organization or institution?
_____
_____

b. What staffing would it have?
_____
_____

c. What facilities would it have?
_____
_____

d. How would it be supported financially?
_____
_____

REFERENCES

Diamond, Robert M., et al. *Instructional Development for Individualized Learning in Higher Education* (Englewood Cliffs, NJ: Educational Technology Publications, 1975).

Durzo, Joseph J. "Getting Down to Business: Instructional Development for a Profit," *Journal of Instructional Development,* 6 (Winter 1983), 2–7.

————. "The Organization and Implementation of Instructional Development Programs in Higher Education: A Review of the Literature," in *Instructional Development: The State of the Art,* Ronald K. Bass, and D.B. Lumsden, eds. (Columbus, OH: Collegiate Publishing, 1978).

Forman, David C., and Penny Richardson. "Course Development by Team: Some Advice on How Many Cooks Does It Take to Spoil the Broth?" *Educational Technology,* 17 (December 1977), 30–35.

Gropper, George L. "On Gaining Acceptance for Instructional Design in a University Setting," *Educational Technology,* 17 (December 1977), 7–13.

Hammons, James O., and Terry H. Smith Wallace. "Sixteen Ways to Kill a College Faculty Development Program," *Educational Technology,* 16 (December 1976), 16–20.

chapter *16*

Summative Evaluation
Determining Program Outcomes

"How can an instructional designer provide evidence that systematic instructional planning does pay off?"

"What is the actual cost of an instructional course?"

"How can a training program be of value if it doesn't directly produce income for the company?"

"Can the important results of a college course really be measured?"

"How do I show that a new training program may be superior to one it replaced?"

Too often an instructional designer or an instructor may intuitively be convinced that what is being accomplished is worthwhile and successful. It is often assumed by persons in education and training that the merits of a program are obvious to other persons in the institution or organization. Unfortunately, rarely is either of these conclusions true.

A summative evaluation permits you to reach unbiased, objective answers to questions such as those above and then to decide whether the program is achieving the goals it was originally intended to reach. With this evidence, your intuition can be supported or rejected, and you have the facts for correctly informing others about the program results.

The following important issues can be examined through summative evaluation procedures:

- Effectiveness of learner or trainee learning
- Efficiency of learner or trainee learning

- Cost of program development and continuing expenses in relation to effectiveness and efficiency
- Attitudes and reactions to the program by learners, faculty, and staff
- Long-term benefits of the instructional program

In this final chapter we will examine methods for gathering data which can lead to a conclusion for each of the five issues stated above. Attention to these matters may be essential in proving the value of a new instructional program and then insuring its continued support.

A summative evaluation of a course or program is more than a *one-time* activity. Immediately after each course or training program is concluded, some or all of the assessment methods to be described should be utilized. By accumulating summative data, continuing positive trends in a program can be tracked over time, or deficiencies can be noted as they show up, with possible corrections being made immediately.

EVALUATION VERSUS RESEARCH

One way of measuring the value of a new program is to compare the results obtained with those of a conventionally conducted course in the same subject. Most often this comparison cannot be fairly made because the two courses were planned to achieve entirely different objectives. It is very likely that there are no stated, measurable objectives for the conventional course that are used as a basis for the comparison. Also, the subject matter treated in the two programs may be significantly different, with the content of the conventional course often being limited to a lower cognitive domain level than that of the new program.

In some situations, evaluation is performed by using a formal research framework. This means that a carefully designed comparison study is based upon control and experimental groups or classes. One or more hypotheses are stated as anticipated outcomes. Then, after instruction takes place, statistical methods are employed to gather data and report the evidence collected about learning outcomes. Conclusions are drawn which support or reject the initial hypotheses.

Such a research methodology is feasible if a theory is to be established which may have widespread application for improving education. For example, as a result of carefully designed research studies, conclusions such as the following are now accepted and applied in instructional programs:

- In a self-paced learning program, when learners are informed of the objectives they will study, they progress through an instructional unit in less time than do learners not informed of the objectives.[1]
- Significantly greater learning often results when media are integrated into an instructional program.[2]

[1]As reported in Davies, *Objectives in Curriculum Design,* p. 90.
[2]Gene Wilkinson, *Media in Instruction.*

● Skill learning will better take place when practice periods are spaced over intervals of time rather than when they are massed together.[3]

Most instructional design projects are not planned to result in broadly applicable theories. Their purpose is to find out how well the needs that have been identified can be met. Growth in learner knowledge or skill activity, as measured by the difference between pretest and posttest results or by observing behavior before and after instruction, provides evidence of learning that can be directly attributable to the instructional program.

Sometimes the success in learning can be shown only in following up on-the-job work being done by individuals after instruction. For example, after completing a safety course, if accidents involving employees working with equipment are appreciably reduced (say, by over 30 percent), then the training can be considered to be successful. Or, if company operating expenses decrease and revenues increase from the pretraining to the posttraining periods, then we could say that direct benefits are due to the results of training. On the other hand, when results do not meet goals, the evaluation evidence would indicate the shortcomings. Steps can then be taken to improve the program before its next use.

In summary, for evaluating instructional design projects, it is not necessary or even appropriate to perform formal research involving control/experimental groups and detailed statistical analysis. All that must be done is to gather evidence relative to accomplishments or change from preinstruction to postinstruction for as many of the five components listed above (effectiveness, efficiency, costs, and so on) as are considered important for that course, then to interpret the information to reach conclusions about the success or failure of the instructional program.

A special note: For some of the procedures considered here, it is advisable (or even essential) to start collecting data from the time the program is *initially planned.* By doing this, you will have the necessary information to determine costs, time, and other facts pertinent to the evaluation. It may come as a surprise to have this pointed out in the last chapter of the book! Hopefully you are reading this as an overview of the process before starting to work on a project requiring summative evaluation.

PROGRAM EFFECTIVENESS

Effectiveness answers the question, "To what degree did students accomplish the learning objectives prescribed for each unit of the course?" Measurement of effectiveness can be ascertained from test scores, ratings of projects and performance, and records of observations of learners' behavior.

An analysis of scores can be prepared by hand or through a computer data-processing service. The data may show the change from pre- to posttest results. Then a summary may be presented in tabular form. See Figure 16.1 on the next page. An examination of the table in this figure will reveal that the group, comprised of six learners, accomplished 90 percent of the objectives. This figure is calculated by totaling the number of objectives satisfied—the X

[3]As reported in DeCecco and Crawford, *The Psychology of Learning and Instruction,* p. 275.

a. Unit Objectives | **Test Questions**

Unit Objectives	Test Questions
A	2, 4, 11
B	1, 7
C	3, 5, 12
D	8, 10
E	5, 9

b. Learner

Learner	1	2	3	4	5	6	7	8	9	10	11	12
					Correct Answers to Questions							
AJ	X	X	X	X		X	X	X	X	X		X
SF	X		X		X		X	X	X	X		X
TY	X	X	X	X	X	X	X	X	X	X	X	
LM	X	X	X	X	X	X	X	X	X	X		X
RW	X	X		X	X	X	X	X	X	X	X	X
WB	X		X	X	X	X	X		X	X		X

c. Learner

Learner	A	B	C	D	E
	Objectives Satisfied				
AJ	X	X	X	X	
SF		X	X	X	X
TY	X	X	X	X	X
LM	X	X	X	X	X
RW	X	X	X	X	X
WB		X	X	X	X

Figure 16.1 A sample analysis of test questions measuring cognitive objectives

marks in c. The total is 27. Divide by 6, the number of learners; 4.5 is the average number of objectives accomplished per learner; 4.5 is what percent of the 5 objectives? 90 percent. This result can be interpreted as a measure of the effectiveness of the instructional design plan for this group of learners. The percentage may be considered as an *effectiveness index* representing: .

1. The percent of learners reaching a preset level of mastery (satisfying each objective)
2. The average percent of objectives satisfied by all learners

If *all* learners accomplished *all* objectives, the effectiveness of the program would be excellent. If 90 percent of the learners accomplish 90 percent of the objectives, could you report that the program has been effective? To answer this question, the instructor, along with the administrator or training director, must have previously decided the level at which to accept the program as effective. In a systematically planned academic course, attainment of the 80 percent level by at least 80 percent of the learners in a class could be acceptable as a highly effective program. In a vocational or skill area, 90–90 (90 percent of the trainees accomplishing 90 percent of the objectives) might be the accepted success level. Similar courses (for example, in biology or electronics assembly) can be compared with respect to effectiveness indices and conclusions drawn for judging program effectiveness.

Realistically, it is very likely that because of individual differences among learners and your inability to design ideal learning experiences, you cannot hope to reach the absolute standard of mastery or competency—100 percent—in all instructional situations. (Some training programs for which life and safety are critical—medical areas, airline pilot training—may require the 100 percent level of mastery learning.)

Then another question must be asked. Assume that your performance standard requires all learners to accomplish 85 percent of the objectives, but that as a group they actually satisfy 82 percent of them. What time, effort, and expense are required to redesign the weak areas of the program in order to raise the learning level to 85 percent. Is the effort to reach the 85 percent level worth the cost? There may be circumstances that would make this achievement almost prohibitive. You may have to settle for a somewhat lower level of accomplishment until someone can design a revision of the program that will make it possible to reach the desired level of performance with reasonable effort and cost.

When we evaluate effectiveness of an instructional program, we must recognize that there may be intangible outcomes (often expressed as affective objectives) and longterm consequences that would become apparent only after the program is concluded and learners are at work. Both of these matters are given attention in the following sections as part of other summative evaluation components. Here, the evaluation of effectiveness is limited to those learning objectives that can be immediately measured.

PROGRAM EFFICIENCY

In evaluating efficiency, the main considerations refer to *time, personnel,* and *space* utilization. These three aspects of a program require attention:

- Time required for learners to achieve unit objectives
- Number of instructors and support staff members required for instruction and the time they devote to the program
- Use of facilities assigned to the program

Learner Time Required

Educational programs are designed typically in terms of available time periods—semesters, quarters, or other fixed time intervals (week, weekend, and so on). It is only when some flexibility is permitted that efficiency can be measured. If a conventional training program can be reduced from a period of possibly 6 to 5 weeks, with the same or increased effectiveness in learning, the program can be considered to be *efficient.*

Efficiency can be used for measuring outcomes primarily of programs that give major emphasis to individualized or self-paced learning activities. From the learner's standpoint, the time required to satisfy unit or program objectives would be a measure of efficiency. Mathematically, this measurement is the ratio of the number of objectives a learner achieves compared to the time the learner takes to achieve them. Learners can be asked to keep records of time (a time log) spent studying a unit or set of objectives. Or, in a more subjective fashion, an instructor can observe and make notations to indicate the number of learners at work in a study area during time periods.

For example, Bill satisfies seven objectives in 4.2 hours of study and work. By dividing the number of objectives Bill achieves by the amount of time it takes him to accomplish them, we find that his *efficiency index* is 1.7 (7 ÷ 4.2). Mary achieves the seven objectives in 5.4 hours. Her efficiency index is therefore 1.3. Thus, *the higher the index, the more efficient* the learning. Such an index can be calculated for each unit, then averaged for each learner to give an efficiency index for the course.

When the index is calculated on a class basis, the information can be used to evaluate the efficiency both of the learners and of the activities and resources in the instructional program. Subjective decisions must be made for accepting the level of an efficiency index or recognizing the need to raise the index through revision of activities and materials.

Faculty and Staff Required

The number of faculty and staff positions required for instruction, supervision, or support of an instructional program also relates to efficiency. The question is, "How many learners are being served by the staff?" If a course requires a half-time faculty position plus the equivalent of one full-time position in assistants and technicians to serve 48 learners, then the faculty/learner ratio would be 1:32 (1.5:48). If the institution-wide ratio of faculty-to-student load is 1:20, then this higher ratio indicates a more efficient use of faculty and staff personnel.

The above ratio of 1:32 may be reported on paper, but the actual working time of faculty and staff in the program can give another indication of efficiency. Let us assume that the instructor and support staff indicated above (1.5 positions) are spending 60 hours a week on the program (preparation, teaching, consulting with learners, evaluating performance, marking tests, providing resources, and so forth). If normal time devoted to a course is 45 hours per week for a staff of similar size, then some revision in the procedures may be necessary. Too much time is being spent and this may be considered an inefficiency on a staff-time basis.

Use of Facilities

Another factor of efficiency is the time that learning facilities—classrooms, learning labs, and so forth—are available during a day, a week, or other period of time. If a facility is used for 12 hours a day, this may be considered an efficient use of space. By obtaining these data as a program is expanded, the need to increase use or to provide for additional training space can be evaluated.

A second component of efficient space utilization is the number of learners making use of the facility during a time period. When 110 learners are being served in a 15-station microcomputer lab, on a weekly basis, this may be determined to be an efficient use of space.

Keep records so that the time spent by learners and staff in the program and facility use can be calculated and objectively related to this factor of efficiency.

PROGRAM COSTS

Historically, a major concern in educational programs is the cost of instruction. The establishment of expense categories such as personnel, equipment, and supplies, is designed to aid the administration in the control and reporting of programs. Standard bases that are frequently used for allocating funds in educational budgets are average daily attendance (ADA) in public schools, full-time equivalent (FTE, meaning the number of students equated for taking a full course load) in higher education, the number of faculty assigned in terms of FTE, and student credit hours or student/faculty contact hours. These bases for allocating funds are mainly accounting methods. They provide little information about the real costs of a single program.

Although a school or college is not the same as a business operation, for both we can identify specific factors affecting costs which can be controlled. The literature on education and training contains numerous explanations and reports on how program costs can be derived. Formulas that consider many of the variables which affect costs are presented in detail and their complexities are interpreted. Such terms as cost effectiveness, cost efficiency, and cost benefits are frequently used. Our concern here is to simply answer the question, "What does it cost to develop and operate a specific program for the number of learners served?" Once we have this essential information, we are able to relate costs to effectiveness, efficiency, and resulting benefits, and thus be able to judge the acceptibility of program costs.

Any new course, or a program being revised, requires attention to the two major categories of costs: **developmental** and **operational.**

Developmental Costs

As an instructional project is being planned and developed, some or all of the following costs may be incurred. They are sometimes called "start-up costs":

- Planning time (percentage of salary for time spent by each member of the planning team on the project, or number of hours spent by each member, multiplied by his or her hourly or monthly salary rate, and fees for consultants)
- Staff time (percentage of salary for time spent by each member engaged in planning and production and in gathering materials, or the number of hours spent by each person, multiplied by his or her hourly salary rate)
- Supplies and materials for preparing print and audiovisual materials
- Outside services for producing or purchasing materials
- Construction or renovation of facilities
- Equipment purchased for instructional uses
- Expenses for installing equipment

- Testing, redesign, and final reproduction of resources in sufficient quantity for operational uses (includes personnel time and costs of materials and services)
- Orientation and training of personnel who will conduct instruction
- Indirect costs (personnel benefits such as retirement and insurance, related to time and salary charged to project; this information available from personnel department)
- Overhead (utilities, furniture, room and building costs or depreciation allowance, proportion of other institutional services changed to project; this information available from business manager or controller of organization)
- Miscellaneous (office supplies, telephone, travel)

Here is an example of the *developmental costs* for a college-level instructional program.

Planning time		
3 people (2 instructors, 1 designer–media specialist), 2 weeks summer @ $1,500		$4,500
Staff time		
Librarian, 1 week summer	$ 600	
Graphic artist/photographer/audio technician @ $12 per hour	1,440	
Secretary, 2 weeks @ $375	750	
		$2,790
Supplies and materials		
Graphic/photo	$ 500	
Audiotape cassettes	75	
Printing guides	200	
Outside services		
Film processing and duplication	$ 500	
Other supplies	300	
		$ 800
Renovating facilities		
Constructing study carrels in lab		$ 600
Equipment		
Ten slide/tape units @ $350		$3,500
Testing and redesign		
Three people, 1 day @ $150	$ 450	
Staff time, 40 hours @ $10	400	
Materials	200	
		$1,050
Orientation for instructional staff		
Three assistants, 6 hours @ $8		$ 144
Indirect costs		
Staff benefits		$2,100
Overhead		
Planning and production facilities		$ 300
Miscellaneous		
Office supplies, car travel		$ 200
Total developmental costs		$16,759

Operational Costs

When the project is fully implemented and instruction is taking place, the recurring operational costs include the following:

- Administrative salaries (based on percentage of time devoted to project)
- Faculty salaries for the time spent in the program (contact hours with groups and individual learners, planning activities, evaluating program, revising activities and materials, personnel benefits)
- Learner or trainee costs (applicable in business-oriented training programs—salary, travel lodging, income for company reduced while trainee not on job, or replacement cost of person substituting for trainee in job)
- Salaries for assistants, maintenance technicians, and others
- Rental charges for classroom or other facilities
- Replacement of consumable and damaged materials
- Repair and maintenance of equipment
- Depreciation of equipment
- Overhead (utilities, facilities, furnishings, custodial services)
- Evaluating and updating materials (time and materials)

Here is an example of the *operational costs* for the college-level course developed above, over a one-semester term:

Administrative salary		
One instructor, 0.20 time @ $14,000	$ 2,800	
Benefits	950	
		$ 3,750
Instructor salaries		
Two instructors, 0.50 time @ $12,000	$12,000	
Benefits	4,000	
		$16,000
Staff salaries		
Assistants, 300 hours @ $10	$ 3,000	
Librarian, 0.20 time @ $10,000	2,000	
Benefits	1,750	
		$ 6,750
Replacements		$ 400
Repair		$ 200
Overhead		$ 500
Updating materials		
Labor 40 hours @ $12	$ 480	
Materials	100	
		$ 580
Total operating cost		**$28,180**

Instructional Cost Index

An attempt at judging whether the costs of an instructional program are acceptable cannot be made by looking solely at the gross amount expended. If it costs a company $1000 to manufacture pencils, this sum must be related to the number of pencils made. Then the price per pencil has meaning and can be compared with the price per unit manufactured by other companies. In an instructional program, costs should be related to the number of learners served in the program.

With data available on developmental and operational costs, we can calculate the cost per learner for a program. This is the important "bottom line" amount which allows for comparison of costs between programs leading to the acceptance of expense levels. Cost per learner or trainee may be labeled an **instructional cost index.** It is determined by the following procedure:

1. Spread the developmental costs over a series of time periods (for example—ten training sessions or five semesters). This would be the anticipated life of the program before it should require major revisions or cease to be useful. This procedure is known as "amortizing" the cost.
2. Add together the above prorated amount of the developmental costs (one-fifth for a five-semester life) and the operational costs for one use period (a complete training class or an academic semester).
3. Determine the average number of learners known or anticipated to be in the program with each use. Divide the total in number 2, above, by this number. The result is the cost per learner or the *instructional cost index.*

An example of an instructional cost index calculated from previous developmental and operational costs:

Total operational costs	$28,180
Portion of developmental cost (one-fifth of 16,759)	3,352
Total cost per semester	$31,532
Number of learners in program—116	
Instructional cost index ($31,532 ÷ 116)	$ 271.83

(This is the total cost for each of the 116 learners over one semester.)

If this program continues beyond five semesters (at which time all developmental costs will have been amortized) and the number of learners remains the same, the instructional cost index will then drop to $242.93 ($28,180 ÷ 116). During this period limited funds are included for minor updating and revision of materials. At the end of five semesters a reexamination of the program for this course may be advisable. The course then may be continued as is, or new developmental costs—hopefully lower than the original ones—would be required. These would affect the ongoing instructional cost index.

The index number itself has little meaning. Calculations could be made in the same way for traditional program costs in a comparable training or subject area. As previously stated, it is difficult (and usually unfair) to make a comparison between a new program with carefully structured objectives and a traditional program based on generalized objectives. It would seem more appropriate to compare two skill-type training programs, two math classes, or a biology and chemistry course if each one has been systematically planned and implemented.

Once an instructional cost index has been calculated, we can ask these questions:

- Is the program *cost effective?*
  Answer: Relate the instructional cost index to the level of learning outcomes (example—90 percent of the learners accomplish 84 percent of the objectives). If a satisfactory learning level is reached and the instructional cost index seems to be within reason, the program would be considered cost effective.
- Is the program *cost efficient?*
  Answer: Relate the instructional cost index to efficiency factors (time required by learners to complete activities, staff time required for instruction and support, level of facilities use). If the efficiency index is acceptable, with a reasonable instructional cost index, the program would be cost efficient.
- Are the costs justified in terms of resulting benefits (*cost/benefit analysis*)?
  Answer: Relate the instructional cost index to the benefits that a company or other organization derives from personnel who complete the training program. (See the following section for details and discussion of potential benefits resulting from training.) If the benefits are high and costs acceptable, then the question can be answered in a positive way.

If the outcomes of a program prove to be acceptable, but the instructional cost index remains *higher* than desired, certain steps might be taken to lower the operational cost portion of the index, as follows:

- Include more learners in the program. This will increase the denominator of the formula.
- Decide whether there are activities for which assistants might replace instructors *without reducing the effectiveness of the program.* This would reduce the higher cost of instructor time.
- Plan to relieve instructors of some learner-contact time by developing additional self-paced learning activities for learners.
- As a last resort, reduce the training time or lower some of the required performance standards. A shorter instructional time would reduce instructor time and thus costs.

SUBJECTIVE MEASURES OF PROGRAM RESULTS

There are many nonquantitative outcomes of an instructional program which need attention during summative evaluation. These include gathering reactions from both learners and the instructional staff as they look back on the program just completed. Three categories of reactions may be given attention:

- *Opinions*—judgments about the level of acceptance of course content, instructional methods, assistance from and relations with instructor and staff, study or work time required, grading procedure, and so forth.
- *Interest*—responses to the value of topics treated, learning activities preferred, and motivation for further study or work in the subject area.
- *Attitude*—reactions to the total program in terms of degree of its being pleasurable, worthwhile, and useful.

During consideration of the evaluation element in the instructional design process (Chapter 11), attention was given to evaluating objectives in the affective domain—attitudinal objectives. Similar methods of developing and using questionnaires, rating scales, and interviews can be applied during summative evaluation. Now, instead of gathering responses for a single topic or unit, you would be interested in asking for participant reactions in order to determine the degree of acceptance of the entire program and its success in their view.

Here are examples of types of questions for gathering subjective reactions:

Checklist

Check each word that tells how you feel about the group projects and oral presentations used in this course.

____ Interesting	____ Informative	____ Difficult
____ Dull	____ Practical	____ Important
____ Exciting	____ Worthless	____ Stimulating
____ Boring	____ Useful	____ Unpleasant

Rating scale

The format used in this experimental class was (check one)

____ more   ____ less   ____ about equally

demanding in terms of study time and energy required of learners as compared with lecture–demonstration classes of the conventional type.

Which statement best describes your feeling about the course now, at the end of the semester? (check one)

____ I still don't like history.

____ I don't care much about history, one way or another.

____ I feel more positive about studying history now than I did when the course started.

____ I have gotten a lot out of the course and now enjoy studying history.

Ranking

Please rank these topics as treated in the *Management* course. Consider their value to you and your job. (Start with number 1 as low.)

____Planning	____Organization and management
____Self-assessment	development
____Stress	____Personnel management
____Labor relations	____Performance appraisal
____Effective presentations	____Internal affairs management
____Budgeting	____Media relations
	____State-of-the-art technology

Semantic differential

I found the quality of the feedback I received from the instructor concerning my work and how I might improve to be:

Not good
at all   1   2   3   4   5   6   7   8   9   Excellent

Open-ended questions

What is your general reaction to this course—the objectives treated, the way it was conducted, your participation, its overall value to you, and so on?

EVALUATION OF FOLLOWUP BENEFITS

There are three general reasons for which instructional programs are most often offered:

- To "educate" individuals so they may participate as informed, cultured, and productive citizens in society
- To prepare individuals for a vocation and gainful employment
- To improve or upgrade competencies of individuals in a specific task or in certain aspects of a job

For each of the above reasons, determining the success of an instructional program requires attention to important outcomes beyond the results of written and performance tests given at the end of a unit or a course. Often the accomplishment of major goals or terminal objectives stated for a program can be assessed only sometime after instruction is concluded.

This can be a complex phase of summative evaluation for a number of reasons. After a course is completed, the learners or trainees move to other courses or work at different locations. Observations of them at work or communication with them may require an extra effort. Some important outcomes are in the affective domain. These may be difficult to identify and measure. Responses for evaluation may be needed from other persons (colleagues, supervisors, and others) who may not be understanding or cooperative. Regardless of these obstacles, attempts should be made to follow up learners after an instructional program has ended. Evidence of followup benefits could be the most important summative results to measure.

Educational Programs

Traditionally, the general, longterm benefits of educational programs are measured through statewide and national standardized tests given to students in public schools; college students take undergraduate and graduate admission examinations; and regional or national opinion surveys are conducted at various times. Such tests measure broad, fairly general objectives. There has been little attempt to examine the longterm outcomes of the objectives of specific courses in other than a casual fashion. Within the framework of the goals and terminal objectives of a program, the following categories of outcomes can be examined concerning learners:

- Capabilities in basic skills (reading, writing, verbal expression, mathematics), as required in following courses
- Knowledge and competencies in a subject as bases for study in subsequent courses
- Proficiencies to carry out job tasks and responsibilities in occupational employment
- Fulfillment of roles as good citizens (law abiding, participating in democratic process, etc.)

As indicated at the beginning of this section, data concerning these outcomes are not easy to obtain. The commonly used methods to gather information are:

- *Completing questionnaires.* Ask former students, present instructors, or employers to respond to a questionnaire designed to indicate learners' present proficiencies as related to competencies derived from the course or program being evaluated.
- *Conducting interviews.* Meet with former learners, present instructors, or employers to inquire about the present proficiencies of learners as related to competencies from the courses or programs being evaluated.
- *Making observations.* Observe learners in new learning or performance situations and judge their capabilities as a followup of competencies acquired in course being evaluated.
- *Examining records.* Check grades and anecdotal records of former students in school files to ascertain how they are now performing in their classes as based on competencies gained in the course being evaluated. (*Note:* Because of privacy laws, this procedure may require permission from the former students before records can be made available.)

These procedures are most helpful for obtaining data about capabilities in basic skills, knowledge and competencies in a subject, and proficiency in job tasks. It is particularly difficult to find means for judging general behaviors such as fulfilling roles as good citizens. Indirect measures, like statistics on juvenile delinquency for the student population in a geographic area and voting records of younger citizens can prove of value.

Training Programs

A training program within a business concern, an industrial company, a health agency, or other organization usually has clearly defined outcomes to be accomplished. These planned results may have initially been identified when a *learning needs assessment* (Chapter 3) was first made. The consequent benefits are expected to result in improved job performance and often can be translated into dollar savings or increased income for the company.

There are three areas which may need attention in posttraining evaluation:

Appropriateness of the training   Although the program was developed according to identified needs, changes in on-the-job operating procedures and in the equipment used could necessitate different job performance from what was taught. Determine whether modifications are required before training is to be conducted the next time.

Competencies of employees   It is one thing to pass written tests and to perform satisfactorily in the controlled environment of a classroom or laboratory, but potentially different to be successful in transferring the learning to a job situation. Determine how well the former trainees now perform the job or tasks they were trained to do.

Benefits to the organization   The advantages need to be measured in terms of the payoff to the organization as well as to the individual. These are some of the criteria which indicate that a training program has been beneficial to the organization:

- Increased safety through reduced number of accidents
- Increased service abilities including both quality of work and speed of performance
- Improved quality of products being produced
- Increased rate of work or production
- Reduced problems with equipment due to malfunctions and breakdowns
- Increased sales of products and greater services, or more income being generated (referred to as "return on training investment")

With respect to affective-type outcomes, the following may be some of the expected results:

- Less employee tardiness and absenteeism
- Less employee turnover on jobs
- Greater job satisfaction
- Higher level of motivation and willingness to assume responsibilities
- Increased respect for the organization

The same methods for gathering information as described for educational programs would apply to measuring the followup benefits of a training program. These include questionnaires, interviews, observations, and examining records. In terms of actual performance levels, if careful records are kept, comparisons can be made between pretraining and posttraining competencies. A key method of followup evaluation can be related to reduction in expenses or greater revenue generated for the company. This requires a comparison of pretraining cost factors with the costs and income data determined at a reasonable time after training is completed. This evidence can be one of the best measures to relate training benefits to the "bottom line" with which a company is most concerned.

REPORTING RESULTS OF SUMMATIVE EVALUATION

The final step that needs to be taken is to prepare a report of the summary evaluation results for others to read and examine. Careful attention should be given to this activity. Future support for the program, as well as the assistance required for additional instructional design projects, can be influenced by the manner in which a summary evaluation is reported.

First, decide for whom the report is to be prepared—administrators/ training manager, instructors, another supporting agency, or whoever. By considering those persons who are to receive the report, emphasis or special attention may have to be given to certain phases of the summative evaluation. Explaining how and where funds have been spent may be of primary interest, or evidence of followup benefits may be of more value than are the efficiencies or effectiveness of instruction.

Second, decide on the format of the report. Should it be on paper for individual reading, or will it be presented to a group with the support of slides or overhead transparencies? In either case, plan to report results attractively. Remember, not everyone would be as highly interested or as well informed about the project as you have been over a period of time. Here are some suggestions:

- Give the report an interesting title:
  Students Respond Positively to New Art History Course; Production Rate Increases 15 Percent After Training of Line Supervisors
- Summarize highlights so the key outcomes can be grasped quickly. Do this by setting them off on a page with white space or with lines forming a box around each statement.
- Describe supporting data in visual ways with graphs rather than as detailed tables; use cartoonlike art work as appropriate.
- If slides or transparencies will be prepared, limit the information on film to only the key points. Prepare printed materials that correlate with the visuals and contain the details of information for the audience to retain.
- End by making appropriate recommendations for continuing, extending, modifying, or terminating the program.

REVIEW AND APPLICATIONS*

A. Recall

1. What does the expression *summative evaluation* mean? How does it differ from *formative evaluation*?

_____
_____
_____

2. What *five* matters should receive attention in summative evaluation?

   a. _____
   _____
   _____

   b. _____
   _____
   _____

   c. _____
   _____
   _____

   d. _____
   _____
   _____

   e. _____
   _____
   _____

3. Which statements relate to:
   a. Effectiveness
   b. Efficiency
   _____ *(1)* Time for students to complete study
   _____ *(2)* Results of test scores and project ratings
   _____ *(3)* Level of learner accomplishment of learning objectives
   _____ *(4)* Amount of use that is made of rooms
   _____ *(5)* Number of staff assigned to a course

4. What are the two categories of program costs?

   a. _____
   _____
   _____

   b. _____
   _____

5. Explain how an *instructional cost index* is calculated.

_____
_____
_____

6. Select the statement that relates to these concepts:
   a. Cost efficient
   b. Cost effective
   c. Cost/benefit analysis
   _____ *(1)* Relating an instructional cost index to changes in employee performance after training

*See answers on page 275.

_____ *(2)* Relating an instructional cost index to length of time required for a training program

_____ *(3)* Relating an instructional cost index to level of learning by learners at end of training

7. Which of the following are feasible procedures in order to *reduce* a *too-high* instructional cost index?

_____ *a.* Reduce instructor time by using more self-paced learning for students

_____ *b.* Drop learners from the program who are failing

_____ *c.* Increase the length of time a program is offered

_____ *d.* Enter more learners in the program

_____ *e.* Require the accomplishment of fewer objectives by learners

8. What are *three* measurement instruments that may be used to gather information on attitudes and opinions about a course?

a. _____

_____

_____

b. _____

_____

_____

c. _____

_____

_____

9. What are *three* techniques which may be used for gathering information when following up learners after the conclusion of an educational program?

a. _____

_____

_____

b. _____

_____

_____

c. _____

_____

_____

10. When you plan to evaluate the results of a training program in an organization, what *three* areas might you examine?

a. _____

_____

_____

b. _____

_____

_____

c. _____

_____

_____

11. What are *five* potential benefits to an organization as the result of personnel training?

a. _____

_____

_____

b. _____
_____
_____

c. _____
_____
_____

d. _____
_____
_____

e. _____
_____
_____

12. When reporting the results of a summative evaluation, what *three* things can be done to attract interest and make the report attractive?

a. _____
_____
_____

b. _____
_____
_____

c. _____
_____
_____

B. Comprehension and Application

1. What is your reaction to the position taken by the author that "program evaluation does not require formal research procedures?"

_____
_____
_____

2. What is the *effectiveness* of instruction for this group?

Student	Objectives Satisfied (total = 10)
1	7
2	9
3	6
4	8
5	8
6	9
7	7
8	10

3. If the above were the results for an academic program, would you most likely accept them as effective?

_____
_____
_____

4. Determine the efficiency index for each learner:

	Time to complete
Learner	*10 required objectives*
1	4.5 hours
2	6.2 hours
3	6.8 hours

5. In question 4, which student's learning was *most efficient?*

_____

_____

_____

6. Determine the *instructional cost index* from these data:

Program development costs	$12,420
Operational costs (1 class)	9,580
Anticipated program use	6 times
Learners in program, each class	40

Instructional cost index: _____

7. What measuring instrument or other data-gathering method might you use to collect information for each of the following?

_____ **a.** To have learners indicate on a list, from the most to the least beneficial activities, they participated in during the course.

_____ **b.** At the end of a school year following a course you wish to evaluate, to check on students' grades in the following courses.

_____ **c.** To determine from employers at distant locations their reactions to abilities of your former students.

_____ **d.** To have learners express themselves about their opinions of the course.

_____ **e.** To determine from employers at nearby locations their reactions to abilities of former students.

_____ **f.** To have learners select from a list of statements the one that indicates their feelings about a certain aspect of the course.

_____ **g.** To have learners indicate their preferences for any of a series of adjectives that describe how a course impressed them.

REFERENCES

Program Evaluation

Berchin, Ervin. *Toward Increased Efficiency in Community Junior College Courses* (Los Angeles: League for Innovation in the Community College, 1972).

Davies, Ivor. *Objectives in Curriculum Design* (New York: McGraw-Hill, 1976), 90.

DeCecco, John P., and William R. Crawford. *The Psychology of Learning and Instruction,* 2d ed. (Englewood Cliffs, NJ: Prentice-Hall, 1974), 275.

Diamond, Robert M., and Richard R. Sedweeks. "A Comprehensive Approach to Course Evaluation." *Journal of Instructional Development,* 4 (Fall 1980), 28–34.

Dick, Walter. "Summative Evaluation," in *Instructional Design: Principles and Applications,* Leslie J. Briggs ed. (Englewood Cliffs, NJ: Educational Technology Publications, 1977), 337–348.

Mezoff, Bob. "Pre-Then-Post Testing: A Tool to Improve the Accuracy of Management Training Program Evaluation," *NSPI Journal,* 20 (October 1981), 10–11,16.

Morris, Lynn Lyons, and Carol Taylor Fitz-Gibbon. *How to Measure Achievement* (Beverly Hills, CA: Sage, 1978).

Smith, Marty, and Al Corbett. "Basic Goals in Evaluating Post-Training," *NSPI Journal,* 15 (September 1976), 12.

Stufflebeam, Daniel L., et al. *Educational Evaluation and Decision Making* (Bloomington, IN: Phi Delta Kappa, 1971).

Tuckman, Bruce Wayne. *Evaluating Instructional Programs* (Boston, Allyn and Bacon, 1979).

Wilkinson, Gene L. *Media in Instruction: 60 Years of Research* (Washington, DC: Association for Educational Communications and Technology, 1980), 11.

Program Costs

Beilby, Albert. "Determining Instructional Costs Through Functional Cost Analysis," *Journal of Instructional Development,* 3 (Winter 1979–80), 29–34.

Doughty, Philip L. "Cost-Effectiveness Analysis Trade-Offs and Pitfalls for Planning and Evaluating Instructional Programs," *Journal of Instructional Development,* 2 (Summer 1979), 17–25.

Doughty, Philip L., Richard Lent, and Albert Beilby. *Cost-Effectiveness Analysis and Instructional Technology* (Syracuse, NY: ERIC Clearinghouse on Information Resources, Syracuse University, 1978).

Head, Glenn, and Charles C. Buchanan. "Cost/Benefit Analysis of Training: A Foundation for Change," *NSPI Journal,* 20 (November 1981), 25–27.

Kearsley, Greg. *Costs, Benefits, and Productivity in Training Systems* (Menlo Park, CA: Addison-Wesley, 1982).

Klein, Jerry, and Philip L. Doughty. "Cost-Effectiveness Evaluation: A Case Study of an Innovative Program in Higher Education," *Journal of Instructional Development,* 3 (Spring 1980), 19–24.

Lent, R. "A Model for Applying Cost-Effectiveness Analysis," *Journal of Instructional Development,* 3 (Fall 1979), 26–32.

Levin, Henry M. *Cost-Effectiveness: A Primer* (Beverly Hills, CA: Sage, 1983).

Nance, John B. "Operations Research Analysis of Audio-Tutorial Systems," *Educational Technology,* 13 (June 1973), 64–72.

Smith, Marty, and Al Corbett. "Pricing the Benefits of Training," *NSPI Journal,* 16 (April 1977), 16–18.

Wilkinson, Gene L. "Cost Evaluation of Instructional Strategies," *AV Communication Review,* 21 (Spring 1973) 11–29.

———. *Educational Media, Technology and Instructional Productivity: A Consideration of Cost and Effectiveness* (Syracuse, NY: ERIC Clearinghouse on Information Resources, Syracuse University, 1980).

appendix *A*

Review and Applications Answers

CHAPTER 1 (PAGE 5)

A. Recall
  1. a. Student acquires knowledge, skills, and attitudes to perform productively
    b. Program has reasonable costs and requires reasonable time
    c. Meaningful and interesting experiences for students who have desire to continue with studies
    d. Satisfactory experiences for faculty and staff
  2. a. Systems approach—a problem-solving procedure that is based on the method of scientific inquiry and that takes into consideration all factors essential to accomplishing the goal
    b. Instructional technology—(1) hardware and software as resources for instruction; (2) process of systematic instructional planning
    c. Instructional development—management of personnel and services within an organization to improve instruction
    d. Instructional design process—application of a systematic planning procedure
  3. a, b, d, f, g, j, k.
B. Comprehension
  1. a. A successful instructional situation may be evidenced by
        —A well-planned course (you were informed as to what was required of you, information was presented logically and clearly, you were tested on what was presented, and so forth)
        —You were successful in your learning and you probably received satisfaction and a degree of pleasure in the work you did
        —The instructor took an interest in you, challenged you intellectually, and made your efforts worthwhile

b. An unsuccessful instructional situation may be evidenced by
—A course that seems to have had little planning or organization (you did not know what was required, presentations were confusing and rambling, time was wasted, your participation was not encouraged, testing may have varied from what was seemingly required or presented)
—The instructor was only casually interested in students, requiring only rote learning, and may have offered little of practical value
(*Note:* Your answers for (a) and (b) may include other facts, but the intent should include at least some of the points made above.)

2. Refer to answers for questions A.1)
   a. (d)   *e.* (b)
   b. (c)   *f.* (d)
   c. (a)   *g.* (a)
   d. (c)
3. *a.* Instructional development
   b. Resources for instruction (hardware and software)
   c. Instructional design process

CHAPTER 2 (PAGE 19)

A. Recall
1. *a.* Student characteristics   *c.* Teaching/learning methods
   b. Learning objectives   *d.* Learning evaluation
2. *a.* Learning needs, goals, priorities, and constraints
   b. Topics, tasks, purposes
   c. Subject content/task analysis
   d. Instructional resources
   e. Support services
   f. Pretesting
3. Revision: To change the content or treatment of any elements of the plan when shown to be weak through tryout or use of the instructional plan.
4. *a.* Has no specific starting point
   b. Elements may be skipped
   c. Elements may be applied in any order
5. Linear
6. Instructional design (or instructional development)
7. *a.* CRI—criterion-referenced instruction
   b. ISD—instructional systems design
   c. LSD—learning systems design
   d. CBI—competency-based instruction
8. *a.* True   *d.* False   *f.* True
   b. False   *e.* False   *g.* True
   c. False
9. *a.* It discourages creativity in teaching.
   b. It is a mechanistic rather than a humanistic approach to instruction.
10. *a.* Training   *c.* Education   *e.* Training
    b. Training   *d.* Education   *f.* Both
11. *a.* Instructional designer   *c.* Subject specialist
    b. Instructor or teacher   *d.* Evaluator
12. Asking questions.

B. Comprehension
  1. Reader's choice
  2. a. 2   *d.* 7   *f.* 5   *h.* 3
     b. 4 or 6   *e.* 1   *g.* 6   *i.* 1
     c. 1
  3. a. Apply elements of planning in whatever order, as desired or necessary. When developing an element, consider various approaches or content treatment that can be suggested or included. Select activities for objectives that are unusual; give students a choice of activities, and allow them to express their own creativity.
     b. Consider various factors concerning individual student or group characteristics and their impact on other planning elements. Develop a program with emphasis on individual, self-paced learning.
  4. Reader's choice.
  5. Reader's choice.
  6. a. Consider learning characteristics early in planning. Relate subject content selection and activities to interests of students; provide variety of activities for motivation. Allow students to know how they are progressing with their learning; provide remedial help; all activities contribute to success with teacher's tests.
     b. Specify learning and performance to be attained. Give major emphasis to content and procedures of selling. Learner performance in selling (through role-playing experiences) should reach acceptable proficiency level before conclusion of course.

CHAPTER 3 (PAGE 30)

A. Recall
  1. a. Find out what is going on in your area of concern or interest.
     b. Decide what should be happening and match data collected against this goal. The difference may justify a new or revised instructional program.
  2. See list on page 26.
  3. See list on page 27.
  4. a. Internal procedures
       See list on page 28.
     b. External procedures
       See list on page 28.
  5. Learning needs assessment or analysis.
  6. a. If an instructional course or training program is warranted, state a general goal.
     b. Consider constraints and priorities that may be appropriate.
  7. a. Goal statement
     b. Learning objective (Chapter 7)
     c. General purpose for a task (Chapter 4)
     d. Goal statement
     e. Goal statement
     f. Not an appropriate statement . . . more like a direction

B. Comprehension
   Situation 1:
   1. Lack of necessary action by employees
      Comments on evaluation forms
      Informal remarks by employees
   2. Yes, since a need for training is strongly indicated.
   3. Comments by district managers
      Observations at staff meetings conducted by supervisors
   4. Yes; similar problem encountered in another company and the effectiveness of a training program
   5. For department supervisors to conduct staff meetings more effectively in a shorter period of time.
   6. None
   Situation 2:
   1. Yes, a learning needs assessment has been made.
   2. The need for a new course in *technical writing* is supported with this evidence:
      a. Survey among companies gives positive results.
      b. Recommended by English department curriculum committee.
      c. Deans of Business and Engineering indicate value of course as elective for students.
      d. Engineering would consider making it a required course for some majors.
   3. To show how specialized subject content can be treated for writing technical reports and other documents. (Other answers with similar intent are acceptable.)
   4. Have course ready for tryout next summer.
      Obtain developmental funds from a foundation.
   Situation 3:
   This may not be a problem that requires a training solution. It would be advisable to talk with the hospital administrator, explaining the supervisor's comments. Administrative decisions might alleviate much of the problem. After this action, depending upon results, training may be reconsidered.

C. Applications
   1. *Sky Diving*
      a. Establishing a need for justification of training
         (1) Through a survey and interviews, determine if there is an interest among members of flying clubs or other groups for training in sky diving.
         (2) Determine from examining medical statistics where there may be an excessive number of accidents in sky diving. If so, the benefits of training might be proposed in a community or even to a state legislature so that anyone wanting to engage in the sport might first be required to complete a training course (as is required for a first-aid or life-saving certificate).
      b. Goal: This training course is for persons interested in becoming proficient in the sport of sky diving. Attention will be given to basic and advanced procedures as well as to safety practices, so you may enjoy the sport, knowing you are performing all maneuvers correctly and safely.
      (*Note:* In this application project on sky diving there can very well be other acceptable answers in addition to those listed here and in subsequent chapters. Judge how reasonable is your own answer as you review those suggested here.)
   2. *Your Subject*
      Reader's activity.

CHAPTER 4 (PAGE 41)

A. Recall
   1. Select topics and specify tasks
      State general purposes
   2. *a.* Topic   *e.* Topic
      b. Topic   *f.* Task
      c. Topic/task   *g.* Task
      d. Task   *h.* Topic/task
   3. See list on page 39
   4. For instructor use
      To clarify thinking and indicate generally what is to be learned in topic or task
   5. *a.* Different: Goal statement relates to overall program; general purpose relates
         to specific topic or task.
      b. Similar: Goal statement is a broad, nonspecific statement; general purpose is
         also a broad, nonspecific statement. The same or similar verbs may be used in
         either one to express anticipated learning results.
B. Comprehension
   1. (*Note:* Your answers may vary from those below according to the way you
      perceive the content and treatment for each unit.)
      a. Topic   *e.* Topic/task
      b. Topic   *f.* Task
      c. Task   *g.* Topic
      d. Task   *h.* Topic/task
   2. *a.* Overall view to detailed consideration
      b. Chronological
      c. Simple to complex
   3. *a.* General purpose   *e.* General purpose
      b. Learning objective   *f.* Learning objective
      c. General purpose   *g.* Learning objective
      d. General purpose
C. Applications
   1. *Sky Diving*
      a. Requirements (an introduction)
         Procedures
         Hazards
         Training and practice
      b. Requirements
         Hazards
         Procedures
         Training and practice
      c. *Requirements:* To determine the kind of person who might become interested
         in sky diving. *Hazards:* To become aware of the procedural and physical
         hazards that must be faced when sky diving. *Procedure:* To learn the free fall
         positions and maneuvers common in sky diving. *Training and practice:* To
         become proficient in the skills of sky diving.
   2. *Your Subject*
      a. Topics and tasks (reader's activity).
      b. General purposes (reader's activity).

CHAPTER 5 (PAGE 53)

A. Recall
  1. a. Academic information
       (Check page 46)
     b. Personal and social characteristics
       (Check page 47)
  2. a. (1) True   *b. (1)* False   *c. (1)* True
        (2) True   *(2)* False   *(2)* False
        (3) True   *(3)* True   *(3)* True
        (4) False   *(4)* True   *(4)* False
        (5) False   *(5)* True   *(5)* False
                                              (6) True
  3. Cognitive style mapping is a method of diagnosing the approach an individual
     prefers to take when engaging in a learning activity.
     This procedure can identify an individual's learning style and assist both the
     instructor and learner to choose a satisfactory method for accomplishing the
     learning most conveniently.

B. Comprehension
  1. (1) e   *(6)* b   *(11)* b
     (2) a   *(7)* a   *(12)* e
     (3) b   *(8)* b   *(13)* c
     (4) c   *(9)* e   *(14)* a
     (5) d   *(10)* c
  2. (1) a   *(4)* b
     (2) b   *(5)* b
     (3) a   *(6)* a and b
  3. (1) d   *(6)* a   *(11)* c   *(16)* e
     (2) b   *(7)* c   *(12)* d   *(17)* a
     (3) c   *(8)* c   *(13)* a   *(18)* e
     (4) d   *(9)* b   *(14)* b   *(19)* e
     (5) b   *(10)* e   *(15)* d   *(20)* a

C. Applications
  1. Sky Diving
     Academic information—educational background (obtain on questionnaire).
     Personal and social characteristics—Age, interest in sky diving, previous experi-
     ence in flying and parachuting (obtain through questionnaire and interviews).
     Health background—general condition, special disabilities or physical problems
     (obtain health report; may require medical examination). *Physical and psycholog-
     ical characteristics*—Physical dexterity, mental attitude, control of self under
     stressful conditions, cooperation with other persons (administer dexterity and
     psychological tests; analyze results with student).
  2. Your Subject
     Reader's activity.

CHAPTER 6 (PAGE 72)

A. Recall
  1. General purpose and learning objectives

2. Teaching/learning activities
   Instructional resources
   Evaluation of learning
3. Robert Gagné
4. *a.* Verbal information   *b.* *(1)* Intellectual skills
         Intellectual skills   *(2)* Verbal information
         Cognitive strategy   *(3)* Intellectual skills
                                (4) Cognitive strategy
                                (5) Verbal information
                                (6) Intellectual skills
5. Diagraming.
6. See description on page 63.
7. *a.* Deductively.
   b. Inductively.
8. While a task analysis gives attention to subject content, it also considers the "doing" part of the skill.
9. Printed references, media, visits to a location.
10. *Detailing*—Listing, in order, all steps or elements that comprise the task. *Flowcharting*—As well as listing all steps, consideration is given to decision points and alternative paths that can be taken for accomplishing the skill.

11. a.

b.

c.

d.

e.

B. Comprehension

1. a, d, e, h, i, j.

2. *a.* Intellectual skill (principle)
d. Intellectual skill (concept)
e. Verbal information
h. Intellectual skill (principle–procedure)
i. Intellectual skill (concept or principle)
j. Verbal information

3. *a.* is *d.* is *g.* cs
b. vi *e.* vi *h.* cs
c. cs *f.* cs *i.* cs

4. Task analysis: *Making a Telephone Call* (In procedural order; * items added.)

 (1) Refer to slip of paper containing person's name and address
 (2) Place telephone book on table for use
 **(3)* Open telephone book
 (4) Locate last name of person on page in alphabetical order
 (5) Locate first name of party
 (6) Point to telephone number beside name
 (7) Write phone number on slip of paper containing person's name
 (8) Close telephone book and return it to storage place
 **(9)* Pick up telephone receiver
 (10) Listen for dial tone
 (11) Dial each of the seven numbers
 (12) Listen for phone ring
 **(13)* Listen for party to answer
 (14) Start conversation

5. (next page)

5. Self-service Gasoline Pumping

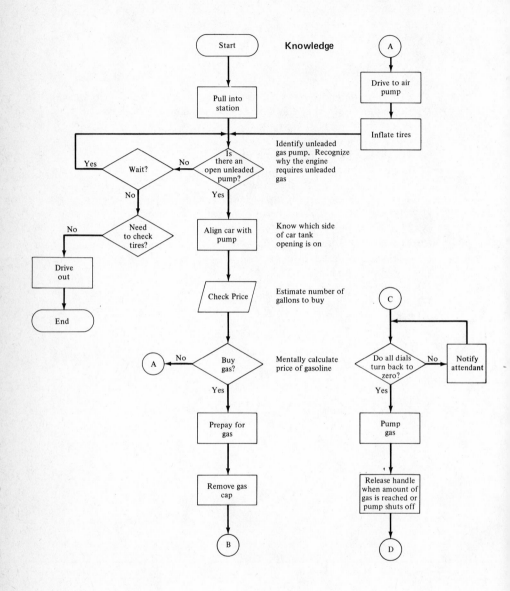

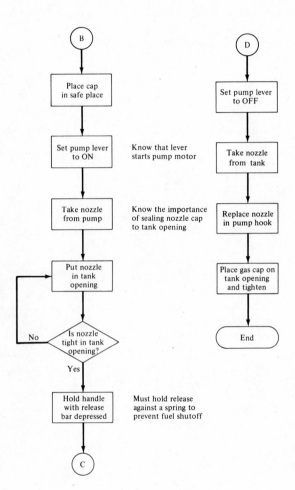

B

Place cap
in safe place

Set pump lever
to ON — Know that lever
starts pump motor

Take nozzle
from pump — Know the importance
of sealing nozzle cap
to tank opening

Put nozzle
in tank
opening

Is nozzle
tight in tank
opening? — No

Yes

Hold handle
with release
bar depressed — Must hold release
against a spring to
prevent fuel shutoff

C

D

Set pump lever
to OFF

Take nozzle
from tank

Replace nozzle
in pump hook

Place gas cap on
tank opening
and tighten

End

C. Applications

    1. *Sky Diving* (Outlines are brief, with only key headings to save space.)

        a. Topic 1: *Requirements*

            A. Reasons for engaging in sky diving

                1. Enjoyment and thrill of errorless performance

                2. Recognition for doing something unusual

                3. Challenge of meeting Nature

            B. Age generally 20 to 30

            C. Mental attitude with panic control

            D. Good muscle tone

        Topic 2: *Procedures*

            A. Achieve stable fall position

                1. Influence of forward speed of aircraft

                2. Overcoming gravity

                    a. Fall rate 16 feet per second each second

                    b. 174 feet per second after 12 seconds

                3. Use resistance to air for descent control and maneuverability

                    a. Body position flat with arms and legs spread

                    b. Clothing a size larger than normal, cotton overalls

            B. Free fall positions

                1. Stable spread—head back, chest raised, and so on

                2. Frog—more comfortable with some stability

                3. Delta—head down attitude for maximum velocity

            C. Maneuvers

                1. Turning (explanation)

                2. Back roll (explanation)

                3. Back roll and front roll combined (explanation)

        Topic 3: *Hazards*

            A. Risk of injury (participation in football 80 times as great)

            B. Improper equipment (seven items)

            C. Lack of observing regulations

            D. Improperly equipped aircraft

            E. Physical hazards

                1. Lack of oxygen at high altitudes

                2. Centrifugal force can cause loss of consciousness

                3. Effects of wind velocity

                4. Body cooling due to low temperature

        b. Task: *Exit Technique*

        Detailing:

        1. Put on training parachute assembly

        2. Hook static line to anchor cable

        3. Shuffle step to doorway

        4. At doorway, position of hands, feet, knees, upper body, head, and eyes

        5. At "go" signal movement of legs up and out

        6. Start of dive—position of knees, toes, head, elbows, upper body

        7. When clear of door—count 1-1000, 2-1000, 3-1000, 4-1000

Flow Charting:

Flow charting   **Content**

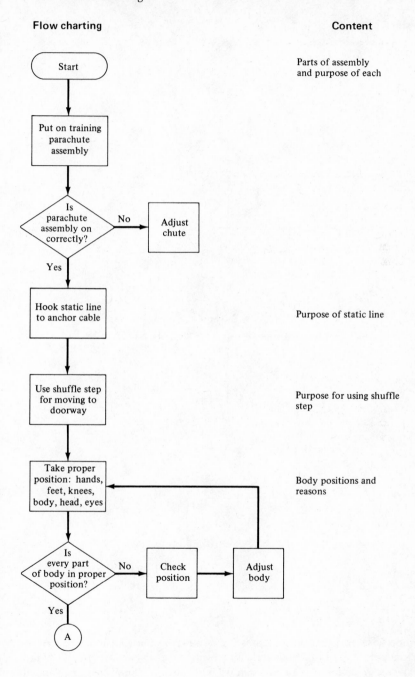

Parts of assembly
and purpose of each

Purpose of static line

Purpose for using shuffle
step

Body positions and
reasons

Flow charting   **Content**

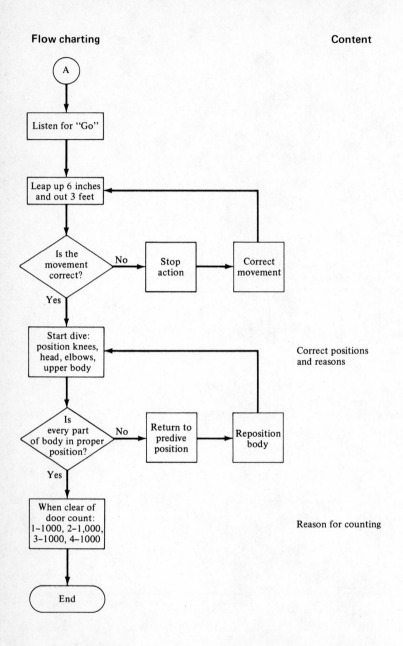

Correct positions
and reasons

Reason for counting

Note: Because each action and movement must be performed exactly right, decision points should be included to evaluate each set of positions and movements. As necessary, a correction or adjustment in action to be performed should be made.

2. *Your Subject*
   Reader's activity.

CHAPTER 7 (PAGE 94)

A. Recall
   1. a. Learners: Lets them know precisely what to do and what to study, and how to prepare for tests
      b. Instructors: Provides basis for selecting instructional activities and resources, and devising tests
   2. a. Cognitive—knowledge, information, thinking, intellectual skills
      b. Psychomotor—Physical activity, motor or muscle skills
      c. Affective—attitudes, appreciations, values
   3. a. Some objectives require learning in more than one domain.
      b. By first giving attention to affective-domain objectives, like creating an interest in a topic, learners can be motivated to become more receptive to pursue cognitive and psychomotor learning activities.
   4. a. Action verb.
      b. Content reference.
   5. a. Performance standard.
      b. Conditions.
   6. a. Approach tendencies—positive behavior by student relative to a subject or situation.
      b. Expressive objectives—important objectives for which outcomes cannot easily be stated.
   7. Grouping objectives in an order according to level of learning behavior required of learners.
   8. a. Terminal/subordinate objectives.
      b. Bloom's taxonomy in the cognitive domain (knowledge, comprehension, application, analysis, synthesis, evaluation).
      c. Gagné's sequence of intellectual skills (facts, concepts, principles, problem solving).

B. Comprehension
   1. a. psychomotor   *f.* cognitive   *k.* psychomotor
      b. affective   *g.* psychomotor   *l.* cognitive
      c. psychomotor   *h.* cognitive   *m.* psychomotor
      d. cognitive   *i.* affective   *n.* cognitive
      e. affective   *j.* cognitive   *o.* cognitive
   2. (d) knowledge   *(l)* knowledge
      (f) higher (comprehension)   *(n)* higher (comprehension)
      (h) higher (evaluation)   *(o)* higher (synthesis)
      (j) higher (application)
   3. to relate   to summarize   to apply
      to compute   to list
   4. a. Acceptable, but desirable to add performance standard, like "8 of 10 problems correct"
      b. OK
      c. OK
      d. Replace verb "express" with more definitive term like "state reasons" or "discuss reasons"; then preferably how many "reasons" are acceptable?
      e. "Compute" a better verb than "master"
      f. OK (affective-domain objective)

   g. OK
   h. Not an objective, an activity
   i. Add performance standard for term "good work habits," like "according to criteria accepted by class"
   j. OK
   k. Replace "demonstrate knowledge of" with measurable verb like "demonstrate" or "explain"
   l. Needs conditions or limitations, like length, format, etc.
   m. More detailed than necessary
   n. OK
   o. Verb may seem too vague, but if a performance standard like "correcting 90 percent of the errors" is added, statement can become acceptable objective
5. *a.* Observed mixing together, conversing, sharing activities, helping one another
   b. Finishes work on time, produces quality products, pleasure in showing work to others; volunteers for additional work
6. *a.* 2   *d.* 3
   b. 1   *e.* 2
   c. 4

C. Applications
   1. *Sky Diving*
      Topic: Requirements.
      Terminal objective: To decide if one is interested in and prepared to engage in sky diving.
      Enabling objectives: (1) To explain the various maneuvers and activities in sky diving. (2) To recognize the mental attitude necessary for becoming a sky diver. (3) To identify the physical abilities necessary for sky diving. (4) To express one's own reason for engaging in sky diving.
      Topic: Procedure.
      Terminal objective: To describe the procedures that must be mastered in successful sky diving.
      Enabling objectives: (1) To describe two aerodynamic principles applied in sky diving. (2) On the ground, to demonstrate three free-fall positions. (3) To explain two basic maneuvers used in sky diving. (4) To explain two advanced maneuvers used in sky diving.

      Topic: Hazards.
      Terminal objective: To describe the seven kinds of hazards which must be overcome for safety in sky diving.
      Enabling objectives: (1) To select seven essential items of equipment. (2) To demonstrate the use of all equipment with 100 percent accuracy. (3) To identify all regulations governing sky diving that must be followed. (4) To list four items that must be provided in an aircraft and their use in sky diving. (5) To recognize at least three atmospheric conditions to avoid.

      Task: Sky diving training and practice.
      Terminal objective: To simulate basic exiting procedures according to established criteria.

Enabling objectives: (1) To dress properly for sky diving. (2) To assemble and prepare to use necessary equipment. (3) To demonstrate correct exit technique with 100 percent accuracy. (4) By using a mock tower, to experience the sensations of falling through space, opening of parachute, and landing safely.
2. *Your Subject*
   Reader's activity.

CHAPTER 8 (PAGE 123)

A. Recall
    1. a. Presentation.
        b. Self-paced learning.
        c. Small-group interaction.
    2. Prelearning—e
       Objectives—a
       Organize content—i
       Individual differences—g
       Motivation—c
       Instructional resources—k
       Participation—l
       Feedback—b
       Reinforcement—d
       Practice—m
       Learning sequence—f
       Application—j
       Instructor's attitude—h

3.	*(1)* e	*(6)* c	*(11)* a	*(16)* d
	(2) b	*(7)* d	*(12)* b	*(17)* e
	(3) a	*(8)* c	*(13)* f	*(18)* b
	(4) f	*(9)* b	*(14)* c	*(19)* d
	(5) a	*(10)* e	*(15)* c	*(20)* d

    4. a. 1   *g.* 1
       b. 2   *h.* 3
       c. 2   *i.* 1
       d. 3   *j.* 1
       e. 2   *k.* 2
       f. 3
    5. a. Active interaction with instructor.
       b. Written work during presentation.
       c. Other mental activity.
    6. a. Self-paced learning—Sequence of required objectives set by instructor; learner may have choice of activities and/or materials to use; all learners move through same program, but at own pace.
       b. Individualized learning—Objectives and learning activities designed for each learner according to individual needs (sometimes called "learner controlled" method); different program for each learner; requires attention to numerous details with use of computer.
    7. a. True   *d.* False
       b. True   *e.* True
       c. False   *f.* True

8. a. 8   *f.* 7   *j.* 7
    b. 6   *g.* 9   *k.* 3
    c. 2   *h.* 8   *l.* 5
    d. 4   *i.* 1   *m.* 3
    e. 5

9. See list on page 117.

10. a. 3   *e.* 4
     b. 6   *f.* 7
     c. 5   *g.* 2
     d. 1   *h.* 1

11. a. What will the instructor do?
     b. What will the learner do?

B. Comprehension

1. a. Instructional resources   *f.* Individual differences   *j.* Reinforcement
    b. Objectives   *g.* Prelearning   *k.* Learning sequence
    c. Feedback   *h.* Practice   *l.* Motivation
    d. Instructor attitude   *i.* Application   *m.* Organize content
    e. Participation

2. a. Self-paced learning   *d.* Presentation
    b. Interaction   *e.* Interaction
    c. Presentation   *f.* Self-paced learning

3. a. Self-instruction book or computer program   *f.* Textbook/worksheets
    b. Audio-tutorial method   *g.* Visuals/guide sheets
    c. Personalized system of instruction   *h.* Audiotape/workbook
    d. Multi-media package   *i.* Self-instructional module
    e. Student contract

4. a. Game   *e.* Panel discussion
    b. Discussion   *f.* Role playing
    c. Case study   *g.* Simulation
    d. Guided design

5. a. 1   *d.* 3
    b. 2   *e.* 3
    c. 1   *f.* 2

C. Applications

1. Sky Diving

Teaching/learning activities *and* resources

Topic: Requirements

Objectives 1, 2, 3:

a. Meet with all 24 learners for introduction to training program. View 10-minute videotape that presents sky diving as an engaging sport and conveys some feeling of those who are active in it. Discuss mental attitude and physical abilities.

b. Observe sky diving demonstration in field.

Objective 4:

Meet with all learners to discuss demonstration along with their reasons for wanting to be sky divers.

Topic: Procedures

Objectives 1, 2, 3, 4:

a. Meet with all learners to view videotape showing free fall positions and maneuvers; learners complete worksheets relating to content and procedures.

b. Divide class into groups of three to practice positions.

Objective 2:
Instructor gives learners self-check exercise on free fall positions, with criteria, so each learner can be judged by another learner.

Topic: Hazards
Objectives 1, 2, 4, 5:
a. Self-paced learning activity with slides/tape and worksheets showing equipment and its use; actual equipment also available; presentation also includes material on aircraft and atmospheric conditions and requires participation on worksheets.
b. Instructor schedules groups of 3 to 4 learners to demonstrate to each other their use of equipment.
Objective 3:
Audiotape and printed regulations studied individually along with worksheet questions and problems for completion.

Task: Training and practice
Objectives 1,2,3,4:
a. Group views videotape on basic procedures for exiting; tape available for individual review.
b. Learners practice dressing and using equipment.
c. Each learner schedules jump from mock tower after instructor demonstration and coaching.
d. Repeated practice for each learner, as necessary.
2. *Your Subject*
Reader's activity.

CHAPTER 9 (PAGE 141)

A. Recall
  1. See list on page 134.
  2. a. (2) Objects and devices
        (3) Models and mock-ups
    b. Audio recordings
        (1) Audiocassette
    c. Nonprojected materials
        (3) Printed paper copies
        (4) Chalkboard and flipchart
        (5) Photographs
    d. (1) Slides
        (2) Filmstrips
        (4) Computer programs
    e. (1) Printed paper/audiotape
        (2) Slides/audiotape
        (5) Interactive computer/videotape or videodisc
    f. Projected motion pictures
        (2) Video recordings

3. *a.* False—Not always; a model or mock-up may be better.
   b. True.
   c. False—printed page.
   d. True.
   e. True.
   f. False—Since pictures are always in order on film, they are not as flexible and cannot be replaced without making a new filmstrip.
   g. True.
   h. False—Being replaced by videotape.
   i. False—Printed paper/audiotape.
   j. True.
   k. True.
4. a, b, d, f, g.
5. *a.* Slides, filmstrip, overhead transparencies.
   b. Video/film or interactive video.
   c. Slide/audiotape or filmstrip/audiotape.
6. a, b, c, e, f.

B. Comprehension
1. *a.* Presentation: (1) Media required? Visual form only? Graphic only? (2) Overhead transparencies.
   b. Self-paced learning: (1) Media required: Audiovisual technique? Motion? (2) Film or video.
   c. Small group interaction: (1) Media required? Simulation activity? (2) Role playing.
   d. Presentation: (1) Media required? Multi-image technique? (2) Slide/slide.
   e. Self-paced learning: (1) Media required? Visual form only? Graphic and photographic combination? Still only? (2) Learning aids.
   f. Self-paced learning: (1) Media required? Audiovisual technique? Still only? (2) Paper/tape.
2. *a.* Small-group interaction—demonstration. Also, self-paced learning—video-tape on equipment.
   b. Presentation—comparison on side-by-side slides (multi-image).
   c. Presentation—overhead transparencies, handout information sheets and self-check quiz for review; may use slide/tape overview of subject highlights for motivation and interest.
   d. Self-paced learning—printed materials with audiotape on law changes; videotape recording or film on new procedures with review questions on paper.
   e. Group interaction—simulation through role playing with followup analysis and discussion.

C. Applications
1. *Sky Diving*
   Instructional resources were selected along with activities in Chapter 8. They include:

   Topic: Requirements
   Objectives 1, 2, 3:
   Videotape for introduction
   Field activity

Topic: Procedures
Objectives 1, 2, 3, 4:
  Videotape showing positions and maneuvers with worksheet

Topic: Hazards
Objectives 1, 2, 4, 5:
  Slides/tape on hazards with worksheet
  Seven items of equipment

Objective 3:
  Audiotape explaining regulations and printed regulations

Task: Training and practice
Objectives 1, 2, 3, 4:
  Videotape on exiting
  Clothing and equipment
  Mock tower facility
2. *Your Subject*
  Reader's activity.

CHAPTER 10 (PAGE 154)

A. Recall
  1. a. Budget   *d.* Equipment
    b. Facilities   *e.* Personnel
    c. Materials   *f.* Time schedule
  2. a. Implementation   *g.* Development
    b. Development   *h.* Implementation
    c. Development   *i.* Development
    d. Implementation   *j.* Development
    e. Development   *k.* Development
    f. Implementation   *l.* Implementation
  3. a. Lecture room or other large-group presentation facility
    b. Self-paced learning study center
    c. Small-group meeting rooms
  4. 80 learners.
  5. Choosing an appropriate resource or form of media to support teaching and learning activities is the purpose of the instructional resource element (Chapter 9). Once the decision has been made, the actual location or preparation of specific items is considered as a support service (Chapter 10).
  6. a. Content outline.   *c.* Script.
    b. Storyboard.   *d.* Final production.
  7. The Audio-Visual Equipment Directory (Fairfax, VA: NAVA (ICIA). Publication available in many libraries and media centers.
  8. a. Media specialist   *h.* Evaluator
    b. Instructor   *i.* Aide
    c. Instructor or subject specialist   *j.* Instructional designer
    d. Instructional designer   *k.* Media technician
    e. Instructor   *l.* Librarian
    f. Media specialist   *m.* Instructor
    g. Instructor or subject content expert   *n.* Evaluator

9. *a.* Planning
   b. Locating and preparing materials
   c. Adapting facilities and installing equipment
   d. Field testing the program
   e. Staff orientation and training
10. Procrastination by putting off assignments and other responsibilities until a later time.

B. Comprehension

Orientation of new employee's problem

1. Materials production costs:

Slides shot on location (26 × .5 hr = 13 hrs @ $20)	$260
Materials (26 × $1)	26
Slides shot in studio (8 × .25 hr = 2 hrs @ $20)	40
Materials (8 × $0.50)	4
Art work 11 pieces (11 × 2 hr = 22 hrs @ $20)	440
Materials (11 × $2)	22
Booklet (15 hrs @ $20)	300
Materials	15
Audio recording (4 hrs @ $25)	100
Materials	10
Total	$1,217

2. Medium selection

(based on material duplication—7 copies to be prepared: 5 for use, 2 spare—and equipment-for-use costs)

a. For slides:

Slides duplicated (63 @ $0.50 = $31.50/set × 7)	$220.50
Slide trays @ $5 × 7	35.00
Equipment @ $500 × 5	2,500.00
Total	$2,755.50

b. For filmstrips:

Master from slides (63 @ $3/frame)	$189.00
Approval prints	25.00
Duplicates (63 @ $0.05/frame = $3.15/set × 7)	22.05
Boxes (7 @ $1)	7.00
Equipment (5 @ $250)	1,250.00
Total	$1,493.05

Filmstrip is the selected medium based on comparable materials costs but much less equipment costs.

3. Filmstrip/audiocassette viewers @ $250 each.

4. Budget

Slide production	$1,217
Filmstrip duplication	250
Filmstrip equipment	1,250
Booklet production	315
Booklet duplication (250 copies @ $2 each)	500
Audio recording	110
Tape duplication	21
Total	$3,663

5. One room with five stations available during working hours. May not require full-time supervisor. A qualified technician (for equipment) and staff member (to answer questions) should be available on call and visit the room periodically.

C. Applications
1. *Sky Diving*
Budget (local production)

Producing 2 videotapes	$500
Slide/tape program	100
Audiotape	10
Printed materials	50
Video equipment	1,200
Slide/tape viewers	1,000
Audiocassette recorders	60
Sky diving equipment	300
Total	$3,220

Facilities
Classroom
Mock tower
Materials
Clothing
Two videotapes
Two sets slide/tape program
Two audiotapes
Printed materials
Equipment
One-half inch videocassette playback and monitor
Two slide/tape viewer units
Two audiocassette recorders
Sky diving equipment
Personnel
Instructor
Assistant
Time Schedule
Requirements—1 hour classroom; 2 hours field
Procedures—2 hours classroom and practice
Hazards—3-day period for individual study
Training and practice—1 week
Learner testing—6 hours classroom
2. *Your Subject*
Reader's activity.

CHAPTER 11 (PAGE 181)

A. Recall
1. a. Written answer.
(1) Short answer.
(2) Essay.
b. Objective type.
(1) Multiple choice.   (3) Matching.
(2) True–False.

2. *a.* False.   *e.* True.
   b. False.   *f.* True.
   c. True.   *g.* False.
   d. True.   *h.* True.

3. *a.* True.
   b. False—Consider constraints before developing test.
   c. True.
   d. False—Also mental skills.
   e. False—A sequence of steps to be checked as performed.
   f. True.
   g. False—Both are important.
   h. True.
   i. True.
   j. False—Also tryout with two to three students.
   k. False—Make anecdotal record.
   l. True.

4. *(1)* a   *(4)* a
   (2) a   *(5)* b
   (3) b   *(6)* a

5. *a.* Student may give desired answer rather than one that expresses true feelings.
   b. Attitude may not be evident until some time after program has ended.

6. *a.* Questionnaire.
   b. Rating scale.
   c. Observation.
   d. Interview.

7. Norm-referenced.

8. Criterion-referenced.

9. Competency-based.
   Performance-based.
   Mastery learning.

10. *a.* False   *e.* True
    b. True   *f.* True
    c. False   *g.* False
    d. True   *h.* True

11. *a.* True.   *e.* True.
    b. False—Should have more test items. *f.* True.
    c. True.   *g.* False—Ensures validity.
    d. False—Important in reliability.   *h.* False—Relates objectives to learning ▶

12. *(1)* Measure student learning
    (2) For student self-evaluation
    (3) Formative evaluation
    (4) Summative evaluation

13. *a.* (c)   *e.* (a, d)
    b. (b)   *f.* (d)
    c. (a, d)   *g.* (b)
    d. (c)

B. Comprehension
   1. a. 3   *d.* 1,4
      b. 2   *e.* 2,3,4
      c. 2,3,4

2. *a.* Matching. *d.* Essay.
   b. Short answer. *e.* True–false.
   c. Multiple choice.
3. *a.* Following the steps in the procedure and performing each one properly.
   b. The resulting good fire that provides heat and light.
   c. Suitable place to build fire; attention to safety practices; providing sufficient material—paper, kindling, logs.
   d. Realistic since actual product must be judged.
   e. Checklist for process, rating scale for product.
4. *a.* Rating scale. *d.* Open-end questionnaire.
   b. Observation. *e.* Closed-end questionnaire.
   c. Observation.
5. *a.* C *e.* N
   b. C *f.* N
   c. N *g.* N
   d. C *h.* C
6. *a.* Reliability. *d.* Reliability.
   b. Validity. *e.* Validity.
   c. Reliability.
7. *a.* F *f.* F/S
   b. S *g.* S
   c. F *h.* F
   d. F *i.* S
   e. S

C. Applications
   1. Sky Diving
   Student Learning:
   Requirements:
   Objectives 2, 4—write a one-page paper explaining reasons for being interested in sky diving, include a self-analysis of one's mental attitude
   Procedure:
   Objective 1—Respond to a described situation by explaining aerodynamic principles being applied.
   Objective 2—Instructor rates learners on positions, using checklist.
   Objectives 3, 4—Write explanations.
   Hazards:
   Objectives 1, 2—Chooses proper equipment from variety on display; demonstrates use of all equipment; graded by instructor on checklist.
   Objectives 3, 4—Objective test on regulations; list items provided in aircraft and describe use.
   Training and practice:
   Objectives 1, 2, 3, 4—Use checklist as learner performs (dressing, using equipment); use rating scale for jumping from mock tower.

   Learner Self-Check:
   Procedures—free-fall positions.
   Hazards—use of equipment; regulations.
   Training—exiting technique.

Formative evaluation:
Instruct in key parts of program for each set of objectives with two to three potential learners interested in sky diving. Use physical and psychological tests, have them view materials and engage in all learning activities, use self-check tests and evaluate performance for all objectives. Examine results and make necessary revisions in program.

2. *Your Subject*
Reader's activity.

CHAPTER 12 (PAGE 191)

A. Recall
   1. Pretest can best be developed after subject content, learning objectives, and tests to evaluate learning have all been prepared.
   2. Learner characteristics.
   3. Self-paced learning program
   4. a. To measure learner preparation to study the course or topic.
      b. To disclose competencies learners already possess relative to topic's learning objectives.
   5. Use a questionnaire
   Observe performance
   Review learner records
   Talk with persons who have worked with learners
   6. a. Related to some learning objectives.
      b. Pretest may include a sampling of questions from posttest.
      c. When the same or comparable tests are used, the growth in student learning for the topic can be determined.
   7. They need not be. May be similar but composed of different questions to test the same objectives. Pretest may be shorter, testing only a representative sampling of objectives.
   8. When you strongly believe learners have little or no familiarity with a topic and you have good understanding of their background preparation. A secondary reason may be that a pretest could be inappropriate for the learner group— younger children or persons not in a formal instructional program, like adults taking a hobby or recreational-interest course.
   9. See list on page 190.
B. Comprehension
   a. Prerequisite.   *f.* Prerequisite.
   b. Topic pretest.   *g.* Prerequisite.
   c. Prerequisite.   *h.* Prerequisite.
   d. Topic pretest.   *i.* Topic pretest.
   e. Prerequisite.
C. Applications
   1. Sky Diving
      a. Information obtained from the questionnaires, interviews, and tests used in Chapter 5 provide useful pretest data. Physical and mental preparation are important and indicate whether learners can be successful in program.

      In addition, a specific pretest for any learner who indicates previous flight and parachuting experience is advisable. Such persons may be knowledgeable and proficient with certain procedures and can bypass instruction for some objectives.

    b. Use a written test treating equipment used in sky diving, maneuvers performed, regulations, items in aircraft, and atmospheric conditions.

    Use performance test on exiting ability, free-fall positions, use of parachute and landing

  2. *Your Subject*
  Reader's activity.

CHAPTER 13 (PAGE 203)

A. Recall
  1. Adding, deleting, or changing items listed on paper is difficult while with cards there is a flexibility as changes are easily made.
  2. *a.* Convenient for persons to see the planning pattern as it is developed.
    b. Easy to shift, add, or remove cards without disturbing other parts of a plan.
  3. Cardboard strips—advantage: easily available; limitations: exerts little pressure on cards, writing low on card may not be seen

  Heavy-weight clear plastic—advantage: can see writing low on card; limitation: exerts little pressure on card

  Lightweight acetate—advantages: easily available, exerts firmer pressure that thinner material when folded limitation: still not firm enough pressure

  Weather stripping—advantage: holds cards securely; limitation: more expensive than other materials

  Plastic carpet runner—advantages: holds cards securely, is easy to use; limitation: may not be easily available for purchase
  4. *a.* Wall type.
    b. Portable with handle or cord for carrying.
    c. Fold-up type.
B. Applications
  1. *and* **2.** *Sky Diving*
      Sample of cards displayed on planning board.
  3. *Your Subject*
  Sample of cards displayed on planning board.

CHAPTER 14 (PAGE 215)

A. Recall
  1. *a.* False—The instructional design function is a specialized one that requires capabilities that many instructors do not have and which would be of interest to them.
    b. True.
    c. False—Ideas should be organized with specificity.
    d. True.
    e. False—Needs patience and persistence to stay with a difficult problem.
    f. False—Is willing to admit mistakes.
    g. True.

   h. False—In addition to areas listed, needs training or experience in media, evaluation methods, and writing skills.
   i. True.
   j. True.
   k. True.
   l. False—It is not necessary for the designer to be competent in the subject.
   m. True.
2. *a.* False—Cooperative approach.
   b. False—Obtain background information *before* first meeting.
   c. True.
   d. False—Approval is often necessary from one or more administrators.
   e. True.
   f. False—Try not to use specialized terminology or to introduce it gradually if needed.
   g. True.
   h. True.
   i. False—Help the instructor to participate in the process of planning and hold off decisions about media until later.
   j. True.
   k. True.
   l. False—Use praise and encouragement all through the planning process.
   m. False—Most valuable to obtain reactions from potential learners.
   n. True.
   o. True.
   p. False—Distribute a summary as soon after the meeting is concluded as possible.
   q. True.
   r. False—In a cooperative approach a disagreement should be resolved through group consensus.
   s. False—First talk with the individual instructor, then if it cannot be resolved, with the supervisor.
3. *a.* +
   b. +
   c. Program is not available until formative evaluation is concluded.
   d. +
   e. +
   f. +
4. *a.* +
   b. +
   c. No. Be flexible to adjust a position if shown to be wrong.
   d. +
   e. +
5. *a.* True.
   b. False—Involve staff in project at earliest appropriate time.
   c. True.
   d. False—While this procedure is acceptable, it would be better to allow members of the staff to see their materials in use and judge for themselves the successes or shortcomings.

6. *a.* +
   b. +
   c. +
   d. +
   e. +
   f. Evaluator should do this.
   g. +
   h. Maintain followup contact to check how things progress during use of program.
7. Position of *evaluator* has been missed. This person is responsible for:
   a. Assisting the instructor to develop tests and interpret results.
   b. Working on formative evaluation procedures and summaries if requested.
   c. Developing and administering the summative evaluation and reporting its results.

B. Applications
How did you rate yourself as an instructional designer?

CHAPTER 15 (PAGE 224)

A. Recall
1. Contributions for improving instruction and learning through effective, efficient, and cost-saving procedures
2. *a.* School or college—Directly under chief academic officer (curriculum director or vice-president for academic affairs).
   b. Company—Directly responsible to training director.
3. *a.* False—Assign subject specialist as needed to work on specific projects.
   b. False—In addition, a conference room.
   c. True.
   d. True.
   e. False—These persons usually are assigned to separate, although closely related, media services.
   f. True.
   g. True.
   h. False—There are both informational and public relations values for reports.
4. *a.* Funds directly budgeted by the organization.
   b. Funds provided by departments within the organization requesting services.
   c. Funds obtained through grants from outside the organization.
5. See list on page 223.

B. Application
Reader's activity.

CHAPTER 16 (PAGE 243)

A. Recall
1. Summative evaluation—By examining the results of an instructional program, to determine how well it has achieved the goals it was established to accomplish. Differs from formative evaluation in that a summative evaluation takes place *at the end* of a course or training program, while formative evaluation is performed when the program is being "formed" and tried out before implementation.
2. *a.* Effectiveness of learning.
   b. Efficiency of learning.

    c. Program costs.
    d. Attitudes toward program of learners and staff.
    e. Long-term benefits.

3. *(1)* b
    (2) a
    (3) a
    (4) b
    (5) b

4. *a.* Developmental.
    b. Operational during program implementation.

5. First, divide developmental costs by number of times program is anticipated to be used during its lifetime. Second, add together this prorated amount of developmental cost and the operating cost for one use period. Third, divide the total amount by average number of learners served by a program use.

6. *(1)* c
    (2) b
    (3) a

7. a, d, e.

8. Checklists
    Rating scales
    Rankings
    Semantic differential
    Open-ended questions

9. Completing questionnaires
    Conducting interviews
    Making observations
    Examining student records

10. *a.* Appropriateness of the training.
    b. Competencies of employees.
    c. Benefits to the organization.

11. See list on page 241.

12. Interesting title
    Summarize highlights
    Describe data in visual form
    Conclude with recommendations

B. Comprehension and Applications

1. Reader's choice.

2. 80 percent effective.

3. Yes.

4. *(1)* 2.22 efficiency index
    (2) 1.61 efficiency index
    (3) 1.48 efficiency index

5. (1).

6. $291.25 instructional cost index.

7. *a.* Ranking
    b. Examine student records
    c. Questionnaire
    d. Open-ended question
    e. Interview
    f. Rating scale
    g. Checklist

appendix B

Information on Sky Diving

Sky diving is a sport in which maneuvers are executed with the body while falling free in the air before the parachute opens. In competition, points are awarded for free-fall style. A person should always be proficient in basic parachuting *before* starting sky diving. The four skills in parachuting include exiting from an aircraft, opening the parachute, controlling the parachute during descent, and landing.

Why?

When you ask sky divers why they engage in this apparently dangerous sport you receive various replies. To some it is purely enjoyment of the pleasure of falling and the thrill of having to perform without error. For others, the experience is an identity and recognition one receives for doing something unusual and dangerous. Most sky divers love the adventure of life and want the challenge of meeting the forces of nature while refusing to be cramped in by form and convention.

Anyone might become a skydiver, but the sport has its greatest appeal among young men 20 to 30 years of age. Mental attitude and what might be called "panic control" are of more importance to the sky jumper than above-average physical requirements. But strength and agility can be necessary. Exercises to develop muscle tone are beneficial—knee benders, squats, push-ups, sit-ups, body twists, and so forth.

Procedure

It is essential to achieve a stable fall position as quickly as possible after exiting from the airplane. By doing this the jumper has control of his fall at all times. He utilizes the same aerodynamic principles that make the flight of airplanes possible—air flow and air resistance against his body to give him maneuverability and control in his rate of descent.

For the first moment of free fall, the forward speed of the aircraft is the controlling factor for the parachutist. Then gravity takes over. During the first second of descent, the fall is about 16 feet. The jumper's speed will accelerate until he reaches a velocity of 174 feet per second or 120 miles per hour in about 12 seconds.

A most important factor influencing the jumper's rate of fall is his body position. If he is falling vertically, he offers only about 2 square feet of air resistance, but in a "flat" stabilized fall, with arms and legs spread apart, there are about ten square feet of body surface to resist the air. Clothing can also have an effect on stability and control. Cotton overalls, a size larger than normal, add resistance and contribute to stability control.

A number of free-fall positions can be used:

1. The basic *stable spread* position: Head thrown back, eyes toward the horizon, chest raised, back arched, legs spread apart with knees slightly bent, and arms arched back (see diagram 1).
2. The *frog* position: Head straight, chest raised and arched, arms forward and bent with hands at shoulder level, and legs spread apart with knees slightly bent (see diagram 2). The frog position is more comfortable than the basic stable spread but still allows excellent stability and opportunity for maneuverability.
3. The *delta* position: Body as straight as possible, arms straight and drawn back along the body, shoulders pulled forward, and legs straight and slightly spread with toes pointed (see diagram 3). This position allows the jumper to travel at maximum velocity (sometimes up to 200 miles per hour) and in a head-down attitude.

The sky diver should not attempt any aerial maneuvers until he has maintained stability for at least 15 seconds. The arched stable fall position should be perfected first, and then tries can be made at the other stable positions.

Here are some maneuvers that can be made:

1. *Turning* is the basic sky diving maneuver. The jumper looks in the direction in which he desires to turn and then drops or lowers the arm or shoulder on that side. This produces a slow turn in the desired direction. Stop the turn by raising the arm and lowering the other one. Watch the ground and straighten out as soon as the turn stops.
2. The *back roll* is started from a stable spread. Bring the feet together, and at the same time, the right arm across the chest. This causes the jumper to roll over on his back. By bringing in the left arm and putting out the right one, the jumper will roll over to a facing-earth position again. For a left barrel roll, just reverse the procedure. Advanced jumpers can learn the back and front loops and baton-passing.
3. The *back roll* and the *front roll* are advanced maneuvers that are performed by variations of bringing the knees up to the chest and arms straight out, forward and pushed down (see sequence in diagram 4).

Maneuvers involving two or more jumpers include *hook-ups* (joining hands) and *baton-passing*.

Hazards of Sky Diving

There are certain hazards in sky diving which should be of concern to those considering taking up the sport. Statistics indicate that the risk of injury in sky diving is about 80 times that of participation in a football game. Of 40,000 persons engaged in sky diving each year, there have been an average of 30 to 50 fatal accidents.

These hazards include:

1. Use of improper equipment (should include main and reserve chutes, coveralls, helmet, goggles, boots, automatic opening device or altimeter
2. Lack of observing regulations governing sky diving (see manual)
3. Use of an improperly equipped aircraft (properly with one door removed, a static line for training, approved step and handholds outside the door)
4. Centrifugal force in a flat body spin that can cause loss of consciousness

Atmospheric conditions that can be hazardous include:

1. Lack of oxygen at higher elevations
2. Wind velocity that can affect the free fall
3. Air temperature that can cool exposed body parts and cause injury

Training and Practice

A ground-training program is essential to familiarize the novice jumper with as many phases of parachuting, as part of sky diving, as possible. In part, this training should include:

1. Basic fundamentals—proper dress, nomenclature of equipment, properly fitting equipment, check of parachute assembly, safety precautions.
2. Exit technique—practice position and movement from the doorway of a plane on the ground or through two uprights simulating an exit door. Following is the proper exit procedure:

    A learner is equipped with a training parachute assembly and static line hooked to the anchor cable in the aircraft to insure the safe opening of the parachute. Use "shuffle" step for moving to doorway to avoid losing balance or tripping; slide feet rather than lift them. Hold static line with one hand, while moving. At doorway, place hands outside of doorway, place one foot 2 inches over edge, the other foot 6 inches behind. Bend knees, upper body straight, head and eyes straight ahead.

    At command "Go," straighten legs, spring up 6 inches and out 3 feet. Place legs together, knees locked and toes pointed down. Drop head with chin against chest. Pull elbows to sides with hands on end of reserve parachute (on chest) and right palm over rip-cord handle. Bend body to see toes of boots. Once clear of the door, count 1-1000, 2-1000, 3-1000, 4-1000. At that point, the parachute should open!

3. Using mock tower—a 34 foot tower with a replica jump door and modified parachute harness for simulating the way to clear the door, jump into and falling through space, overcoming fear of height and sensation of shock of parachute opening. Learner lands on mound of soft dirt.
4. Errors to overcome during practice:
    a. A weak exit: falling, diving, stepping out
    b. Head up, knees bent, feet apart
    c. Closing eyes
    d. Slow or hurried count

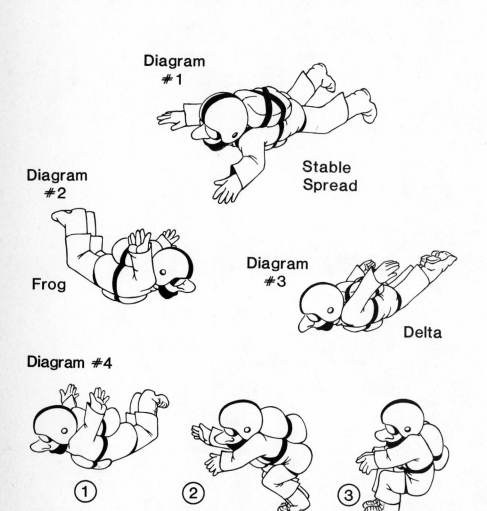

Diagram #1

Stable Spread

Diagram #2

Frog

Diagram #3

Delta

Diagram #4

① ② ③

④ ⑤ ⑥

Figure B.1

appendix **C**

Glossary

affective learning   developing attitudes, values, or appreciations

andragogy   field of adult learning

behaviorism   learning theory in which subject content is divided into a series of small steps; the learner participates actively, receives feedback on effort, and is guided to success

client   person for whom instruction is being planned and who may serve as subject specialist when working with the instructional designer

cognitive learning   acquiring information, knowledge and intellectual abilities relative to a subject or topic

cognitive strategies   highest level of cognitive learning, typified by problem solving (from Gagné)

competency-based instruction   providing and evaluating instruction against a specific standard as indicated by the learning objectives for the topic or task

concept   name or expression given to a class of facts, objects, or events, all of which have common features

criterion-referenced instruction   *See* competency-based instruction

developmental costs   all personnel, resources, and services costs required to plan and develop an instructional program

domains of learning   cognitive, psychomotor, and affective categories

efficiency   measuring the amount of learner time, of personnel services, and of facilities use required to carry out an instructional program, and then deciding if these amounts are acceptable or excessive

effectiveness   measuring the degree to which learners accomplish objectives for each unit or a total course

enabling objective   subobjective that leads to accomplishing a terminal objective, also called supporting objective

evaluator   person responsible for assisting the instructor in designing tests to measure student learning, to conduct formative and summative evaluation, and to analyze results

feedback   providing the learner with answers to exercises and other information relative to progress in learning

flow chart   visual description of the sequence necessary for performing a task, including decision points and alternate paths

formative evaluation   testing a new instructional program with a sampling of learners during the development phase, and using the results to improve the program

front-end analysis   *See* learning needs assessment

general purpose   broad statement of what is to be taught within a topic or job task

goal statement   broad statement describing what should take place in an instructional course or training program

individualized learning   allowing learners to learn by providing each one with objectives and activities appropriate to his or her own characteristics, preparation, needs, and interests

instructional cost index   mathematical calculation of the cost per learner or trainee to accomplish objectives for a topic or course, taking into account a portion of the developmental cost and full implementation costs

instructional design process   systematic planning of instruction in which attention is given to ten related elements

instructional designer   person responsible for carrying out and coordinating the systematic design procedure

instructional development   managing the planning, development, and implementation procedure for instruction or training

instructional systems   another expression for the instructional design concept

instructional technology   (1) resources (machines and materials) used for instruction, and (2) process of systematic instructional planning

intellectual skills   organizing and structuring facts for learning to form concepts, principles, rules, and laws (from Gagné)

interaction learning   learners, with or without an instructor, work together in group activities which may include pursuing projects, discussing, and reporting

job tasks   major physical actions or skills to be accomplished within a course

learner characteristics   factors relating to personal and social traits of individuals and learner groups which need consideration during planning

learning needs assessment or analysis   procedure of gathering information before deciding whether there is a substantive need for instruction or training

learning objective   statement describing what the learner is specifically required to learn or accomplish relative to a topic or task

learning styles   recognizing various methods of learning as preferred by individuals or which may be more effective with different individuals

learning systems design   another expression for the instructional design concept

mastery learning   indicating whether a learner successfully accomplishes the necessary level of learning for required objectives

module   a self-instructional package treating a single topic or unit of a course

nonconventional learners   individuals that have characteristics differing from those of typical learners or employees, including ethnic minorities, disabled persons, and adults

norm-referenced testing   evaluating the results of instruction in a relative fashion by comparing test scores of each learner with those of other learners in the class

objective-type tests   consisting of questions for which a learner must select an answer from two or more alternatives and persons scoring the test can easily agree on the correct answer

operant conditioning   result of applying behavioralist psychology, including the use of active learner participation, feedback, and reinforcement

operational costs   all personnel, resources, and services costs incurred as an instructional program is being implemented

performance-based instruction   *See* competency-based instruction

performance technology   another expression for the instructional design concept

planning board   surface on which cards can be displayed as planning elements are completed and relationships are examined

posttest   final examination given at the end of a course or training program (differs from pretest)

prerequisite test   portion of a pretest that measures content or skill preparation a learner has for starting the course or unit

presentation teaching method   instructor disseminating subject content to a group of learners, often in a lecture setting

pretest   testing learners prior to the start of instruction in order to determine level of preparation relative to a topic or task

principle   high level generalization derived from a set of concepts

psychomotor learning   becoming proficient in performing a physical action or skill involving muscles of the body

reinforcement   learner receiving feedback on success in learning, thus being encouraged to continue learning

reliability   ability of a test to produce consistent results when used with comparable learners

self-paced learning   allowing the learner to satisfy required learning activities by accomplishing them at his or her own speed or convenience

subject matter expert (SME)   person qualified to provide content and resources information relating to topics and tasks for which instruction is being designed

summative evaluation   measuring how well the major outcomes of a course or program are attained at the conclusion of instruction (posttest) or thereafter on the job

support services   matters such as budget, facilities, equipment, and materials that require attention for the successful preparation and implementation of a new instructional program

supporting objective   *See* enabling objective

systems approach   an overall plan to problem solving that gives attention to all essential elements

task analysis   listing, often in the form of a flow chart, of the sequential skill components of a task and related knowledge

taxonomies of learning   sequential classifications of learning in cognitive and affective domains on progressively higher levels

technology of instruction   *See* instructional technology

terminal objective   statement of a major outcome for a topic or a task

topics   units or major subject content divisions specified within a course or instructional program

validity   direct relationship between test questions and the learning objectives they are intended to measure

verbal information   lowest level of learning requiring only memorization and recall of facts (from Gagné)

Applications of the Instructional Design Process

APPLICATION #1—INSTRUCTIONAL DESIGN PROCESS

Course: Introduction to Meteorology

Goal: To gain understanding of the essential facts and principles that can lead to prediction of weather conditions

Learning Needs Assessment: There is a need to expand the physical science course offerings at this college. A survey of science faculty and an examination of catalogs of other institutions reveals that attention should be given to the field of meteorology in the curriculum. This will be the first course.

Priorities/Constraints: Because this is a new course, staff time will be limited. There is also an interest in exploring nontraditional instructional methods. Therefore self-paced student learning activities should be planned for a portion of the course.

Student Group: Freshmen and sophomores 60 students IQ: 105–133 Reading: 10th–college Fulfilling general education requirements Some background in physical science principles

Topic: Air Masses

General Purpose: To know the characteristics and sources of air masses.

Subject Content

1. Definition of air mass: Widespread body of air with similar properties throughout.
2. Source regions:
   a. Land—Alaska, Canada, Arctic
   b. Water—North Pacific, Caribbean
3. Symbols for air masses:
   mP—maritime Polar
   cP—continental Polar
   mT—maritime Tropical
4. General characteristics of air mass:
   a. Tropical
   Warmer than land below
   High moisture content
   Limited visibility
   Stratus-type clouds
   Drizzle, dew
   Moves north and east
   b. Polar
   Colder than land below
   Low moisture content
   Good visibility
   Cumulus-type clouds
   Showers, thunderstorms
   Moves south and east
(and so on)

Learning Objectives

1. To write a definition of the term air mass
2. On a map of North America, to locate the source region for three types of air masses and show direction of movement with arrows with 90 percent accuracy
3. To use the correct symbol designation for each air mass
4. When given temperature, wind direction, and humidity, to select the name and symbol of an air mass, at least four out of five times
5. To relate cloud types and other weather factors to the appropriate air mass
6. At assigned times, to observe local weather conditions and indicate the air mass affecting the area

Activities and Resources

Instructor Activities	Learner Activities
1. Present 5-minute animated film showing how air masses form, source regions, and movement. Follow with overhead transparencies to review source regions, indicate symbols and show movements. 2. Participate with groups of students to review activities, answer questions, and discuss local air mass reports.	1. Take notes on handout sheet during presentation. 2. At Learning Center, study 30 frame filmstrip/audio recording on air masses relating to objectives. 2 to 5. Complete accompanying worksheets. Check answers. 3. Make local weather observations for 2-week period using report form. 4. Sign up for discussion group and prepare for activity according to handout sheet.

Support Services	Evaluation

Budget—$150
 3 transparencies
 8 copies filmstrip and audiotape
 Printed material

Personnel
 Instructor (presentation, 3 discussion
   groups)
 Artists/photographer (10 hours)
 Recording technician (2 hours)
 Learning center aide (12 hours)

Equipment
 16mm projector
 Overhead projector
 6 filmstrip viewers/recorders

Facilities
 Classroom (1 period)
 Discussion room (3 periods)
 Learning center (6 stations, 12 hours)

Schedule
 1 class period
 6 discussion periods

1. Describe the term air mass in 20
   words or less.
2. On the map below, mark the source
   region for three major air masses and
   show direction of movement during
   the winter with arrows.
3. Flying in lower levels would be
   bumpy in mP, mT, cP?
4. On the East Coast in winter, weather
   is—fog, temp. 62°F, dew point 62°F,
   wind SE 10. Give symbol for air mass.
5. What kind of air mass is affecting our
   local area today? Justify your answer
   with at least four facts.
6. Listen to the tape recording marked
   "Weather Reports." You will hear
   three sample broadcasts to pilots in
   flight.
   a. Is this a continental polar or
      maritime tropical air mass?
   b. What flying conditions would you
      expect in this air mass?
   c. What is the name and symbol for
      this air mass?

Pretest

1. What does each symbol mean?
   mP   cP   mT
2. Which area(s) may be source regions
   for tropical air?
   a. Gulf of Mexico
   b. Southeast Asia
   c. Africa
   d. Mid-Atlantic Ocean
3. Characteristics of polar air mass are in
   which group:
   a. Warmer than land
      Cumulus clouds
   b. Good visibility
      Showers
   c. High moisture
      Poor visibility
4. Cumulus clouds are associated with
   which air mass?
   a. Tropical
   b. Polar

APPLICATION #2—INSTRUCTIONAL DESIGN PROCESS

Training Program:
Woodworking Machine Operation

Goal: To operate five kinds of woodworking machines in a safe and efficient manner for constructing storage and display units.

Learning Needs Assessment: Management has directed that services previously contracted with a vendor be performed within the company. The shop supervisor requires that six employees from the electronics area become proficient with woodworking skills.

Priority/Constraints: Training will take place within 3 months so construction work can start a month later. Employee training will be on an individual basis, under supervision of an experienced woodworking specialist.

Trainees: Six presently employed technicians who volunteered for these newly classified jobs. Must satisfactorily complete a dexterity and physical ability test. Have at least an 8th-grade English reading level.

Task: Operate the Drill Press

General Purpose: To use the drill press safely for drilling holes and boring holes to predetermined depths in wood.

Learning Objectives

1. Identify all nine parts of a drill press.
2. State the purpose served by each part with 100 percent accuracy.
3. Demonstrate eight safety precautions with complete precision when setting up and using a drill press.
4. Set up a drill press for drilling various size holes into and through wood from 1/2 to 2-inch thicknesses.
5. Drill sets marked, spaced holes in wood of three different thicknesses.

Subject Content

1. Parts of the drill press

quill	quill lock
chuck	table locking
table	clamp
guard	table height
feed	adjustment
clamp	
lever	depth stop

2. Safety precautions
   Wear eye protection.
   Use correct motor speed:
   large bits—slow speed
   medium bits—medium speed
   small bits—high speed
   Fasten drill securely in chuck.
   Keep hands clear from line of travel of drill.
   (and so on)
3. Basic use:
   (see next page)

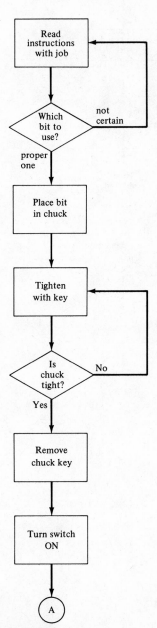

Figure D.1

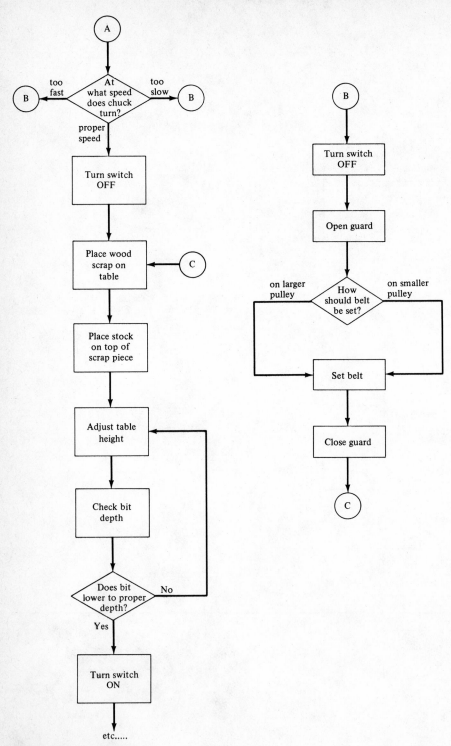

Figure D.1 (continued)

292

Activities and Resources

Trainee Activities	Supervisor Activities
1. Study diagram of drill press with parts labels and functions explained. Relate parts to ones on drill press. Complete review on worksheet. Repeat study as necessary.	1. Check replies on worksheet. Clear up misunderstandings with trainee.
2. View video recording on setting up and using drill press. Note safety precautions. Practice safety precautions. Request check-out when ready.	2. Review safety practice with trainee.
3. View video recording again. Give attention to set-up procedure. Request check-out when ready.	3. Review set-up procedure with trainee.
4. Practice drilling sample holes in wood of various thicknesses.	4. Observe trainee using drill press and examine product. Critique procedure and results with trainee.

Support Services	Evaluation

Equipment
  Drill press
  Video player and monitor
 	
Personnel
  Supervisor on call
 	
Schedule
  1 week training
 	
Facility
  New wood shop
 	
Budget—$500
  Video production
  Printed materials
  Wood samples
	1. On a drill press, locate each part and explain purpose. Supervisor uses checksheet.
	2. Set up drill press for use and carry out drilling procedure on six samples of wood. Supervisor uses rating scale to judge set-up procedure, safety practices, drilling procedure, and quality of products.

Pretest

1. Explain to supervisor how a drill press is used. With acceptance, demonstrate use in drilling holes.
2. With success in above, complete posttest evaluation. Supervisor corrects any misconceptions.

Index